The African Experience:
From "Lucy" to Mandela
Part III

Professor Kenneth P. Vickery

THE TEACHING COMPANY ®

PUBLISHED BY:

THE TEACHING COMPANY
4151 Lafayette Center Drive, Suite 100
Chantilly, Virginia 20151-1232
1-800-TEACH-12
Fax—703-378-3819
www.teach12.com

ISBN 1-59803-226-7

Kenneth P. Vickery, Ph.D.

Alumni Distinguished Undergraduate Professor,
North Carolina State University

Ken Vickery was born in Washington, D.C., and raised in Virginia and Mississippi. He received his B.A. degree with Phi Beta Kappa honors at Duke University in 1970. He went on to study sub-Saharan African history at Yale University under the late South African historian Leonard Thompson. His dissertation, a study of the political economy of southern Zambia in the colonial period, involved both archival and extensive oral-historical fieldwork. Yale awarded him the Ph.D. degree in 1978.

Professor Vickery joined the history faculty at North Carolina State University in 1977, where he continues to teach and serves as the department's Director of Undergraduate Advising. He has been a visiting professor on several occasions at the University of North Carolina at Chapel Hill and at Meredith College. In 1993, he was awarded a Fulbright teaching fellowship and spent the entire year of 1994 as Fulbright Visiting Associate Professor in the Department of Economic History of the University of Zimbabwe in Harare.

Dr. Vickery was inducted into the Academy of Outstanding Teachers at NC State in 1986. In 2005, he was named Alumni Distinguished Undergraduate Professor, the university's highest teaching honor.

Professor Vickery has continued to conduct research during his 11 journeys to Africa. His book *Black and White in Southern Zambia: The Tonga Plateau Economy and British Imperialism, 1890–1939* (1986) was a finalist for the Herskovits Prize, given annually by the African Studies Association for the outstanding book in African studies in any discipline. He has published numerous articles and reviews in *Comparative Studies in Society and History*, *International Journal of African Historical Studies*, *Journal of Southern African Studies*, *American Historical Review*, and other journals. In 2006, in honor of the anthropologist Elizabeth Colson, he edited and prepared a collection of 15 essays, *The Tonga-Speaking Peoples of Zambia and Zimbabwe*. Professor Vickery is also preparing a biography of Sir Roy Welensky, Prime Minister of the Federation of the Rhodesias and Nyasaland (1956–1963), set in the context of Southern African labor history.

Table of Contents

The African Experience: From "Lucy" to Mandela
Part III

The African Experience: From "Lucy" to Mandela

Scope:

This course of 36 lectures is intended to provide a general introduction to Africa and its history. To many in the West, Africa has often seemed to be the Lost Continent—"lost" in two senses. The first would be *lost from view*: Many of us simply don't hear much or know much about the place and its past. The second would be "lost" in the sense of *hopelessly lost*: What we do hear seems overwhelmingly negative, dominated by poverty, disease, disasters, violence, and tyranny. Our aim is certainly not to sugarcoat, explain away, or make excuses; there is enough reality behind these images to make doing so a genuine disservice. Our objective is to provide a fuller and more balanced view, a greater appreciation and understanding of the complexity of the African experience.

This course will focus primarily on Africa south of the Sahara Desert. This reflects the training, research interests, and teaching concentration of the instructor. Indeed, for related reasons, if there is a privileged subcontinent in the course's coverage, it would be Southern Africa. The Republic of South Africa, in particular, features prominently, in part because it is by far the most developed and powerful country within our scope, but also because its history at many junctures yields fascinating comparisons with the history of the United States. Nonetheless, we will devote plenty of attention to themes and developments centered in West, Central, and East Africa. Although the sequence of lectures is essentially chronological and based on dynamics unfolding in the whole continent or in a major subregion, at several points, we will devote a lecture to a specific country, such as Ethiopia, the Congo, or Zimbabwe, in addition to South Africa.

History is often described as drama; if true, it is played out on a stage. Our original "stage" comprises the many natural environments of the African continent. Following an introductory lecture, we begin our course with descriptions of the basic ecological zones of Africa, then sample some of the more spectacular specific places, such as Mt. Kilimanjaro and the Victoria Falls (one of the seven natural wonders of the world). We continue by considering African history in the truly long run. This, after all, is the so-called "cradle of mankind," and we examine not only the evidence concerning human origins but the transformation of human society from hunting and gathering to agriculture and the Iron Age. We analyze the emergence of essential social categories related to kinship, ethnic identity (what is a "tribe"?), and politics—the groundwork for African states and kingdoms.

We pause in Lecture Seven to mark an exception to our sub-Saharan focus by looking briefly at ancient Egypt and its connections to Africa further south, upstream on the Nile.

Lecture Eight surveys the enduring importance of religion—indigenous, as well as Islam and Christianity—and the following lecture provides an overview of the ancient outpost of Christianity, the Ethiopian kingdom. We then encounter some recurring themes of the course—statebuilding and the connection with long-distance trade—by exploring the "golden age" in the West African savanna, the rise of the Swahili city-states on the east coast, and the massive ruins of Great Zimbabwe in the south.

Some 500 years ago, global history reached a turning point, symbolized rather well by Columbus's voyage. In Africa as elsewhere, from this point forward, relations with Western powers become increasingly relevant. Over a span of six lectures, we illustrate this by investigating two absolutely critical developments: West Africa's long, deep, and tragic involvement in the Atlantic slave trade and the origins of modern South Africa, beginning with the Cape Colony in the 17th century and culminating in the discoveries of diamonds and gold in the late 19th.

By that point, Africa's encounter with Europe reaches another crucial juncture. Important as the slave trade and proto-South Africa were, most of Africa retained its independence and was not colonized until the late 19th century. Then, in a very short space of time, it was—in fact, virtually the entire continent was carved up and added to one or another European empire. We look at the reasons for this sudden imposition, African resistance, and the commonalities and differences in various colonial systems.

By the mid-20th century, however, under intense pressure from African nationalists, the colonial edifice began to crumble nearly as fast as it had been built. But the paths to independence varied dramatically from colony to colony, especially between those that achieved decolonization peacefully and those where bloody liberation wars emerged. Nonetheless, with the final triumph of Nelson Mandela and his movement in South Africa, by the 1990s, colonialism and/or white minority rule were things of the past.

The drive to independence engendered great hopes and great expectations. After an initial period with genuine achievements, things began to turn sour—a bitter disappointment for so many. We analyze the factors—both internal and external—contributing to this downturn. We consider particularly appalling situations, to wit, the Rwanda genocide and the HIV/AIDS pandemic.

Yet we observe as well not only the South African "miracle" but also a revival of democratic spirit in many corners of Africa. We conclude with an assessment of Africa at the start of the millennium, mixing sobering reality with some reasons for hope, however cautious.

Lecture Twenty-Five
The Congo—Promise and Pain

Scope:

We pause here to devote a lecture to a single, vast, and crucial country: the Congo. The Congo's history seems to throw into stark relief the processes we have been examining: conquest, colonization, decolonization. Henry Stanley supervised the creation of a colonial regime that was initially the possession, not of the Belgian state, but of Belgian King Leopold II *alone*. So vicious were the means used by Leopold's agents to extract red rubber from the Congo rain forest that an international protest movement arose in response. Much later, the Belgians abandoned a more paternalistic rule with a haste that suggests panic. This move set the stage for the *Congo crisis* of the early 1960s, and all manner of foreign intervention. Visionaries, such as Patrice Lumumba, lost out to the iron hand of Mobutu Sese Seko, who in 32 years of power set the African standard for incompetence and corruption. Today, the country wallows in civil war. This is not a story for the fainthearted.

Outline

I. *Congo*, like *Timbuktu* or *Zulu*, conjures up all sorts of images in the Western mind. Whatever their validity, there is no getting around the significance of the place.

   A. We pause to focus on the Congo at this particular point because it provides vivid illustrations of the processes we have been examining: conquest, colonization, and decolonization.

   B. For continuity's sake, we will carry the Congo story further, up to the present. Thus, this lecture is something of a bridge between past and future lectures.

II. We need to clarify first that there are two countries marked "Congo" on Africa's map.

   A. First is the more northerly Republic of Congo, whose capital is Brazzaville. It was a French colony that gained its independence in 1960.

B. The second is the Democratic Republic of Congo, whose capital is Kinshasa. The name of this country was changed to Zaïre in 1971, then back to Congo in 1997. It is this country on which we will focus in this lecture.

III. The Congo is a huge place—as big as the United States east of the Mississippi.

  A. It encompasses much of a gigantic rain forest, vast savanna belts, and mountain and lake environments.

  B. It includes scores of ethnic groups and languages and was home to numerous major kingdoms, such as the Luba, Lunda, and Kuba. Perhaps it is little wonder that it has proven such a challenge.

IV. The modern Congo originates with the rather amazing and still shocking tale of Belgian King Leopold II, a man of gargantuan appetites and ambitions and—let us state it plainly—greed. He never set foot in the Congo but was ultimately responsible for devastating the lives of millions and starting the country down a path from which, in some ways, it has never recovered.

  A. His first vehicle in getting his share of the "magnificent African cake," as he called it, began with his founding of the International African Association, which he promoted as a philanthropic project with a civilizing mission.

  B. In reality, his aims were more material, and his first means of building a fortune was through ivory.

  C. Eventually, however, he turned to rubber, needed, of course, for the new electrical and automobile industries. Leopold's economic bounty perfectly illustrates the relation between the scramble for Africa and the industrial age.

  D. Leopold's "Congo Free State" was something unique. This was *his* project, his colony, not the possession of the Belgian government. His principal henchman was none other than Henry Stanley—yes, *that* Henry Stanley.

   1. One of Stanley's tactics was "treaty-making": Accompanied by a well-armed force, Stanley persuaded indigenous rulers to agree to a legal document giving certain rights to the king.

   2. Most of these rulers were illiterate and had little understanding of what they were agreeing to.

E. To get the rubber, Leopold unleashed an army of agents—rogues and sadists—who forced the population to collect the wild rubber, which was difficult and dangerous work in itself. At times, these agents took family members of the workers as hostages and insisted on getting quotas of rubber from the workers. Failure to meet the assigned quota often resulted in the loss of one's hand, foot, ears, nose, or head.

F. Eventually, the Western world—a world that had, obviously, no objection to colonialism per se—became so appalled by the excesses

that what might be seen as the world's first international human rights movement arose. The pressure finally led to Leopold turning the Congo over to the Belgian government in 1908. One reputable scholar estimates that Leopold's mayhem had depopulated the Congo by some 10 million.

V. For the next half-century, the Belgians reigned over a generally quiet colony. In fact, the Belgian government delegated a substantial amount of its responsibility.

A. The Catholic Church played an unusually large, quasi-public role, especially but not exclusively in education and health.

B. The Belgians granted gigantic monopoly concessions over vast regions to private firms. Union Minière, for instance, held exclusive rights over the colony's most lucrative resource, copper from the Katanga region.

C. At its best, the system represented a reasonably benevolent though firm paternalism. Union Minière led the way, for instance, in the "stabilization" of its labor, allowing workers to reside with their families in company towns, with company provision of services.

D. None of the colonial powers was fond of Africans engaging in politics, because this was equated with "troublemaking." But the Belgians were especially resistant to any notion of African involvement in decision making. Theirs was a "direct rule" with little place for notions of "assimilation."

E. As a result, when the winds of African nationalism began to blow in the 1950s, the Belgians, at first, cracked down hard, then permitted only the most modest exercises in local elections. Political parties were legalized only in August

1959; then, astonishingly, the Belgians announced in January 1960 that independence would be granted in six months.

VI. The Belgians had done virtually nothing to prepare the nation for independence. If France and Britain eventually showed a haste to decolonize, Belgium showed a panic. Given the size and the diversity of a country with fewer than a dozen university graduates, what followed was perhaps predictable.

A. The country's first leader, the former clerk Patrice Lumumba, was almost immediately faced with a series of secession crises. His charisma combined with his radical agenda did not endear him to the West. Although he was killed by Congolese assassins in 1961, after only six months in power, it has now been established that external Western powers were involved in his murder.

B. There ensued a half-decade of incredibly complex chaos, which saw the country remain a single entity of sorts mainly through the efforts of a United Nations intervention.

C. Behind the scenes, a shrewd young army officer, Joseph Mobutu, was consolidating his power. In November 1965, he pulled off a bloodless coup d'état.

VII. Thus began 32 years, no less, of Mobutu's regime. We asked in the last lecture what Africa's new rulers would do with their power, and we will see that the answers vary and change. In Mobutu's case, the answers are clear and disheartening.

A. Internally, Mobutu was quite prepared to hammer any opposition, but he also showed considerable political acuity, rewarding allies or buying off rivals, adept at wielding both carrot and stick.

B. Internationally, he played the geopolitical game rather cleverly, adroitly positioning himself as a friend of the West to keep the Cold War-era aid coming.

C. Above all, he lined his pocket, on a colossal scale, becoming literally one of the richest men in the world. Most of the wealth wound up in European banks and real estate.

D. Eventually, the center could not hold. De facto, "Zaïre" (as Mobutu had renamed the country), had largely ceased to exist by the 1990s. A rebellion launched from the east in 1997 quickly drove him into exile, where he died shortly thereafter.

VIII. Since Mobutu's fall, alas, the situation is little better.

- **A.** A major civil war, complicated by spillover from Rwanda and other Great Lakes countries, has festered.
- **B.** Congo has always been a target of external interest because of its enormous resources, including *coltan*, an element used in cell phones.
- **C.** With Congo's always considerable mineral wealth the prize, in fact, numerous nations, including several from Africa, have descended in force on the country, a perverse rendition, in a sense, of the era of Leopold and the scramble.

Suggested Reading:

Bill Berkeley, *The Graves Are Not Yet Full: Race, Tribe and Power in the Heart of Africa*, chapter 3.

Howard French, *A Continent for the Taking: The Tragedy and Hope of Africa*, chapters 3, 6–7, 10–11.

Adam Hochschild, *King Leopold's Ghost: A Story of Greed, Terror, and Heroism in Colonial Africa*.

Georges Nzongola-Ntalaja, *The Congo from Leopold to Kabila: A People's History*.

Michaela Wrong, *In the Footsteps of Mr. Kurtz: Living on the Brink of Disaster in Mobutu's Congo*.

Questions to Consider:

1. Author Adam Hochschild finds something distinctly modern in the fact that Leopold never set foot in "his" Congo—pain or misery inflicted impersonally, from a distance. Do you agree?
2. How did the Cold War affect the course of Congo/Zaïre's history?

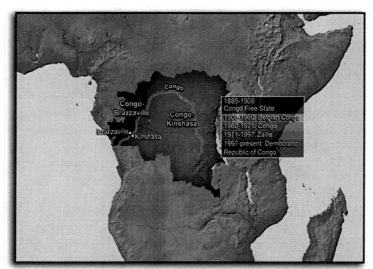

The Congo across History: When we speak of the Congo in this series, we are usually speaking of what might be called Congo-Kinshasa, as opposed to Congo-Brazzaville. Congo-Kinshasa has a storied littany of names and rulers across time, as the key shows.

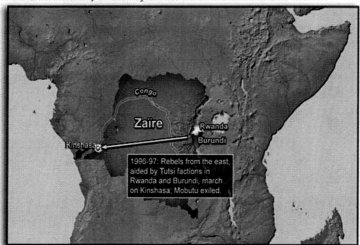

The Fall of Mobutu: Joseph Mobutu, later Mobutu Sese Seko, was among the most savvy but also most ruinous of Africa's autocrats, ruling Congo (which he renamed Zaïre in 1971) for 32 years. This map, displaying his overthrow with the help of factions from Rwanda and Burundi, underscores the regional interconnectedness of African history, a theme of this course.

Lecture Twenty-Five—Transcript
The Congo—Promise and Pain

Welcome. The word "Congo," like the words "Timbuktu" or "Zulu," conjures up all sorts of images in the minds of many of us in the Western world. Whatever the validity or reality behind those images might be, there is no getting around the place's tremendous significance. We pause to focus on the Congo at this particular point because it provides vivid illustrations of the processes we have been examining: conquest, colonization, and decolonization.

In fact, for continuity's sake, we will carry the Congo story further, up to very recent history—up to the present—in other words to another great theme, which would have to be described as the disappointments of the independence era. In general, the reason for devoting a full lecture to the Congo, as we did to Ethiopia, is partly because the vividness of its history—its experience with all of these things—its history of conquest, of colonization, of decolonization— its experience since independence—seems to be writ large. It's as if the characters and the events in the Congo versions of these general processes are under a magnifying glass or something. They seem larger than life. If you were going to invent a country that wanted to throw into stark relief all of the great themes of modern African history, the Congo might be a good choice to base it on.

I'm going to pause here for a moment to make a geographical clarification. If you've looked at the map of central Africa, and I certainly hope you have, like most maps it tells many stories. You may have noticed that there are, in fact, on most political maps of modern Africa, two countries labeled or marked "Congo."

So, let us sort these out first of all. There are in fact two. One, the more northerly country, is the Republic of Congo. The more southerly one is the Democratic Republic of Congo. The Republic of Congo, which is more easily referred to as Congo-Brazzaville, after its capital city, was a French colony created during the Scramble and one of the territories that fell to France as part of French Equatorial Africa.

The other—again, perhaps easiest to refer to as Congo-Kinshasa— was begun, as we'll see in a moment, by Belgian's King Leopold and eventually became the Belgian Congo. After independence, it was known as the Congo for a time. Its name, just to further muddy the waters, was changed in 1971 by its ruler at the time to Zaïre, which is a corrupted version of a name for the Congo, or Zaïre, River. It stayed Zaïre for about a quarter of a century until the ruler, who we'll meet, was evicted from power and the country's name changed back to Congo.

So, I will be referring in this lecture to the Congo-Kinshasa, the former Belgian Congo, the country known as Zaïre, and now known again as Democratic Republic of Congo.

Perhaps the place to start is with some geographical realities. The Congo is a huge place. It straddles the equator and, as most of you know, the countries that are in that bulge of the earth's middle often get underrepresented, in a sense, in two-dimensional maps. In fact, the Congo (Congo-Kinshasa) is as big as the United States east of the Mississippi River. It encompasses a great portion of the world's second largest rain forest and vast savanna belts that run below that rain forest. In the east, we see some of the manifestations of the Great Rift that we talked about early in the course. Major mountain ranges and lakes are a part of the geography in the east.

In terms of its human geography and history, this vast region was home to numerous major Bantu kingdoms, such as the Luba, the Lunda, and the Kuba. With all of this diversity and with this massive scale, perhaps it is little wonder that the Congo has proven to be such a challenge.

The modern Congo originates with the rather amazing, almost incredible, and still shocking tale of Belgian's King Leopold II. A man of gargantuan appetites, of huge ambition, Leopold never set foot in the Congo or in Africa, but was ultimately responsible for the devastation of the lives of millions. I hope to show that. I don't believe that's an exaggeration. In some respects, he started the country down a path from which, in some respects, it has never recovered.

Leopold ascended the throne of Belgium in 1865 upon his father's death, after a childhood in which he appears to have been, or at least felt, starved of love. As you can imagine, like Shaka Zulu and Cecil Rhodes, he's been the stuff or the object of a number of amateur psycho-historical treatments.

I mentioned gargantuan ambitions. He was a man of gargantuan appetites in the most literal sense. His usual breakfast consisted of six poached eggs, an entire rack of toast, and an entire jar of marmalade, matched by lunches and dinner of equal scale.

In modern terms, he would probably be called an obsessive compulsive. He was one of those who washed his hands dozens of times a day and who insisted that the tablecloths be boiled after each meal. Perhaps most curiously, he wrapped a bag around his quite lengthy beard when he went out in public if there was dampness or rain.

It may be that the felt deprivations or hollowness of his childhood led him to seek fulfillment or validity with grandiose projects. Apparently the kingship of Belgium was not enough. It was a small country, after all, and nothing on the scale of the power of Britain or France.

To pursue these dreams, then, Leopold increasingly turned toward Africa and becomes a major player—a major figure—in the "Scramble for Africa," which we looked at earlier in the course. As early as 1877, before the Scramble really has taken off, he wrote to one associate: "I mean to miss no chance to get my share of this magnificent African cake."

"This magnificent African cake": It's a rather nice image—a useful image, I think—for the era of the "Scramble for Africa."

His first vehicle in doing this was an association that he founded called the International African Association. He put it forth in a series of meetings, very adroitly. Again, whatever one says about Leopold's record or personality, he was a man of great intelligence and great cleverness and with the ability to attract to him support, or at least tolerance, for his projects from those with the force of his considerable intellect and considerable charm.

He put the International African Association forward as essentially a philanthropic project. This would be an association that in Central Africa would, for instance, combat the slave trade—in this case, the ongoing slave trade connected to the east coast and usually referred to as the Arab-Swahili slave trade. It would bring moral uplift. It would bring the advancement of science. It would bring, in other words, the civilizing mission. As we've seen earlier in the course, this is very much the order of the day—the agenda. He was putting on the table an additional version of a project justified, in precisely those terms, in a lot of different places in Africa at that time.

In reality—and I will put it that way—his objects were far more material and far more mundane. He sought a fortune in Africa. That his first means of building that fortune was through one of Africa's age-old commodities will not surprise us, and that is ivory.

But, eventually, Leopold's project in Africa would be associated with a quite different commodity and that would be rubber—in this case wild rubber. As we saw in the case of palm oil, for instance, in the "oil rivers" and other parts of Nigeria ("oil rivers" not named for petroleum, which comes out of there now, but for the palm oil that was used to lubricate the rapidly multiplying machines of the industrial age). As with palm oil, then, rubber is almost a perfect fit between a product coming out of Africa and the requirements of that industrial age. Obviously, its principal uses, exploding at precisely the time (the last decades of the 1800s and first of the 1900s), would be in the automobile and electrical industries.

Leopold's territory in Africa came to be known as the "Congo Free State," and it was something unique. This was his colony. It was not the possession, until later in the story (from 1908 on). It was his personal colony in the center of Africa. So, this is not an example of a competition as part of that Scramble between governments as it is a remarkable individual's role in carving out his own Central African territory.

His principal agent was none other than someone we've met before. He was born John Rowlands, out of wedlock in Wales, but eventually, after travels in America and in Africa, was known to the world as Henry Morton Stanley. Of course, he was the man who found Livingstone, and we met him before in that case.

Stanley had become frustrated in his efforts to get the British government to back his own efforts in launching the Scramble. The British obviously came on board at a certain point, but he offered his services to Leopold, and a very convenient partnership was born.

Stanley's first step in creating the Congo Free State was something we can see as part of the "Scramble for Africa" in many parts, and that was what we might call "treaty-making." The notion was to go in with a very well-armed force to chiefs and indigenous rulers and persuade them one way or another to agree to a legal document—a treaty—giving certain rights (usually rather shadily defined rights) to the outside power, in this case to King Leopold. It is fair to say that most of the indigenous rulers he was dealing with were illiterate and probably had very little indication or understanding of what they were, in fact, signing or getting into.

In any case, the orders or instructions from Leopold himself to Stanley were quite clear. I use Leopold's words here: "The treaties must be as brief as possible, and in a couple of articles must grant us everything." These treaties gave Leopold the ability to put a case forward to have his possession in Central Africa recognized by the other national powers involved in the Scramble. That was really the purpose for doing them.

To establish genuine occupation on the ground, on the other hand, Stanley obviously had more difficult work involved, but began to recruit a service of not just Belgians, but frankly a large army of adventurers, in some cases rogues, I think we could say, who began to man what the Congo Free State called the "stations of the interior." They were backed, of course, by military force, and in this case that force came to be called the *Force Publique*, which, in fact, remained the name for the police and military forces in the country until independence in 1960.

This was a force that meant business. It introduced Congolese to, for instance, one instrument that was known as the *chicotte*. It was a longish whip made of hippopotamus hide and shredded at the end in a sort of corkscrew style. It was used to deliver the corporal punishment that Stanley and his followers utilized effectively to get the resources that they were after.

Rubber is essentially coagulated sap in the wild form. It's now, of course, been replaced first by domesticated production of rubber and, then, obviously comes from petroleum today. But in the wild form, it essentially is available in the rubber trees plentiful in the Congo rainforest, but often up quite high. It's difficult and dangerous work to collect wild rubber. In a lot of respects, the great obstacle here or the great object of the game was to create the labor force that would collect this wild rubber.

Here is where the facts of this matter become rather graphic indeed. In order to get men to ascend the rubber trees and deliver the rubber to the agents of the Congo Free State, essentially the agents took hostages, predominantly women, and in some cases children, usually the wives or relatives of those, and then insisted upon quotas for the delivery of rubber from the related males.

I mentioned the latitude given to the "man on the spot" in colonial administration generally a lecture or two ago. But this was the man on the spot latitude with a vengeance. Failure to meet the assigned quota resulted often in the loss of one's hand, foot, ears, nose, or in some cases, head.

Eventually, whistles began to be blown. One of the most remarkable of these was the African-American journalist, later historian, George Washington Williams, who actually bought into Leopold's project quite a bit. But he went in 1889 to prepare a journalistic report and returned with a bitter open letter, which he published about the king, suggesting that the king had, in fact, been engaging in the slave trade himself internally there.

As Williams said: "His name produces a shudder among these simple folk when mentioned. They remember the broken promises, his copious profanity, his hot temper, his heavy blows, his severe and rigorous measures, by which they were mulcted of their lands."

Williams was followed by others: E.D. Morel, who wrote the book *Red Rubber*; Roger Casement. Eventually what emerged is what you might say is sort of the first international human rights movement. Obviously, the Western world had no objection to colonialism per se at this time, but became so appalled by these excesses that, indeed, this first human rights movement arose. The pressure eventually led to Leopold turning the Congo over to the Belgian government in 1908.

The depopulation from killings—from starvation, from exhaustion, from disease, from plummeting birth rates—was estimated by one scholar (this is Jan Vansina, one of the very senior scholars and formerly a professor at University of Wisconsin). He considered that the Congo's population may have been cut in half between 1880 and 1920. That, in turn, based on later estimates, would mean a loss of population of something on the order of 10 million.

For the next half-century, the Belgians reigned over a generally quiet colony. In fact, the Belgian government delegated a substantial amount of its responsibility. The Catholic Church played a huge role, even greater than missionaries played in other places, not just in education, but certainly in health as well.

The Belgians granted gigantic monopoly concessions over vast regions to private firms. Most importantly, Union Minière held exclusive rights over the colony's most lucrative source: copper from the Katanga region.

At its best, the system represented a reasonably benevolent, though firm, paternalism. Union Minière, for instance, led the way in the "stabilization," so called, of labor and did, indeed, undertake the creation of, in many respects, quite well-run company towns where education, and healthcare, and so forth was available. This was, in a way, the Belgian version of the developmentalist state that we saw in the case of the late French and British empires.

The Belgians, however, were not interested, probably even far less than others, in so-called "troublemaking," and were particularly resistant to the notion of African involvement in politics. As a result, when the winds of African Nationalism began to blow in the 1950s, the Belgians at first cracked down hard and then permitted only the most modest exercises in local elections. Political parties were legalized only in August of 1959.

Then, astonishingly, the Belgians announced in January 1960 that independence would be granted in *six months*. The Belgians had done virtually nothing to prepare the nation for independence. If France and Britain eventually showed a haste to decolonize, Belgium showed something close to panic. The notion that they might be faced for another generation or two with constantly escalating demands and so forth led them to make the political turnover in the hope, as we've seen before, of retaining as much of the economic possibilities as they could.

Given the size and the diversity of a country with less than a dozen university graduates in 1960, what followed was perhaps predictable. The first person elected in these hastily organized elections was a former clerk named Patrice Lumumba. Lumumba was, in many respects, a radical. He voiced a vision of a genuine revolutionary sort. As you might imagine, this did not endear him to either the departing Belgians or those in the West.

The context we must introduce here, of course, is the Cold War. The year 1960 is in the heart of this epochal competition between the Western bloc and the old Soviet Union bloc, of course, for influence all over the world. Eventually, both the Soviet Union and Western powers, including the United States, would install, or support, or back up, or give aid to leadership leading to situations that can hardly be called admirable.

The first proverb I ever learned out of Africa was something like this: "When two elephants fight, it's the grass beneath the feet that suffers." It was directly put forward in reference to the Cold War.

Lumumba immediately faced crises. The army mutinied within the first two weeks when the old Belgian officer wrote on a blackboard in front of them: "Before independence = after independence." In other words, "We're going to continue to have Belgian officers," and so forth. The younger members of that army wanted promotions and wanted to see the fruits of this hastily arranged independence immediately, and Lumumba was faced with a crisis.

Soon enough, the Katanga, the copper-bearing region in the far south, declared its independence—again, in this case, with quite direct Belgian support—the landing of official Belgian troops—to try to break away from the Congo. They were supported by numerous mercenaries drawn from South Africa and Southern Rhodesia.

Certainly, the attitudes and ideologies of Lumumba, as I said, earned him the enmity of not just the Belgians, but the Americans. These were amply documented in the church hearings between 1975 and 1978 on the Central Intelligence Agency. President Eisenhower, for instance, is reported at one meeting after a briefing asking if, "We can't get rid of this guy?"

The Belgian foreign minister, in a document unearthed later, said that: "Responsible authorities had the duty to render Lumumba harmless."

Eventually, the triggers are pulled by Congolese themselves, given the support of the external powers. Lumumba was assassinated in early 1961 after something like six months in office.

There ensued a half-decade of incredibly complex chaos. If you lived through the early 1960s, the headlines each day seemed to be a kind of revolving door of movements, and secessions, and interventions, and different leadership, and so forth. Behind the scenes, though, a shrewd, young army officer originally known as Joseph Désiré Mobutu was consolidating his power. He visited Washington and actually met with President Kennedy in 1963.

In November of 1965, he pulled off a bloodless coup d'état. Thus began 32 years, no less, of Mobutu's regime. We asked in the last lecture what Africa's new rulers would do with their power, and we will see that the answers to that are variable and changeable. In Mobutu's case, the answers are clear and disheartening.

Internally, Mobutu is quite prepared to hammer any opposition, but he also—again, a man of great intelligence and political skill—is rewarding allies and buying off rivals—adept at both the carrot and the stick.

Internationally, he played the geopolitical game very cleverly again, adroitly positioning himself as a friend of the West to keep the Cold War-era aid coming. He developed a cult of his own personality. He, in fact, dropped the Joseph Désiré to his name and became known officially as—listen for all of it—Mobutu Sese Seko Koko Ngbendu Wa Za Banga, meaning "the all-conquering warrior who triumphs over all obstacles." An alternative translation that I actually think is more accurate is, "The strutting rooster who covers all the hens, going from battle to battle, leaving enemies in his wake."

Above all, Mobutu lined his pocket on a colossal scale, becoming literally one of the richest men in the world—a fortune estimated at certainly over $4 billion. Most of the wealth wound up in European banks and real estate.

Eventually, the center could not hold. The corruption at the top percolated to every level of Congolese society. Mobutu had become, by the 1990s, something of a caricature, even an embarrassment to his Western supporters. "Zaïre" (as he had renamed the country) I would say essentially ceased to exist by the 1990s.

A rebellion launched from the east in 1997, again with some external participation, in this case by neighboring African countries, quickly drove him into exile, and he died shortly thereafter.

Since Mobutu's fall, alas, things are little better: a major civil war, complicated by spillover from Rwanda and Rwanda's genocide in 1994. Another Great Lakes country has festered. Congo has always been a target for external interest because of its enormous mineral resources in things like copper, diamond, and, these days, in coltan, a crucial element that is found, for instance, in every cell phone. I don't have to tell you how strategic that has become in the last decade or so.

In fact, in the civil war that has emerged in the Congo in the 1990s and essentially continues off and on with sporadic cease fires and breakdowns again, there are numerous nations that have forces inside the Congo, including at least five other African nations. We have, in a sort of perverse sense here, a kind of perverse rendition of the era of Leopold and of the Scramble.

As you might imagine, over the years I've had a great number of students in my ordinary undergraduate classes from Africa. As you might imagine, I rely on them. I turn to them. I ask them to supplement my obviously limited knowledge. I often ask them to give presentations about their country.

I have to say, the only ones I've ever seen break down in tears for their home countries are the students who have begun to tell their fellow students about the Congo. Let us hope that the next generation brings better times.

Lecture Twenty-Six
Segregation to Apartheid in South Africa

Scope:

We last touched South Africa at a stage where colonial conquest was complete, the country unified, and mining-based modernization well underway in a context of white supremacy: the age of segregation. In the years following World War II, when the sun began to set on European colonial rule in much of Africa and on America's own version of segregation, South Africa moved in the opposite direction. When the Afrikaner National Party came to power in 1948, it took numerous bold steps to entrench and intensify white supremacy— forever—though not without challenge, of course. Such leaders as Nelson Mandela organized incessantly for the rights of the black majority. All such efforts were crushed ruthlessly, and by 1960, Mandela and others concluded that armed revolution was the only course. In 1964, Mandela was given a life sentence. White supremacy was in the saddle. What combination of forces would end it?

Outline

I. In the years following the Second World War, when other parts of the world, such as the French and British colonies in Africa and the United States, began to move with some seriousness toward racial equality, the country of South Africa moved, with great seriousness, in the opposite direction. We can call this the transition from segregation to *apartheid*—a word from Afrikaans meaning literally "apartness," a word I am sure you have heard many times. It was apartheid, of course, that made South Africa notorious in the later 20th century.

II. Let us begin by offering what may be a rather different perspective on segregation. I will rely largely on the work— brilliant work, in my view, certainly stimulating—of the late John Cell.

    A. Cell, a son of the American South himself, wondered why systems called segregation emerged in the United States and in South Africa at about the same time—the early 20th century. The word did not exist before then.

B. Like me, and like many of you perhaps, Cell assumed that segregation—what he called the "highest stage of white supremacy"—was the product of a rural past, created by ignorant, backward people, the opposite of progressive. Modernization, development was fundamentally at odds with such irrationality and would gradually erode segregation.

C. His research and his reading—especially of a younger generation of South African historians—led him in a quite different direction. Cell began to conclude that segregation was not a throwback, a leftover from a frontier past but, rather, a response—an innovative, even creative response— to conditions of turbulent change: the onset of substantial urbanization and industrialization, in both South Africa and the U.S. South.

D. Segregation, then, represented the *modernization of white supremacy*. Racial discrimination was not necessarily incompatible with overall economic development; indeed, it might actually contribute to growth—through the creation of a cheap supply of labor, for instance. There was certainly separation in numerous spheres, but at the macro-level, the societies were actually becoming more, not less, intertwined—integrated, if you like.

E. In the South African case, the racial pillars of the segregated society—a society increasingly driven by an urban, industrial dynamic—were a radically unequal division of land, a resultant cheap migrant labor system, and a white monopoly on political power, symbolized by the voting franchise.

III. What, then, was the significance of the move from segregation to apartheid?

A. It is common to refer to the South African election of 1948, which brought the "purified" Afrikaner Nationalist Party to power and marks the onset of apartheid, as a "watershed" in South African history. I do not accept the metaphor.

B. The notion of the watershed is based on the assertion that the "water"—events, ideas, history—is running in a fundamentally different direction on one side of the divide compared to the other side.

1. But the trend in South Africa after 1948 was not fundamentally different from the trend before that date, as evidenced in a speech by Jan Smuts, prime minister of South Africa in 1919 and again in 1939.

2. The pillars of apartheid—land, labor, and power—were the same as the pillars of segregation, and they had been solidly erected in the segregation era.

C. What was different was the deadly serious effort by South Africa's apartheid-era rulers to intensify every form of racial discrimination and, most important, in my view, to make white supremacy *permanent*. It was a project to seal off the future, to craft a "final solution" (I realize the gravity of the term) to the country's "racial problem."

1. To this end, the National Party government passed an avalanche of new legislation in the 1950s, designed to regulate every aspect of race relations: Miscegenation and intermarriage were outlawed; total separation in every form of public amenity and in urban residential areas was enforced.

2. "Bantu education" emasculated the mission-based but open-ended schooling available to blacks and imposed what one critic called "education for servitude."

3. Under Prime Ministers Verwoerd (1958–1966, considered the system's greatest theorist) and Vorster (1966–1978), the government pursued its vision of "grand apartheid."

   a. Each of South Africa's 10 major Bantu ethnic groups (Zulu, Xhosa, Venda, and so on) would ultimately find its political destiny in its own "homeland," its portion of the land set aside as "reserves" for blacks in the land laws of 1913 and 1936.

   b. This was "divide and rule" with a vengeance. There was to be no common political future.

      c. Given that all 10 homelands combined constituted 13 percent of South Africa's total land area, designed in theory to accommodate 75 percent of the population, there was, in fact, no possibility that all the "tribes people" assigned to a given homeland could actually make a living there; they would have to continue to migrate and work in white South Africa.

      d. The architects of apartheid, therefore, never entertained the notion of ending their dependence on black labor. This was not true and total separation but an elaboration on continued *unequal integration.*

IV. Needless to say, South Africa's nonwhite population (blacks, "coloureds," and Asians) did not take all this lying down.

  A. A new generation of black activists, coming of age in the 1940s and 1950s, injected a new strain of militancy and—understandably, as apartheid set in—urgency to protests in the name of equality. Within the African National Congress (ANC), founded in 1912 as the petitioning organ of the elite, this change was symbolized by the mass-party but nonviolent vision of the Youth League and one of its founders, Nelson Mandela.

  B. Throughout the 1950s, these activists constantly escalated their own campaigns in response to the government's measures. In 1955, the ANC and allied organizations adopted the Freedom Charter, a virtual constitution for a future nonracial, egalitarian South Africa.

  C. The dialectic of move/countermove on both sides reached a climax at Sharpeville, south of Johannesburg, in 1960.

      1. Police opened fire on unarmed protestors of the hated "pass laws," which required that Africans carry booklets documenting their right to be and/or work in an urban area. In all, 69 protesters were shot dead.

      2. In the aftermath, the government took off its gloves, banning the ANC and many other movements and moving to detention without trial.

  D. For their part, Mandela and his peers concluded that they had "closed a chapter" on the question of nonviolence and that armed struggle was now the only option left to them.

E. After some initial successes in a sabotage campaign, Mandela and other top leaders were caught, tried for treason, and sentenced to life in prison in 1964.

V. White supremacy seemed securely in the saddle. Indeed, the rest of the 1960s and early 1970s were eerily quiet. Economically, South Africa prospered as never before, demonstrating again, perhaps, that racial oppression could be quite compatible with "development."

Suggested Reading:

John Cell, *The Highest Stage of White Supremacy: The Origins of Segregation in South Africa and the American South.*

George Fredrickson, *Black Liberation: A Comparative History of Black Ideologies in the United States and South Africa*, chapter 6.

George Fredrickson, *White Supremacy: A Comparative Study in American and South African History*, chapters V–VI.

Nelson Mandela, *Long Walk to Freedom: The Autobiography of Nelson Mandela*, parts 1–7.

Leonard Thompson, *A History of South Africa*, chapters 5–6.

Questions to Consider:

1. What does the term *segregation* mean? Why wasn't it simply *separation*?

2. What is the significance of the 1948 elections in South Africa?

Lecture Twenty-Six—Transcript
Segregation to Apartheid in South Africa

Hello. The history of the Congo, which we surveyed in the last lecture, seems to represent some of the great themes of 20th-century African history in magnified form and in inversions writ large—themes like colonial conquest, the realities of colonial rule, decolonization, and the disappointments of independence.

In this lecture, we're going to turn to a different case altogether—a country whose history in the 20th century seems to run at a quite different trajectory. We know that even before the 20th century, South Africa's history was exceptional in Africa, especially in the very early establishment of substantial European (that is, Dutch and British) settlement and a subsequent frontier history quite reminiscent of that of the United States.

We last touched South Africa at a stage where colonial conquest was complete, the country unified, and mining-based modernization well underway in a context of white supremacy. This was the beginnings of what we can call today "the age of segregation."

To move slightly forward, in the years following the Second World War, when the sun began to set on colonial rule in places like the French and British empires in Africa, and when the colonies of the French and the British along with other parts of the world like the United States began to move with some seriousness towards an end to formalized white supremacy, the country of South Africa moved with great seriousness in the opposite direction.

We can call this the transition from segregation to "apartheid." It's a word from Afrikaans literally meaning "apartness." I'm sure that you've seen it and heard it many times, often pronounced "apar-thide" or what have you—technically "apar-tate." But, in any case, it was apartheid, of course, that made South Africa notorious and eventually something of an international pariah in the late 20th century.

Let me turn back a bit and begin by offering what may be a rather different perspective on segregation, at least one that I think you may find stimulating. I will rely here largely on the work—in my view brilliant work—of the late John Cell and, in particular, his book entitled *The Highest Stage of White Supremacy: The Origins of Segregation in South Africa and the American South*. It's a work of comparative history.

Let me confess here to a certain personal bias. John Cell was my teacher at my undergraduate institution and the supervisor of my senior thesis, etc. He certainly remained my friend, teacher, and critic (believe me, he could be a critic) until his unfortunate and premature death in 2001.

It turns out that I have a more direct connection with Cell, which I hope will also have some relevance here. I teach at North Carolina State University, and if you go two floors up in my building (I didn't know this until I took the job there), you will find a library that says: "The John W. Cell Memorial Library." Now it is, in fact, not created in honor of the man I'm drawing on today—his work—but that of his father, who was a mathematics professor for 30 years or so at North Carolina State.

Here's where I think this may have some relevance. My point is simply that Cell grew up in Raleigh, North Carolina. He grew up in the American South. He was a son of the South. He grew up during the age when segregation went from being very much in the saddle, of course, to being dismantled, certainly in the legal sense. He himself was a historian predominantly of British colonial administration, but he found himself, partly because of his own background, to the subjects that I mentioned in the title of his book.

Even as a young man, Cell was questioning things. He was a fine athlete and at one point in the 1950s, he found himself playing for the high school basketball championship in North Carolina against a team—I have to mention this—that included Sonny Jurgensen. The reason I have to mention this is because I grew up in Northern Virginia, and I'm quite fond of the Washington football team. But even then, after they had lost to Jurgensen's team, Cell was asking himself, at least in his reminiscences to me, why it was that the high school champions, so called, of North Carolina were the winners, of course, of games played entirely by white North Carolina high school students.

He wondered then about segregation because he grew up in it and because he had the kind of mind that wondered and was curious about a lot of things. He wondered first of all, before he began this study, about the word itself. The word "segregation" does not appear in dictionaries, for instance, before approximately the first decade of the 20th century. It's a new coinage, in other words, and that struck Cell as slightly curious. He wondered why it emerged not only at that time but particularly, some would say almost exclusively, in two great places—in two particular places: in the American South and in the newly formed country of South Africa.

Cell had assumed, growing up and even later, like I had assumed, like perhaps many of you had assumed, that segregation—what he called the "highest stage of white supremacy"—was the product of a rural past created by ignorant, backward people, if you like—that it was the legacy left behind by slavery and by that frontier past—that it was the opposite of anything like progress—the opposite of progressive. Modernization, development, and progress were fundamentally at odds with such irrationality, so the arguments seemed to him, and would gradually erode segregation. Indeed, these were the arguments made by liberals, if you will, in both South Africa and in the United States in the early to mid years of the 20th century.

His research and his reading, particularly his reading of a younger generation of South African historians beginning to publish their material in the very late '60s into the '70s and the '80s—his research in reading led him in a quite different direction. Cell began to conclude that segregation was not after all just a throwback—a leftover from a frontier past—but rather a response—indeed an innovative, even creative, response—to conditions of turbulent social, economic, and political change, spurred in both cases—in both the South African case and the southern American case—by the onset of substantial urbanization and industrialization.

Again, I don't want to suggest that Cell overstated this. He states quite clearly in the first pages of the book that it was the ideology of white supremacy—of white racism, if you like—that was the driving force of segregation, but he wondered why it didn't result in other kinds of alternatives that might have been entertained after the ending of slavery, for instance, such as deportation. At one point, he even wondered about genocide. When his editors, he told me, questioned that this was really not remotely conceivable in the case of the U.S. case, for instance, he had an answer I think born from the 20th century. That was, "How many did Hitler kill?"

In other words, segregation represented one path that white supremacy might take. It was his discovery that it seems to emerge and be identified not so much with these cultural atavisms—with these throwbacks, these leftovers—but rather with the emergence of cities and the emergence of factories, with modern infrastructure, and even with progressive politics in many cases.

Segregation then, he concluded, represented, in a nutshell, the modernization of white supremacy. Racial discrimination was not necessarily incompatible—it was not necessarily any irrationality that would be eroded by economic development—not incompatible with that. Indeed, it might actually contribute to economic growth and development (and this was an idea that he definitely did take from the South African scholars I mentioned a moment ago), for instance through the creation of an inexpensive supply of labor as a factor fueling economic growth and development at the macro level.

Segregation, of course, often taken to be separation, again he asked himself, and I ask you to ask yourselves why it is that there was a coinage of a different word, then, if it was simply separation. Now, don't get me wrong or get Cell wrong. There was obviously separation in many and numerous spheres. There was clearly separation in legal ownership of land, in residential life, in education, and so on.

But his argument is that, again, at the macro-level, in the overall view of these societies in the stages of history that they were going through, these societies were actually being knit together more closely than they had been in the past. They were becoming more, not less, intertwined—that there were greater levels of mutual dependency, particularly in South Africa perhaps, with its dependence on labor, than had been the case in the past. More intertwined—more (if I can use the word) "integrated," if you like— but integrated unequally.

He asked us to think of segregation, then, as unequal integration. At one point, he puts it this way: If the groups that compose these societies were truly separate, if they really lived their lives apart, if economy and society were truly plural or dual, then there would be no need for segregation.

In the South African case, the racial pillars of the segregated society—a society, again, in the aftermath of the discoveries of gold and diamonds—a society increasingly driven by an urban industrial dynamic—the racial pillars were, I would suggest, three. There was a radically unequal division of land, yes, and that is a form of separation, but what flows from that? The second pillar is a resultant low-wage, migrant labor system, which we examined in Lecture Eighteen. The necessity for oscillating migrancy out of the limited amounts of space and land reserved under the segregation division of land (the land laws in South Africa of 1913 and 1936, for instance)—the resultant cheap labor migrancy system is a direct consequence of that division of land.

The third pillar, of course, is a white monopoly on political power, again, in the constitution of 1910, although in a couple of exceptional cases—in the old Cape Colony, now part of this unified country—they still had a color-blind franchise. That was not the case in the other provinces of South Africa, except very theoretically in Natal. In the Orange Free State and in the Transvaal, there was a straightforward racial exclusion on voting.

Even if you could vote for members of parliament, let's say, and you were an African or a so-called "coloured" (and a few could for a number of years still, based on income, education, and so forth), you could vote only for white candidates. Again, by law in that 1910 constitution, all members of parliament were required to be white.

Three pillars of segregation: the unequal division of land, the migrant labor system, and the white monopoly on political power.

If that's the case of segregation, or if that is a capsule characterization of segregation, what then is the significance of the move from segregation to apartheid? The shift is usually marked with the South African election of 1948, which brought the so-called "purified" Afrikaner Nationalist Party to power and marks the onset of apartheid, as the official policy of the Union of South Africa.

It is common to refer to that election of 1948 and to that year of 1948, in many analyses I have heard and read, as a "watershed" in

South African history. I do not accept the watershed metaphor. After all, the watershed metaphor is based on the assertion that the "water," if you like—that is, events, ideas, the tide of history, trends—call it what you like—that the water in those senses is running in a fundamentally different direction on one side of the divide compared to the other. It's obviously an image drawn from geography, and ridges, and watersheds, and so forth. So, again, the notion of a watershed: that the tide of history, events, or ideas running in fundamentally one direction on one side of the watershed event, or year, or marker, and running in a fundamentally different way on the other.

But I would argue that the trend in South Africa after 1948 was not fundamentally different from before that time. The pillars of apartheid—the land, labor, and power features I just mentioned—were the same pillars of segregation and had been solidly erected in the segregation era. I would like to try to demonstrate that by going back to the segregation era to a speech by Jan Christian Smuts, who was the loser in the 1948 election—that is, he lost to those who were interested in imposing apartheid.

But this is a speech that Smuts made long, long ago. Smuts had a very long and distinguished career. He first made a name fighting the British in the Boer War back in 1899 to 1902. He went on to become a distinguished philosopher of science and eventually a world statesman. This was from a speech he made in 1917 in London while on a visit there. He outlined the future South Africa towards which they were working.

His words: "You will have large areas cultivated by blacks and governed by blacks, where they will look after themselves in all their forms of living and development, while in the rest of the country, you will have your white communities, which will govern themselves separately according to the accepted European principles. The natives will, of course, be free to go and work in the white areas, but, as far as possible, the administration in white and black areas will be separated such that each will be satisfied and developed according to its own proper lines."

This notion of development along your own lines is very typical of the language of segregation. But, of course, the crucial sentence there is: "The natives will, of course, be free to go and work in the white areas." By the million! These were societies that were becoming more interdependent, more intertwined, and again, at the macro level, being integrated, although obviously unequally.

Cell commented that not even Dr. Hendrik Verwoerd, who was considered the great theorist of apartheid in the 1950s and 1960s, really improved upon General Smuts's formulation.

So, I think that the pillars are there. We can ask, then, what is the significance of 1948? I would say that what *was* different was the deadly serious effort by South Africa's new rulers to intensify every form of racial discrimination, but more important—in my view, most important—to make white supremacy permanent. This was a project to seal off the future, as it were—to craft a "final solution." I'm aware of the gravity of that term, "final solution." I'm obviously not discussing genocide here. Again, that's not the name of the game here under segregation or apartheid in anything like the literal sense, precisely because of the mutual dependency. But I do mean it was intended to seal off the future and to create a final bearing—a set of final parameters, if you like—in which South African life and history would go forward.

To these ends, the National Party government passed an avalanche of new legislation in the 1950s, designed to regulate every aspect of race relations. Miscegenation and intermarriage were outlawed. There was to be total separation of every form of public amenity and in urban residential areas. So, this is the era when the park benches begin to be painted over, or the signs pointing people to toilets or the water fountains, let alone the buses, restaurants, etc., with literally "whites only" ("*blankes* only" in Afrikaans), or "*nie-blankes* (non-whites) only," "Bantu, coloured, and Asian only": This is the apartheid of the signs—that is, what some analysts call "petty apartheid." Not that it's unimportant, although its importance is less than what I'll call "grand apartheid" in a moment.

In the education sphere, so-called "Bantu education" under the new rulers in the 1950s emasculated the admission-based but quite open-ended—that is, no ceiling for the rise of black students under those admission-based systems—emasculated that schooling available to blacks and imposed what one critic, Trevor Huddleston, the Anglican bishop during the 1950s, called "education for servitude."

Prime Minister Verwoerd served from 1958 to 1966, when he was assassinated, actually, dramatically by a stabbing in parliament by a deranged white. It seemed to have very little to do with his politics. Under the great theorist Verwoerd and under his successor, J.B. Vorster, who ruled from 1966-1978, the government pursued its vision of grand apartheid. Each of South Africa's 10 major Bantu ethnic groups, or "tribes," if you like—the Zulu, the Xhosa, the Venda, the Ndebele, etc.—would ultimately find its political destiny in its own "homeland"—that is, its portion of the land originally set aside for "reserves" for blacks in the land laws of 1913 and 1936. The terminology here went from "reserves," to so-called "Bantustans," and ultimately to "homelands."

Again, you can hear the echoes there from Smuts's formulation much, much earlier of the ultimate political destiny being devolved away from South Africa proper into these homelands. Indeed, four of the homelands eventually were declared to be independent by the South African government. No other country in the world recognized them, but South Africans literally lost their citizenship, including millions of people who had never actually seen the homelands because they and their parents and grandparents had lived in the cities.

This was "divide and rule" with a vengeance. Again, I repeat: There was to be no common political future. Since all 10 homelands combined constituted only 13% of South Africa's total land area, designed in theory to accommodate 75% of the population, there was, in fact, no actual possibility that all of the "tribes people" (so-called) assigned to a given homeland could actually make a living there. They would need to continue to migrate and work in so-called "white South Africa." The architects of apartheid, therefore, never entertained the notion of ending their dependence on black labor. This was not true total separation, but an elaboration on continued *unequal integration*.

Needless to say, South Africa's non-white population (the so-called blacks, so-called "coloureds," and Asians) did not take all of this lying down. A new generation of black activists, coming of age in the 1940s and 1950s, injected a new strain of militance and—understandably, as apartheid set in—a new tone of urgency to protests in the name of equality.

Within the African National Congress, which had been founded way back in 1912 and was part of that first generation of petitioning, elite style of protests—within the ANC, this change was symbolized by the mass party but non-violent vision of the Youth League and of one of its founders. At this point, I'd like to quote Mandela speaking of this point of his life when he became politicized at some length. This is from his autobiography. He says:

> I cannot pinpoint a moment when I became politicized, when I knew that I would spend my life in the liberation struggle. To be an African in South Africa means that one is politicized from the moment of one's birth whether one acknowledges it or not. An African child is born in an "Africans only" hospital, taken home in an "Africans only" bus, lives in an "Africans only" area, and attends "Africans only" schools, if he attends schools at all.

> When he grows up, he can hold "Africans only" jobs, rent a house in "Africans only" townships, ride "Africans only" trains, and be stopped at any time of the day or night and be ordered to produce a pass, failing which he will be arrested and thrown in jail. His life is circumscribed by racist laws and regulations that cripple his growth, dim his potential, and stunt his life.

> This was the reality, and one could deal with it in myriad ways. I had no epiphany, no singular revelation, no moment of truth, but a steady accumulation of a thousand slights, a thousand indignities. A thousand unremembered moments produced in me an anger, a rebelliousness, a desire to fight the system that imprisoned my people. There was no particular day on which I said, "From henceforth I will devote myself to the liberation of my people." Instead, I simply found myself doing so and could not do otherwise.

Throughout the 1950s, these activists constantly escalated their own campaigns in response to the government measures. They had names like "The Program of Action" and "The Defiance Campaign." In 1955, the ANC and allied organizations adopted the Freedom Charter, a virtual constitution for a future non-racial, egalitarian South Africa.

The dialectic going on here of move and countermove—government moves, protesters' response; opposition moves, government response; and so on—this dialectic reached a climax at a place called Sharpeville, south of Johannesburg in 1960, where police opened fire on unarmed protesters of the hated "pass laws" (this was the identity booklet that all South Africans had to carry, giving them the right to be in a city, for instance, or not). They opened fire and shot 69 dead, many of them in the back.

In the aftermath, the government took all gloves off, banning the ANC and many other movements: the PAC, the Communist Party, and so on. They moved with a great deal of firmness towards tactics they had not utilized before: detention without trial, increasing use of interrogation involving torture, and so on.

For their part, Mandela and his peers concluded that they had "closed a chapter" on the question of non-violence. Indeed, I'll turn again to his own explanation of this. He said: "[They] had come to the conclusion that as violence in this country was inevitable, it would be unrealistic and wrong for African leaders to continue preaching peace and non-violence at a time when the government met our peaceful demands with force. This conclusion was not easily arrived at. It was only when all else had failed—when all channels of peaceful protest had been barred to us—that the decision was made to embark on violent forms of political struggle and to form *Umkhonto we Sizwe*.

Umkhonto we Sizwe means "the Spear of the Nation" ("MK" for short in its abbreviations). *Umkhonto we Sizwe* became the military arm—the military wing, if you like—of the ANC from the early 1960s on. This obviously represented a very sharp turn, indeed, for that historic organization.

There was now, then, a very thorough-going polarization in South Africa. The notion that non-violent, or constitutional, or peaceful avenues of protest might get anywhere seemed to have reached a dead end. Again, both sides shift their tactics and their strategies quite dramatically at this turning point around 1960 or so. Again, compare that with what's going on in so much of Africa to the north around 1960 or so—polarization.

After some initial successes and a sabotage campaign, Mandela and other top leaders were caught, tried for treason, and sentenced to life in 1964. Again, I'm just quoting, one more time, his statement at the time of his sentencing:

> During my lifetime, I have dedicated myself to this struggle of the African people. I have fought against white domination, and I have fought against black domination. I have cherished the ideal of a democratic and free society in which all persons live together in harmony and with equal opportunities. It is an ideal which I hope to live for and to achieve. But if needs be, it is an ideal for which I am prepared to die.

In fact, it was very possible that he and his fellow ANC members on trial could have been sentenced to death.

With the imprisonment of Mandela and others, with the banning of the ANC, and so on, white supremacy seemed securely in the saddle. Indeed, in the rest of the 1960s and 1970s, things were eerily quiet. I started this with a comparison between the United States and South Africa, but if you compare them in the late 1960s and early 1970s, they're completely different. There's the era of very strident protest, for instance, in the U.S. and very little upfront in South Africa.

Economically, South Africa prospered as never before, demonstrating again, perhaps, that racial oppression could be quite compatible with economic growth and one form of "development." Thank you.

Lecture Twenty-Seven
The Armed Struggles for Independence

Scope:

South Africa's descent into the rigid white supremacy of apartheid suggested that the "winds of change" sweeping Africa were perhaps not, after all, irresistible. And South Africa was not alone. The most critical difference among various colonies was the size and entrenchment of permanent European settlement. Settlers had something quite tangible to defend—a lifestyle almost always superior to what they could have enjoyed back in Europe—and they were prepared to fight for it. That, in turn, impelled African nationalists to take up arms themselves. One example was Southern Rhodesia (now Zimbabwe), where whites declared themselves independent of the British Empire and where a bitter liberation war raged all through the 1970s. In Angola and Mozambique, Portugal, lacking the economic muscle of a Britain or France, held on desperately in support of its colonial settlers against multiple armed African movements. The scars from these conflicts have been slow to heal.

Outline

I.   The case of South Africa, which we surveyed in the last lecture, demonstrates that the "winds of change" sweeping Africa in the 1950s and 1960s were not, in the shorter run at least, irresistible. South Africa was not alone. The march of majority-rule independence, beginning in West Africa, moving east, then wheeling south, came to a halt—the Zambezi River might serve as symbolic barrier.

II. All of the African territories that resisted rule by Africans were what we have defined as settler colonies—those where substantial numbers of Europeans came to take up land and livelihoods, with the expectation that they and their descendants would stay.

III. It should hardly surprise us that most settlers had little sympathy for majority rule.

A. Typically, they enjoyed a far better lifestyle than they could have dreamed of back in the metropole. The garden, the verandah, the pool, and maybe best of all, the servants, were all possible, even for the artisanal, let alone the middle classes.

B. Thus they felt they had something to hold on to. And, increasingly, they believed that, in the face of African demands, they—or their metropolitan sponsors—would have to fight for it.

IV. The territories of Angola and Mozambique were, of course, settler colonies. But they were also the colonies of Portugal, and this made a difference.

A. Under such dictatorial leaders as António de Oliveira Salazar, Portugal felt no commitment to the virtues of democracy.

B. Portugal was itself a poor country, and this meant that, unlike England or France (or even Belgium), Portugal did not have the benefit of what Nkrumah of Ghana called the "neocolonial option": that is, to go ahead and grant independence and depend on your economic power to obtain what you want from your former colonies.

C. Thus, Portugal concluded that it could not relinquish, or even loosen, the reins on its colonies in response to African nationalism. Lose the empire, this line of thought went, and you lose everything. Needless to say, Portuguese settlers concurred.

D. Nascent African political movements were, therefore, crushed, and early on, in the 1960s, the nationalists took up arms against colonist and settler.

E. Rather like the Belgian Congo, these places were huge territories, parceled out to concessionaires and containing a multitude of ethnicities with little in common except their suffering.

    1. In light of this, it is slightly surprising that in Mozambique a single liberation movement, FRELIMO, dominated the struggle.

    2. Not so in Angola, where three armed movements emerged, each with its own ethnic base.

      a. In the north, there was the Frente Nacional de Libertação de Angola, called the FNLA, led by Holden Roberto. It was based on the Congo ethnicity.

      b. The Movimento Popular de Libertação de Angola, called the MPLA, was based around the capital city of Luanda and in the central belt and drew ethnically on the Kimbundu (or Mbundu) peoples, as well as on *assimilados* and *mestizos*. This was the most avowedly radical and Marxist of the movements.

      c. Based in the central highlands, the eastern portions of the country, and in the south was the UNITA movement (União Nacional para a Independência Total de Angola), led by the charismatic figure Jonas Savimbi. The ethnic base here was the Ovimbundu people.

F. More than a decade of war ensued in both countries. By 1974, young Portuguese military officers had decided the wars were endless and unwinnable and that Portugal's future lay in Europe; they staged a coup in Portugal itself and quickly moved to end more than 400 years of Portuguese colonialism.

    1. In Mozambique, the transition went quite smoothly. FRELIMO was the clear heir apparent and came to power under the charismatic socialist Samora Machel.

    2. Again, the transition did not go so smoothly in Angola. As independence day approached, a veritable free-for-all broke out, with several foreign powers—South Africa, Cuba, the United States—backing their favored movements. The socialist MPLA came out on top, but its position was exceedingly shaky.

G. Alas, in neither country did independence signal the end of conflict.

    1. Remember that apartheid South Africa had regarded the Portuguese colonies as buffers against the southward tide of majority rule. If anything, the Portuguese exit prompted much greater South African intervention.

    2. In Mozambique, a movement that drew support both ethnically and from resentment over radical FRELIMO measures quickly got South African backing as well.

After a further decade of war and the end of South African participation after 1990, the sides negotiated a settlement. Since then, Mozambique has forged a rather remarkable recovery and is often cited as one of Africa's success stories today.

3. Angola, once again, was left considerably worse. With hardly a break after independence in 1975, civil war continued for another quarter-century; there are many Angolans today who have *never* known peace until the last couple of years. Perhaps Mozambique will prove an inspiration.

V. Let us turn to Southern Rhodesia, now Zimbabwe.

   A. From 1953 to 1963, Southern Rhodesia had been joined with Northern Rhodesia and Nyasaland (now Zambia and Malawi) in the Central African Federation.

   1. The Federation experiment, driven by the region's white settlers (most of whom were in Southern Rhodesia), created an economically advantageous bloc and advertised itself as an alternative to either majority rule to the north or rigid apartheid to the south.

   2. It is fair to say that most Africans saw the Federation's "partnership" policy, however, as moderated white supremacy.

   B. The Federation foundered on the shoals of African nationalism. The British acceded to African demands and granted independence to Malawi in 1963 and Zambia in 1964.

   C. Southern Rhodesia's settlers had other ideas. Led by the redoubtable Ian Smith, they declared independence from Britain in 1965.

   D. Soon, both major African nationalist parties, the Zimbabwe African National Union (ZANU) and the Zimbabwe African Peoples' Union (ZAPU), which had different ethnic bases, were banned and the leadership was imprisoned or exiled.

   1. For a time, Smith enjoyed a honeymoon, but a genuine guerilla war developed in the early 1970s.

   2. The war picked up steam after 1975, when the ZANU was able to begin using bases in adjoining and now-independent Mozambique.

E. The two liberation movements forged a paper alliance, the Patriotic Front, but never cooperated. After a vicious war resulting in 30,000 dead and a million refugees, Smith negotiated an agreement permitting an open election.

F. To the surprise of some, ZANU won an impressive victory, and its leader, Robert Mugabe, assumed the presidency of what was now Zimbabwe, where he remains today. We will continue Zimbabwe's story in Lecture Thirty-Five.

VI. Finally, we must mention South West Africa, now Namibia. South Africa had run the place since the German defeat in 1918.

A. Not surprisingly, a protracted, low-level liberation war developed in this largely empty land as well.

B. The United Nations, which considered South Africa's occupation illegal, supervised elections leading to independence in 1990, but there is no doubt that the change was mostly due to the dramatic changes unfolding by that time in South Africa itself.

VII. All these former settler colonies eventually won their independence. But the scars left by their struggles run particularly deep, as we shall see in our later discussion of Zimbabwe's current crisis.

Suggested Reading:

Frederick Cooper, *Africa since 1940: The Past of the Present*, chapter 6.

Martin Meredith, *The Past Is Another Country: Rhodesia, UDI to Independence*.

William Minter, *King Solomon's Mines Revisited: Western Interests and the Burdened History of Southern Africa*, chapters 7–8.

Questions to Consider:

1. "Mozambique and Angola had the misfortune to be colonized by one of Europe's poorest empires," wrote author Frederick Cooper. Why was this a "misfortune"?

2. America's 13 colonies were, like Southern Rhodesia, possessions of the British Empire. How would you compare the American and the Rhodesian declarations of independence?

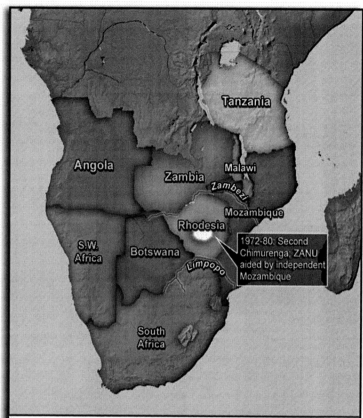

Tanzania

Angola

Zambia

Malawi

Zambezi

Mozambique

Rhodesia

1972-80: Second Chimurenga; ZANU aided by independent Mozambique

S.W. Africa

Botswana

Limpopo

South Africa

Regional Conflicts in Africa, 1970s

Before the abrupt abdication of colonial rule by Portugal in 1974, both Angola and Mozambique were battlegrounds for liberation wars that drew other parties into the conflict. Cuba and South Africa backed various sides in the Angolan War, and South Africa also interfered in Mozambique. Upon independence, Mozambique assisted guerillas in Rhodesia. Zambia's Kenneth Kaunda also provided bases for ZAPU (and for a time ZANU), drawing retaliatory airstrikes from Ian Smith's Rhodesian government. Even Tanzania played a role as the sole rail route for copper out of Zambia not blockaded ran through that country.

Lecture Twenty-Seven—Transcript
The Armed Struggles for Independence

Welcome. The case of South Africa, which we examined in the last lecture, demonstrates that the "winds of change" sweeping Africa in the 1950s and 1960s were not, after all, irresistible, at least in the shorter, or even medium, run.

South Africa was not alone. The march of majority rule independence beginning in West Africa, moving east, then eventually wheeling south, came to a halt. The Zambezi River might serve as a symbolic barrier. As we mentioned in Lecture Twenty-Four, the Zambezi separating Northern Rhodesia from Southern Rhodesia, Zambia becoming independent under African rule in 1964, and Southern Rhodesia pursuing a very different course as we will describe in a few minutes.

Virtually all of the African territories that resisted rule by Africans were what we have defined as "settler colonies"—those where substantial numbers of Europeans—of whites—came to take up land—and livelihoods—with the expectation that they and their descendents would stay—that they were a permanently immigrant—a permanently transplanted—fraction from the mother country.

It should hardly surprise us that most European (or white) settlers had rather little sympathy for majority rule. There were certainly exceptions. But, typically, they enjoyed a far better lifestyle than they could have dreamed of back in the metropole. The weather was better. I sometimes ask my students to imagine—or better yet, go spend—a winter in London and then spend one in say Harare, capital of Zimbabwe, and see which you prefer.

On a more substantive level, the large yard, the veranda, the swimming pool, and maybe best of all the servants (the housekeeper, the gardener): All of this was possible in the settler colonies and available not just to the upper or middle classes. The semi-skilled—the artisanal people—could enjoy some of the amenities and some of the lifestyle that I just described, again under quite sunny skies very often. This was something that was a possibility for the mechanic, the builder, the guy who lays concrete, and the telephone repairman—things that would hardly have been dreamed of in the metropolitan capitals.

So, these people understandably felt that they had something to hold on to. Increasingly, they concluded in the face of what was happening in many parts of Africa—all over Africa, really—in the middle of the 20th century, they increasingly concluded that they or their metropolitan sponsors (both perhaps, or preferably) would have to fight for it.

The territories of Angola and Mozambique were, of course, settler colonies. In fact, they became more settler after the Second World War, when tens of thousands of additional settlers from Portugal came there to live. But as I just implied, they were also the colonies of Portugal, and this fact made a difference—I mean of Portugal vis-a-vis France and Britain, for instance. You can argue that it was the fact of Portuguese possession that was equally important, or perhaps more important, than the realities of settler rule. I think *both* were very important.

But why is the factor of Portuguese possession important in understanding these cases of the so-called delayed decolonizations? First of all, Portugal back in Portugal was ruled in quite authoritarian—some would say dictatorial—fashion for a very substantial portion of the early, middle, and into the late years of the 20th century. The rulers of Portugal, such as Salazar, showed very considerable sympathy—I'm not putting words in their mouths—for fascism and could be fairly described as at least quasi-fascist in their methods of rule.

The significance of this is that compared to Britain or France, there was an absence of even a theoretical commitment, as it were, to the virtues of democracy, for instance. There was not the rhetoric of democracy at the very least in the case of Portugal and its colonies. So, there was no pretense of the sort of thing that Britain and France certainly claimed they were doing and in some respects were doing, certainly by the 1950s, at least late in the day of the colonial regimes in the case of the French and the British: that is, bequeathing parliamentary institutions, bequeathing the best of ideas and practices of Western democracy to the colonies, which they increasingly knew they were going to be departing.

There's no pretense of doing that sort of thing—of leaving that sort of legacy of colonialism behind in the Portuguese colonies. That, in turn, perhaps even more important, meant that the ability of African nationalists to exploit that rhetoric—to exploit that commitment to democracy—was absent. When we looked at decolonization—the Nationalist movements in the French Empire, for instance, the way in which politicians from West Africa like Senghor or Houphouët would seize upon French talk whenever it arose about citizenship, for instance—"a greater citizenship for a greater France," and so on— and in a sense challenged them to match their words with their actions—to put their money where their mouth was—there were no such spaces for the utilization of the colonizers' own superficial, at least, stance to exploit.

Unlike England or France again, Portugal, to turn to the economic side of this, was itself a poor country. This meant that unlike England or France, or indeed even like Belgium, Portugal did not have the benefit of what someone like Kwame Nkrumah from Ghana would have called, with some accuracy perhaps, the "neocolonial option": that is, go ahead, grant independence, and depend on your economic power—or at least hope that your economic power can continue to permit you and allow you to gain at least some benefits from the resources and markets of your former colonies.

So Portugal concluded, unlike these more economically muscular colonizing powers in Africa, that it could not relinquish its empire. It couldn't even loosen the reigns on its colonies in response to African nationalism. This line of thought went: "Lose the empire, and you lose everything. We don't have that option of turning to other means of getting the things we may want or need."

Needless to say, Portuguese settlers—again, increasing numbers of settlers—concurred in this view that to give up the empire, of course, threatened everything that they had gone to Africa for in the first place.

So, whereas earlier we made an assertion—a judgment—that the yoke or burden of colonialism in comparative terms was relatively heavy in the Portuguese territories in terms of the longevity of forced cultivation, or forced labor, or what have you, it's also true that they were particularly heavy-handed on nascent African political movements when this emerged in the very late 1950s and early 1960s.

To put it bluntly, those movements were crushed and banned. Early on, certainly by the early 1960s, the Nationalists had decided to take up arms against the colonists (the Portuguese) and against the settlers.

There are echoes in that dynamic with what we saw in the last lecture in South Africa, of course, of this polarization and the embrace, essentially, of very militant approaches on both sides. In a sense, there was never the phase in the Portuguese colonies of the open constitutional protests, mass demonstrations, and so forth that was a feature of South African life in the 1950s. We go very quickly to the completely polarized situation.

Rather like the Belgian Congo, both Angola and Mozambique were huge territories. They were vast. Like the Belgian Congo, they had been parceled out to various concessionaires—private companies that were responsible and given the exclusive rights, very often, to take out the cotton, or tin, or what have you.

Like the Belgian Congo and a feature of the tremendous size here, it contained a multitude of ethnicities with little in common except for, perhaps, their common suffering.

In light of all this, it's slightly surprising that in Mozambique a single liberation movement known as FRELIMO ("The Front for the Liberation of Mozambique" in Portuguese, the acronym FRELIMO)—in Mozambique, a single liberation movement came to dominate the anti-Portuguese struggle.

This was not the case in Angola, where three different armed movements emerged, each with its own ethnic base and also showing considerable ideological differences. They were the FNLA in the north, based on the old Congo ethnicity and led by Holden Roberto; the MPLA, the Popular Movement for the Liberation of Angola, around the capital city of Luanda and in the central belt based ethnically on the Kimbundu (or Mbundu) peoples, but also drawing a lot of support from the tiny category or class in Angola known as the *assimilados*, that is, highly educated intellectuals—the *intelligentsia*, if you like. Some of those, in turn, were drawn from the *mestizos*, those of mixed Portuguese and African descent, a fact that in some cases was a sort of easy target for the rival Nationalist movements, and certainly the MPLA was the one that gave its greatest embrace to more radical approaches and, indeed, called itself a Marxist movement.

Then based in the central highlands, the eastern portions of the country, and in the south was the UNITA movement (The Union for Total Independence in Angola) led by a very charismatic figure, a large man with a tremendous amount of command and charm in the view of many, Jonas Savimbi. The ethnic base here was the Ovimbundu people.

In both Mozambique and Angola, beginning in the 1960s, war ensued. By 1974, however, the tide was turned not by events that unfolded within Africa itself, but back in Portugal. Young Portuguese military officers had concluded and decided that these wars were endless and unwinnable as they looked at the rest of the 20th century, and that perhaps equally, or maybe more, important, that Portugal's future ought to lie with Europe. They looked at things like the burgeoning Common Market (and, of course, that has developed into the European Union) and stressed that the new Portugal should find its economic and, indeed, its political destiny there—that empires, after all, were outdated, atavistic remnants of the past.

They staged a military coup in Portugal itself, and very quickly, within 12 months or so, moved to end something over 400 years, at least at the coastal areas, of Portuguese colonialism.

In Mozambique, at first, certainly at the time of these actions in 1974 and 1975 (the Portuguese coup and within a year or so of that the withdrawal of Portuguese political power), in Mozambique, that transition went quite smoothly. After all, as we noted before, FRELIMO was the clear heir apparent and came to power under another very charismatic figure, although his ideology is very different from Jonas Savimbi's on the other side of the continent, in the sense that Machel also was a self-styled socialist.

The transition did not go smoothly in Angola. Again, we see a distinction between these two territories. As independence day approached in November of 1975, a veritable free-for-all broke out.

I remember these days very clearly. I was working actually on Capitol Hill and trying to avoid doing my dissertation at that point and working for—it was called the Washington Office on Africa, an information center. There on Capitol Hill, there were these late night sessions of Congress, and reports from the U.N., and so forth—all of this focusing on the coming independence day in Angola, and nobody, frankly, was really sure what was going to happen. These three rivals were still very much at it—at this point not so much with the departing Portuguese, of course, as with each other.

It's at this point that we must introduce again, as we did in Lecture Twenty-Five on the Belgian Congo, the all-important context of the Cold War, this ongoing competition for world prestige, power, etc., between the Western powers and the Soviet Union and its satellite powers.

In the weeks and months leading up to the independence day set for November of 1975, several foreign powers quite clearly and openly backed their favorite movements, and the most visible examples of this were an invasion from South Africa in support of UNITA and Jonas Savimbi's at least alleged conservatism. Cuba, on the other hand, intervened with thousands of troops in support of the MPLA, their fellow Marxists. The Soviet Union played a supporting role in that. Finally, the United States certainly provided financial assistance and materiel also at first in favor of the FNLA but later also on the same side as South Africa on behalf of UNITA.

In the short run, the socialist MPLA came out on top, but its position was exceedingly shaky. Alas, in neither Angola or Mozambique did independence signal the end of conflict.

Remember that apartheid South Africa had regarded the Portuguese colonies as buffers against the southward tide of majority rule. After all, the Portuguese territories, which in one case (Mozambique) bordered South Africa, and in the other bordered the South Africa controlled territory of South-West Africa. These were, indeed, seen as buffers against this tide rolling southward of majority rule.

If anything, the Portuguese exit, then, prompted much greater South African intervention. Again, the first indication of a South African willingness to play a much-expanded role in these former buffer states was the entry into Angola in 1975, which was not successful in the shorter run—or in the long run, for that matter.

Nonetheless, it was echoed soon enough in Mozambique. In Mozambique, a movement that drew some support both ethnically and from resentment over radical measures instituted by FRELIMO, such as collective farms and so forth—very Soviet bloc style measures in some cases carried out or attempted to be carried out by Samora Machel and his ruling FRELIMO party. The movement entitled RENAMO, or MNR (the Mozambique National Resistance) developed, again capitalized on certain perceived-to-be-excluded ethnic bases alienated from the FRELIMO government, and also tapped into resentment over these radical measures.

South Africa began to back RENAMO quite heavily as well, and—after a further decade of war (essentially the 1980s) and the end of South African participation in 1990—the sides negotiated a settlement.

Since then, Mozambique has forged a rather remarkable recovery. After all, this was a country that certainly was one of the poorest countries in the world, and in some respects remains that. But, nonetheless, it is often cited today as one of Africa's success stories.

Angola, once again, was considerably worse. With hardly a break after independence in 1975, civil war continued for another quarter of a century. There are many Angolans today who had never known peace until the last couple of years when finally—with the capture and killing of Jonas Savimbi—something like a cease-fire and truce ensued. Perhaps Mozambique will serve as an inspiration for the rebuilding of Angola.

Let us now turn to Southern Rhodesia, which is, of course, now known as Zimbabwe. From 1953 to 1963, Southern Rhodesia had been joined with Northern Rhodesia and Nyasaland (for now Zambia and Malawi) in the Central African Federation. The Federation experiment driven by the region's white settlers (most of whom were in Southern Rhodesia) created an economically advantageous bloc, certainly. It also advertised itself as an alternative to either majority rule to the north or the rigidity of apartheid to its south.

I do think this is fair to say, however, that most Africans in the Federation saw the official policy of so-called "partnership" as a form, but a moderated form, of white supremacy. The Federation broke apart, as we saw in an earlier lecture, on the shoals of African nationalism. The British acceded to African demands and granted independence to Malawi in 1963, Zambia in 1964, and might well have done the same in Southern Rhodesia.

However, Southern Rhodesia's settlers had other ideas. If you recall for a moment the case in Kenya where there were white settlers, but not nearly of the numbers that we find in Southern Rhodesia, the settlers in Kenya lacked the power to defy Great Britain when the moment came that Britain decided that it would negotiate with African nationalists and grant independence.

In Southern Rhodesia, things took a very different turn. Led by the redoubtable Ian Smith, a former RAF pilot, a cattle rancher in the southern part of the country, and a guy with a very considerable streak of defiant toughness to him, the settler government in Southern Rhodesia declared the so-called Unilateral Declaration of Independence (UDI) in 1965.

I'd like to read you a couple of phrases from the UDI (the Unilateral Declaration of Independence) issued on November 11, 1965. It begins this way:

> Whereas in the course of human affairs, history has shown that it may be necessary for a people to resolve the political affiliations which have connected them with another people, and to assume among other nations the separate and equal status to which they are entitled; and whereas in such event a respect for the opinions of mankind requires them to declare to other nations the causes which impel them to assume full responsibility for their own affairs... [It goes on:] We now sever our connection with Britain.

The language, I'm sure, rings a bell with you. It is borrowed very directly from the U.S. Declaration of Independence. Despite the fact that it's two centuries later and, of course, the context is completely different, structurally speaking there is some similarity here. You have prominent settlers, or descendents of settlers, in a colonial situation declaring that they are going to sever their connections with the old empire.

In the aftermath of the U.S. Declaration, of course, there was a war— the Revolutionary War. We know that. This was threatened in the case of Rhodesia, but it never materialized. What did materialize were international sanctions proposed by Britain and eventually adopted by the United Nations and so forth—economic sanctions. It was essentially a boycott—or cordon, if you like—around Rhodesia.

In the aftermath of UDI, soon the major African nationalist parties, which were ZANU (the Zimbabwe African National Union) and ZAPU (the Zimbabwe African Peoples' Union), were banned, and the leadership imprisoned. That leadership included Robert Mugabe, who was put into jail in 1965, where he stayed for a decade.

For a time, Ian Smith enjoyed a honeymoon. Indeed, the sort of self-sufficiency that sanctions imposed on Rhodesia as it now called itself (there was no need to call it Southern Rhodesia anymore since Northern Rhodesia had become Zambia). Rhodesia actually did rather well economically in the early years.

This was not to last. In the early 1970s, a genuine guerilla war: This came to be known as the Second Chimurenga—the second "struggle" in the Shona language. The first, of course, was the rebellion against Rhodes's British South Africa Company in the 1890s. That war picked up steam after 1975, and it did so especially on the part of ZANU, Mugabe's movement, because they were now able to take advantage of Mozambique's independence from Portugal.

The ways in which all of these processes—all of these stories—are unfolded in a regional context, and indeed in a global context, is something that I think we need to emphasize here. These are not simply internal processes, in any case. They are increasingly regional, cross-border, internationalized cases of politics and decolonization.

The two liberation movements in Zimbabwe forged a paper alliance, the Patriotic Front, but in fact they never cooperated. The war deepened, and it was a terrible war. Atrocities were committed on all sides in this war. Some people were put in impossible positions. Village headmen or chiefs were approached by the government forces from Smith's government during the day and asked and challenged if they were giving support to the guerillas. If the evidence were not forthcoming that they were refusing to do so, the

©2006 The Teaching Company Limited Partnership

punishment could be very severe, indeed, in terms of torture and killing.

The same night, you could be visited by the emissaries from the local guerillas operating in the bush. This is what they were called in the capital: the "boys in the bush" (the *Bosjesman*). They would literally pull the entire village out of the their homes and announce a *pungwe*. Today, this means an all-night party with music and everything, but at that time, it was musical, but these were enforced sessions where people were forced to sing the liberation songs, and so on, and so on. Again, this "man in the middle"—the notion of "You better not provide support to the guerillas, or we may shoot you," and being approached by the other side—by ZANU or ZAPU—and being told that "If you don't provide us support, we may shoot you."

This war ultimately resulted in 30,000 dead and a million refugees. Eventually Smith negotiated an agreement, and to some people's surprise, ZANU, Robert Mugabe's movement, won an impressive victory in what is generally considered to be a free and fair election and assumed the leadership—the premiership—of what was renamed in April of 1980 "Zimbabwe."

That, of course, is where he remains today. We will look at the Zimbabwean situation in Lecture Thirty-Five, but I think we can see some of the important roots of the contemporary crisis in what we've just been talking about.

Finally, we should mention South-West Africa, now known as Namibia. South Africa, after all, had run the place under a League of Nations mandate originally since the German defeat in 1918. Not surprisingly, a protracted, low-level liberation war developed in this country as well, although it was low-level partly because the population in this largely desert country is slight.

The Namibian or South-Western African struggle overlapped very much with the Angolan one. The interpenetration around the border between Angola and Namibia was almost inexplicable in some instances.

The United Nations, which inherited the old League of Nations mandate and which considered South Africa's occupation illegal— they had declared it illegal at various points since the 1960s—

eventually supervised elections leading to independence in 1990, but there's no doubt that the big shift that brought that about, as well as in some respects what brought the accommodation in Mozambique, were the shifts in South Africa itself, centered around Mandela's release, the legalization of the ANC, and other changes in South Africa. So, once again, we see this regional context—how what happens in one country affects another—what happens on the global level is played out in these examples of decolonization.

All of these former settler colonies, then, eventually won their independence, but the scars left by their struggles run particularly deep, are especially painful, and have ongoing relevance. We will see that, I think, very clearly in our penultimate lecture in this course: our look at Zimbabwe's current crisis. Thank you.

Lecture Twenty-Eight
The First Taste of Freedom

Scope:

While wars of liberation ravaged the Southern African settler states, most countries in the rest of Africa were enjoying the first years of independence. The exhilaration of the nationalist crescendo carried over into a kind of honeymoon period. The triumphant and often visionary new leaders announced great plans for bringing the fruits of independence home to ordinary citizens, and indeed, in a great many cases, they delivered. Schools and clinics multiplied, roads were paved, dams constructed. An expansionary world economy provided a climate in which real growth and development were achieved. Alas, the honeymoon did not last. Understandably, many Africans look back to these years with nostalgia—and with bitterness over what ensued.

Outline

I. In the 1960s, when Southern Africa began its immersion in violent conflict and/or heightened repression, most Africans were embarking on the first years of freedom from colonial rule. What was this experience like? Let us return to the question posed at the end of Lecture Twenty-Four: What would the new rulers do with the prize they had won—the formerly colonial state apparatus?

II. Anyone who watches film footage of the official ceremonies marking independence—the lowering of the Union Jack or Tricolor, the raising of a brand new flag (for a nation with a brand new name, often enough)—can sense, in the packed-in, surging crowds, one great emotion: Joy! Freedom! Ours at last! Now the world will see the new Africa!

  A. The feeling was genuine and thrilling. But clearly the expectations raised in the heady ride to independence would be a challenge to meet.

  B. Nonetheless, the new citizens were not passively awaiting the delivery of the fruits of freedom. The widespread mobilization of the nationalist movements carried over into a widespread willingness to participate in, to personally work toward, the next great triumph: development.

C. Thus, when Kenyatta cried out at his post-independence rallies, *"Harambee!"*—"Let us all pull together!"—the crowds yelled it back with enthusiasm. And indeed, many of the achievements in these years depended on the self-help initiatives of energized local communities.

III. Nonetheless, there was no getting around the pivotal role of the state. The colonial states had been highly interventionist, sponsoring and orchestrating the colonial economies, especially in the late-colonial developmentalist period. Coolness to free-market approaches, often assumed to begin with socialist or quasi-socialist independent governments, actually had colonial roots.

A. The new leaders had no intention of changing this large state role, except perhaps to make it even larger. "Seek ye first the political kingdom," Nkrumah had said—and use it to add all else, particularly real development.

B. Though Nkrumah (and others) had exploited the resentment of farmers over colonial marketing boards, he was quite prepared to retain them and use the margin created with low producer prices to finance other projects.

C. In the avowedly radical states, such as Ghana and Tanzania (usually proclaiming themselves "African socialist" rather than rigidly Marxist), a good measure of nationalization took place, as well as experiments with state farms.

    1. In Tanzania, Nyerere, whose 1967 Arusha Declaration articulated his vision of socialism built on traditional African values, pushed a disastrous "villagization" scheme, forcing farmers into compact settlements.

    2. Such schemes, like the boards and state farms, expressed, perhaps, an ominous fear of a truly independent, vigorous peasantry—despite the fact that the new leaders had partly ridden that peasantry to power.

D. Even in more conservative regimes, it was common to see a state role inserted or expanded in numerous enterprises;

parastatal—the notion that there was a public/private blend—was a frequently heard term.

IV. Whatever the longer-term weaknesses of these approaches, for a good while, they yielded impressive results.

    A. The economic growth of the late-colonial developmentalist period not only continued but increased.

        1. Gross national product (GNP) per capita for all of sub-Saharan Africa grew each year in the 1960s and the first half of the 1970s, often at rates of a very respectable 2–3 percent.

        2. Kenya's per capita GNP rose 30 percent in the 10 years after independence in 1963; that of the Ivory Coast doubled in the 20 years after its independence in 1960.

    B. Even manufacturing industrialization—the litmus test of modernization and development to many, whether on the right or the left—had its moment: It expanded at twice the rate of overall gross domestic product (GDP) between 1965 and 1973.

    C. Despite this growth, African economies failed to achieve a meaningful diversification. What boom there was rested largely on exports of primary products produced by farmers and miners. In other words, the dependency on an export-import economic base was only marginally altered.

    D. In this respect, the expansionary world economy, with—most importantly—buoyant commodity demand and prices, was a critical part of the successes of these years.

V. Most impressive of all, perhaps, new African governments kept their promises to improve education and health care.

    A. Between 1960 and 1980, sub-Saharan school enrollment percentages rose by more than 50 percent at the primary level and more than 500 percent at the secondary. All the new nations built universities, which had hardly existed before independence.

    B. Such countries as Tanzania made concerted efforts to give rural populations access to clinics. Infant mortality rates dropped and life expectancies rose. Thus, population increased—not a problem at this point perhaps; later, under different conditions, it would be another story.

VI. Allow me to illustrate some of these points with recollections of my earliest visits to the place I know best, Zambia.

    A. When Northern Rhodesia became Zambia in 1964, the new currency was named the *kwacha,* "the dawn,"—which captures perfectly the exhilaration of the times.

    B. The president, Kenneth Kaunda, seemed the epitome of decency. A thoughtful and sincere Christian, Kaunda expounded his political philosophy of "Humanism"—a people-centered vision avoiding the extremes of either capitalism or socialism.

    C. Although obviously still a Third World country, Zambia had an economy that was humming in the mid-1970s: People had work, construction was everywhere, and goods were in the shops. The reason: Zambia, almost totally dependent on copper export, was still riding the long copper boom that had begun in the post–World War II era.

    D. The University of Zambia, with which I was a research affiliate, was a shiny-white, modern complex, full of dedicated teachers (many still expatriates) and idealistic students.

    E. The village where I did much fieldwork enjoyed steady income from maize, cotton, sunflower seeds, and cattle. The pride of the village—and *sine qua non* of the meaning of independence—was the new primary school.

VII. There *was* a dawn, then, in much of Africa, with the coming of independence, and the new rulers deserve considerable credit for it. There were also ill omens, however.

    A. These new rulers rather furtively tried to instill a sense of identity with the new nation—as opposed, especially, to an ethnicity ("One Zambia, One Nation" was Kaunda's mantra). And they had some success; still, it was a tall order.

    B. Still enjoying, and perhaps deserving, considerable popular support, they could afford varying degrees of tolerance. Already, however, there were moves afoot to stifle opposition. Having won power, none of them planned to surrender it.

Suggested Reading:

Frederick Cooper, *Africa since 1940: The Past of the Present*, interlude and chapter 5.

Kevin Shillington, *History of Africa*, chapter 28.

Questions to Consider:

1. Among Africans old enough to remember, why do so many recall the early years of independence with nostalgia—tinged with bitterness?

2. To what extent were the newly independent states' successes—and, later, failures—affected by the systems created during the colonial period?

Independent Africa, 1970

Triggered by the independence of formerly British Ghana (Gold Coast) and formerly French Guinea in 1957 and 1958, respectively, independence swept like a wave across Africa in or soon after 1960, the *annus mirabilis* of African history. By 1968, most countries had gained independence. The significant exceptions were in Southern Africa where the settler colonies of Rhodesia, Southwest Africa, South Africa, Angola, and Mozambique resisted African self-rule, eager as they were to preserve their privileges and prerogatives. The road to independence and the aftermath would prove taxing and usually bloody in these countries.

Lecture Twenty-Eight—Transcript
The First Taste of Freedom

Hello again. In the 1960s, when southern Africa, as we have seen in the last couple of lectures, began its immersion in violent conflicts over decolonization or heightened repression in the case of South Africa, at that time, most Africans and most African countries were embarking on the first years of freedom from colonial rule. We need to return to them—to those situations. After all, this was the majority of the African population and the majority of African countries. What was this experience of independence like?

We need to remind ourselves also of just what the nationalists had won. They had taken control of a colonial apparatus: the state (of course, formerly colonial at this stage). Finally, we need to ask the question with which we ended Lecture Twenty-Four: What would they do with this new prize?

Anyone who watches film footage of the official ceremonies marking independence—typically the lowering, as national anthems are played—"God Save the Queen" is played in the background—the Union Jack is lowered, and then the new flag of Zambia, or Kenya, or Nigeria, or Ghana is raised. The same for the Tricolor of the French and so on. Very often, of course, a new flag for a nation with a new name: Ghana, instead of the Gold Coast; or eventually Zimbabwe instead of Southern Rhodesia; certainly, Zambia instead of Northern Rhodesia in the period I'm referring to.

When you see those packed-in crowds and the surging, you're taken with one great emotion: joy. Freedom! Ours at last! Now the world will see the New Africa! The feeling was genuine, and it was thrilling. I'm reminded, again, of that very simple statement by the great Guinean historian opening an article on the period from his own reminiscence: "It was certainly great to be alive in those days."

Clearly, the expectations raised in the heady ride to independence would be a challenge to meet. It's worth repeating a point we made earlier in looking at decolonization in Lecture Twenty-Four, and that is that in the late-colonial period, some of the officials in places like France and Britain concluded that disappointment was coming, and that it would be better for it to be directed at African rulers as opposed to themselves.

Nonetheless, the new citizens were not passively awaiting the delivery of the fruits of freedom. The widespread mobilization of the nationalist movements during the 1940s and 1950s carried over into widespread willingness to pitch in, to participate in, to personally work toward the next great triumph: development. In this case, they don't mean the sort of halfway house—the halfhearted development—of the "developmentalist" states that Britain and France turned to in the late-colonial period.

"No! We want the full measure—the real thing! And we want it under our own direction, our own supervision, and not yours." So there's a tremendous amount of energy that is apparent in the early years after independence in country after country. In Kenya, Jomo Kenyatta, who had been in jail, after all, up until 1959, when he cried out at his post-independence rallies, "*Harambee!*" (Swahili for "Let's pull together!"). The crowds yelled it back, and they meant it. They yelled it back with enthusiasm.

Indeed, many of the achievements of these years depended on the self-help initiatives of energized local communities. Efforts to build the new school, to clear the way, and create or build the new road—or repair the old one, the bridge that needs the same sort of work: Often we saw this in a sort of work-party atmosphere punctuated with songs from the nationalist struggle, and so on.

Despite this popular participation, which was real, widespread, and again, genuine and enthusiastic, still there was no getting around the pivotal role of the state. The colonial states had been highly interventionist, sponsoring and orchestrating the colonial economies, perhaps especially in the late-colonial, "developmentalist" period.

I often find that people assume—and it's a natural assumption—that coolness in independent Africa—coolness toward what we might call "free-market" approaches—hesitations towards that—people assume that that largely stems from having a socialist or quasi-socialist perspective and, of course, that would be correct. But, in fact, some of this coolness or hesitation comes from the colonial roots. Those state apparatuses that the nationalists had inherited, of course, had deeply interventionist, often counter-market (certainly counter-free-market) tendencies and character.

The new leaders had no intention of changing this large, interventionist state role except perhaps to make it even larger. Remember Nkrumah's mantra, the "Father of African Nationalism," the first to become president of an independent sub-Saharan state (Ghana) in 1957: "Seek ye first the political kingdom," Nkrumah had said, "And use it to add all else."

Nkrumah, of course, had spent his Sundays when he was a student at Lincoln University in Pennsylvania attending African-American churches. He borrowed some of his rhetorical style from what he saw there. As you can see, he also learned some scripture. He's paraphrasing there, of course, seeking ye first the kingdom of God. "Seek ye first the political kingdom." Seize the apparatus of the state; turn it to add the other things that we seek—above all, real development.

Although Nkrumah and others had, in fact, exploited during the nationalist crescendo the resentment of farmers over colonial marketing boards, after he took power, he was quite prepared to retain them. Again, the notion of the board was a monopsony—a sole buyer that bought (in this case especially cocoa, in a situation like Ghana) at a given price and sold it on the world market at another price. This was a resentment during the colonial period, because, of course, they felt that the margin was going in essence into the colonists' hands.

In the independence period, Nkrumah retains the boards and uses the margin, or at least says he will use the margin—promises to use the margin—to finance other projects.

In the validly radical states like Ghana, and like Tanzania in East Africa, usually proclaiming themselves to be "African socialists," as opposed to rigidly Marxist, a good measure of nationalization took place as well as some experiments with state farms, and so on.

Take the case of Tanzania, where Julius Nyerere, the former teacher who had earned the affectionate nickname of *Mwalimu* (or "Teacher" in Swahili) and had studied overseas, and so forth, Nyerere issued, in a sense, his African socialist manifesto, if you like, in 1967, the Arusha Declaration. It's still an eloquent and impressive document, essentially articulating a vision of socialism built on traditional African values. It's, in a sense, the sort of economic side of his articulation of the one-party state, which we'll turn to in the next lecture.

What I'm trying to get at is an approach that blends ideas from the outside—in this case, socialism—with ideas generated from African culture itself.

But in the name of his African socialism, Nyerere pushed a disastrous "villagization" scheme, the *Ujamaa* scheme. It comes back to a notion of family-hood, if you like, in Tanzania. The *Ujamaa* villages, forcing farmers into compact settlements: It did not work. Such schemes like the state marketing boards and state farms expressed, perhaps, an ominous fear of a truly independent, vigorous peasantry—despite the fact, again, that quite a number of the new leaders had ridden to power precisely on the grievances of such peasantries.

I have been stressing a state role—an interventionist role—the overall orchestration and management of an economy. We've seen, as we would expect, that in the more radical regimes, the quasi-socialist or African socialist regimes, we would expect that. But it was also common to see a state role inserted or expanded into numerous enterprises in conservative regimes—those, for instance, of Senegal, or the Ivory Coast, or indeed of Kenya.

A word that often came up this time was "parastatal," meaning precisely the notion that there's a kind of public/private blend here— a partnership between a substantial state role, whether it's owning shares in the name of the government or the insertion of publicly paid officials into the steel production, or the textile industry, or what have you.

Whatever the longer-term weaknesses of these approaches, for a while (and it was a good while, it wasn't simply a moment), they yielded some impressive results. The economic growth of the late-colonial, developmentalist period—and certainly in macro terms, there had been substantial economic growth in the late-colonial periods—this not only continued, but, in fact, increased and accelerated in quite a number of cases.

Overall, the GNP (gross national product) per capita for all of sub-Saharan Africa grew each year in the 1960s and through the first half, approximately, of the 1970s, often at quite respectable rates of some 2–3% a year. Again, that's an overall per capita rise in GNP after independence.

Kenya, to use one example: Per capita, GNP rose 30% in the 10 years after independence for Kenya in 1963. That of the Ivory Coast doubled in 20 years after its independence in 1960. Even manufacturing industrialization—and this is often taken to be the sort of litmus test—the measuring rod, if you like—of economic modernization and development to many, whether on the right or the left—even manufacturing had its moment. It expanded overall on the continent at twice the rate of the overall GDP improvement or increase between 1965 and 1973.

Despite this, African economies failed to achieve a truly meaningful diversification. What boom there was rested largely on exports of primary products produced by farmers and miners. In other words, the dependency on an export-import economic base forged in the colonial period, as we know and as we've seen, was only marginally altered. This continued to be the basis of the development that we're seeing.

In this respect, we need to go global again to achieve an understanding, just as we introduced the Cold War to look at political developments in places like the old Belgian Congo and places like Angola last time. In this respect, the expansionary world economy of the 1960s—and it was a very expansionary economy, indeed, in that era—was extremely important to this whole process.

In particular, the buoyant commodity demand and prices were the context, if you like, for the sorts of successes that we are seeing, which is not to minimize them. One still must take advantage of even favorable conditions, and country after country, and indeed we must concede that leader after leader, showed some skill in doing that.

Most impressive of all, certainly to ordinary people, the new African governments kept their promises in many cases to improve education and healthcare. Between 1960 and 1980, sub-Saharan school enrollment rose by over 50% at the primary level. It rose by over 500% at the secondary level (that is a five-fold increase in people—African children—attending high school). All the new nations built universities, which, with a handful of exceptions, had not even existed before independence and were symbolically incredibly important.

Countries like Tanzania made concerted efforts to give rural populations access to clinics. Infant mortality rates dropped. Life expectancy rose. Of course, that implied that population was going to rise. At this stage, that was not a particular problem. In fact, one could even count on a rising population from some perspectives as an asset.

Later, under different conditions, these larger populations, of course, may indeed pose a very different question and a very different kind of problem.

I've been generalizing so far about Africa's first decade—the first fruits of freedom—the first tastes of freedom—that Africa experienced with independence in or around 1960. Let me focus this a bit, and let me personalize it a bit and try to illustrate some of these points from my own experiences in the place I know best, my first love in Africa as far as countries go, and that is the country of Zambia.

Northern Rhodesia (of course, the British territory originally created by Cecil Rhodes's British South Africa Company)—when Northern Rhodesia became Zambia in 1964, the new currency that the government adopted and came into general use at that time was called "*kwacha*" (it's still called *kwacha*). "*Kwacha*" was a word from a couple of the languages spoken in Zambia, and the meaning was "dawn." To me that captures perfectly the exhilaration of the times.

The various symbols on the *kwacha*—the sikwaze (the fish eagle)— very reminiscent when you look at it, of course, of the symbolism of the American bald eagle or golden eagle as the symbol of freedom. The portrayals of the statue that stands there in central Lusaka of the very muscular African literally breaking the chains of colonial rule— that appears on the *kwacha*—it appears on the currency itself of Zambia.

Of course, the hero of the nationalist struggle was Kenneth David Kaunda, and he certainly seemed to many, both inside Zambia and outside, as the epitome of decency. Kaunda's father had been an

African missionary. We often forget that many of the missionaries in Africa have been, in fact, Africans themselves. But like a lot of missionaries, he carried his gospel from one place to another. In this case, Kaunda's father had come from Nyasaland next door, now Malawi, where Livingstone's old influence of the Scottish Presbyterian missionaries, in a sense, was reflected. He had come into the northern part of Zambia earlier in the century and settled there as a teacher and a pastor (a preacher) in Zambia.

So, Kaunda, raised in that household, as he very lovingly evokes in his autobiography—again, an autobiography—it's a memoir—it's certainly not his whole life, because Kaunda is very much still with us—but published in 1962, *Zambia Shall Be Free*, his (again) loving portrait of that upbringing with his father and mother in a remote mission station of northern Zambia.

In short, what I'm getting at is that he was a thoughtful and sincere Christian. He is a very devout man, indeed. Eventually he expounded his whole philosophy—his sort of counterpart to Nyerere's Arusha Declaration was the development of Kaunda's philosophy/ideology of "humanism." This was, indeed, a people-centered vision like the Arusha Declaration—quite impressive, eloquent, and an articulation of an approach to public affairs and to life itself—to questions like development centered on people. In Kaunda's own view of it, it was something that avoids the extremes of either capitalism or socialism—it avoids the extremes of right or left.

Kaunda (again) seemed then, and in a lot of respects still seems, to be both dignified and down to earth. I interviewed him once for my own historical research purposes, and like a lot of others who have come away from a personal encounter with Kenneth Kaunda, it was the word "gentleman" that first came to my lips.

Although Zambia was obviously still a third-world country, Zambia's economy when I first went there in the early to mid-1970s was humming. It was fat. You can spell that "f-a-t," or spell it like my students do: "p-h-a-t," but it had a lot going for it. Again, I don't want to overstate this. Obviously, it was a poor country, but people had work. If you went down Cairo Road in central Lusaka, you could see on either side the cranes on the tops of these buildings adding stories and putting up new skyscrapers. There were goods in the shops, and so on.

Again, the reason for this in economic terms, although for a time it had to be managed adequately, and for a time it was managed adequately—the reason behind it, though, was that Zambia, almost totally dependent on copper export, was still riding the long copper boom that began in the post-World War II era. It's not accidental that when they constructed the new parliament house in Zambia—again, a symbol of this new age and the pride of this new age—its roof over this considerable expanse of this building is 100% copper. It's a symbol of the new age.

The University of Zambia: I mentioned the establishment of these new universities as an achievement of this first taste of freedom—this first experience with independence. The University of Zambia, built out on the Great East Road, obviously east of town, in Lusaka, was a citadel. You approach it, and it has this very modern architecture: shiny-white appearance from a distance on a small rise—a small hill.

I was a research affiliate there, and I found the place to be full of dedicated teachers. A number of those—quite a number of those at that point—were still expatriates. They were from many other countries in the world who wanted to be there. They wanted to play their part—at least make a contribution to what they saw as this era of hope taking shape in modern Africa. It was full of idealistic and very committed students. It was an exciting place to be.

To localize this even further, the village where I did much fieldwork was located in southern Zambia in the so-called Tonga ethnic group, or inside the Tonga-dominated area of Zambia. At this point in the early to mid-1970s, the small farmers—and that's what everybody in that village was—they were peasant households—they enjoyed a steady income from sales of maize, cotton, sunflower, seeds, and cattle. Again, I don't want to overstate this. These were not commercial farmers, and they didn't live like commercial farmers. But this was, for a time at least, a prosperous peasantry.

The pride of the village and, perhaps, the one symbol that strikes me still today as representing the promise of the new age—the *sine qua non*, the symbol more than any other, the meaning of independence—was the new primary school—Chiavola Primary School. The construction of this, which was partly a state enterprise but partly (again) this mass participation, local pitch-in construction—became, in essence, the centerpiece of the whole village life. I can't stress enough the fact that this was taken to mean that the fruits of independence had reached us—that we can be part of this new age like anyone else.

So, there was a dawn—there was a *kwacha*—in much of Africa with the coming of independence, and the new rulers deserve considerable credit for it. There were omens on the horizon, however, and we might mention a couple.

I said earlier that a ruler like Nkrumah in Ghana had not dismantled the marketing boards that, of course, he had criticized so vociferously during the nationalist rise. I mentioned that his reason for not doing so was to use the margin between the producer price and the selling price to finance other projects usually said to be development projects.

But it's also true that Nkrumah began to invest some of that margin and numerous other marginal resources that he was able to control, because he controlled the state, in what we can call "showcase projects." The notion of the Volta Dam, which remains a fairly dubious large-scale investment in Ghana, but certainly was the sort of project that puts you on the map—that gets attention. The construction of the new national stadium for the soccer teams that will now be wearing our new national colors…

Back to Nkrumah's case, the construction, which he definitely put resources into, of a new headquarters for the OAU (the Organization of African Unity)—these kinds of showcase projects, again, were symbolic enough, but they did not necessarily represent the same sort of investment in ongoing development that other investments did.

The new rulers rather furtively tried to instill a sense of identity with the new nation as opposed to, especially, an ethnicity. We've mentioned this challenge before. We've said it many times. But all the new nations encompassed a number of different ethnic groups, and they faced a tall order. They had some success with it. The counterpart to Kenyatta's shouting *"Harambee!"* and having it recalled is that Kaunda at his rallies would shout: "One Zambia!" The crowd would shout back: "One Nation!"

"One Zambia, One Nation." People did come to think of themselves as Zambians to a considerable extent, but that was easier to do during these buoyant times.

Finally, still enjoying, perhaps deserving—I would say they did deserve—considerable popular support, the newly independent leaders could afford varying degrees of tolerance. After all, if you don't feel that you're in danger of losing your political office, it creates some room or space for you to allow opposition, whether those are parties, or critics, or what have you.

Already, however, even by the late 1960s and by the early 1970s, during this favorable first boom period in the post-independence years, there were moves afoot to stifle opposition. Having won power, none of these leaders planned to surrender it.

Still despite these omens, the achievement of independence was exactly that. It was impressive, and I refuse to see it cynically. A New Africa had been born. Thank you.

Lecture Twenty-Nine
The Taste Turns Sour

Scope:

Within a decade of independence, the promise of postcolonial freedom began to falter. To the outside world, coups, conflict, and corruption increasingly seemed the order of the day. To get a clearer view, we must examine exactly what it was that African nationalists had won. They inherited countries whose borders were artificial, drawn by outsiders and encompassing many different ethnic groups, religions, and interests. Rather than nations seeking statehood, these were preshaped states seeking to build a sense of nationhood. It should not be surprising that ethnic conflict could sometimes become explosive. The new leaders presided over export-dominated economies with limited capacity to generate real development; many of the elite were quite happy to settle for enriching themselves. When conflict or popular anger threatened stability, rulers turned to one-party states, and armies turned to military coups with alarming frequency.

Outline

I. The honeymoon didn't last; the "dawn" clouded over. Although the degree of decline certainly varied widely and in some places never occurred at all, there is no avoiding the conclusion that in much of Africa, the hope and promise of independence changed to disillusionment. In this lecture, we focus on the political/social aspects of the story; in the next, on the economic.

II. We have seen that state power was central—or more than central—in the overall political economy. Important implications flow from this fact.

   A. In more developed and diversified societies, there are many ways to do quite well financially. A politician or bureaucrat who loses his or her job through elections or otherwise can turn to a host of other occupations: go back to the law practice, become a lobbyist, turn to business.

   B. Such options were far less available in the new African nations. Getting access to the state machinery—at high stations or low—was, in a sense, the only game in town, and that, in turn, meant that it was a game likely to be played with deadly ferocity.

C. If you were inside the "one shelter our former rulers left," as author Chinua Achebe described it, you wanted, and intended, to stay inside. And to those outside, you said, "Stop your clamoring; though you are

there, and I here, we must think of ourselves as one; we are doing everything we can and shall pass you morsels through the window."

D. Or, to change the metaphor, "Our challenges are great; our enemies [often erstwhile imperialists] many; don't rock the boat, else we all shall sink."

E. Thus, opposition, dissent, or competition came increasingly to be seen as threat and, depending on the case, treacherous threat, even treasonous threat.

III. The upshot was the move, almost everywhere, to greater authoritarianism.

A. The open, multiparty parliamentary systems left behind by the departing colonialists began to be abandoned. But remember that these systems had begun life very late in the colonial day, in a sort of deathbed conversion to the virtues of dispensing democracy. With shallow roots, they were rather easily stunted.

B. One option, chosen by a great many rulers, was the declaration of the one-party state.

1. As so often, positively or negatively, Nkrumah of Ghana led the way. But Kenyatta of Kenya, Nyerere of Tanganyika, Kaunda of Zambia, Banda of Malawi, Houphouët-Boigny of the Ivory Coast, and Senghor of Senegal—all the "great ones"—followed suit.

2. At its best and most sophisticated, the one-party state was posited as a more authentically African political model than the imported one. Rather than constant negative competition, it called for positive search for consensus, rather like the village gatherings of old. Nyerere and Kaunda, in particular, argued in this vein and, indeed, permitted a certain amount of dissent *within the party*.

3. And, again, the argument goes, "Our challenges are so great—whether to mobilize for development or to foil the imperialists lurking—that we cannot afford the luxury or the wasted time of disunity."

4. At its worst and crudest, the one-party state was simply a quite transparent cloak for iron dictatorship.

IV. The one-party state was one aspect of what author and professor Ali Mazrui calls "the search for stability." And, indeed, if measured by longevity in office, several of the rulers mentioned above found it. But stability was elusive in a great many places.

A. One threat to stability was certainly ethnic conflict.

1. As we know, almost all the African countries contained numerous "nations"—ethnic groups—and faced a rather daunting task, before and after independence, of building a new and larger sense of national identity based on externally imposed units.

2. There's nothing natural or inevitable about ethnic conflict; tolerance and coexistence are just as common.

a. But it's also not surprising that in a struggle over limited resources, mainly within the arena of the state, people often mobilized along ethnic lines.

b. As we stressed early on, ethnicity is fluid; previously quite separate communities might discover enough cultural similarity to mobilize as an ethnic bloc.

3. In its more benign form, this fluidity could lead to endless varieties of ethnic balancing acts—something instantly familiar to students of, say, American politics.

4. But in certain circumstances, it was dynamite. The most obvious example was Nigeria, the most populous country in all of Africa.

a. Here, three large ethnic blocs coexisted uneasily: Hausa/Fulani in the north, Yoruba in the southwest, and Igbo in the southeast. Igbo, in particular, had taken to Western education with alacrity and often wound up in relatively elevated positions all through the country; thus, they found themselves to be targets of resentment.

b. Anti-Igbo pogroms erupted in the north in 1966. Igbo leaders in the southeast announced that they would secede and form a new nation, Biafra, in 1967.

   c. Nigeria's rulers thought otherwise, and a bloody civil war raged from 1967 to 1970. Nigerian "unity" prevailed, though anyone can see, 35 years later, that it remains precarious.

B. Another threat to stability was the military coup. As Mao said, power comes from the barrel of a gun, and any leader anywhere without a loyal army is vulnerable.

   1. There is a paradox here because coups were often launched in the name of restoring stability, of combating "indiscipline" and corruption, as we will see later in this lecture. The officers involved—often young ones— would set things aright, then return to the barracks.

   2. That rarely happened, though it was not unknown. The problem was, once the precedent was set, a new group of officers would get the idea.

   3. Yet again, Nkrumah was in the lead: The shock of his overthrow in 1966 diminished as coup after coup, more than 150 in all, became a dismally familiar bit of news out of Africa.

V. Finally, and obviously, we must mention corruption. We looked briefly at Congo/Zaïre's Mobutu, the all-time champion, but many, many others found it impossible to resist the temptation once inside the "shelter," albeit on a vastly diminished scale.

A. Some saw themselves as deserving, after all those years of struggle; others, as author and professor Peter Ekeh suggests, saw the state arena as an alien trough, not subject to traditional African mores about accountability and honesty. Eventually, as Ayi Kwei Armah showed brilliantly in his novel *The Beautyful Ones Are Not Yet Born*, given this free-for-all, it simply seemed stupid rather than courageous not to join in.

B. In a way, the larger problem was that it was often dead-end corruption: a payoff to avoid bigger problems, a rip-off of foreign aid funds, not, unfortunately, a commission on a project that might be genuinely productive.

VI. Coups, conflict, and corruption. A picture exaggerated in the West, for sure, but real enough, and it wasn't Westerners who were paying the price.

Suggested Reading:

Chinua Achebe. *The Trouble with Nigeria.*

Ayi Kwei Armah, *The Beautyful Ones Are Not Yet Born.*

Frederick Cooper, *Africa since 1940: The Past of the Present,* interlude and chapters 5, 7.

Samuel Decalo, *Coups and Army Rule in Africa: Motivations and Constraints.*

Questions to Consider:

1. Was the essential precondition for the "coups, conflict, and corruption" that seemed endemic in Africa of the 1970s and 1980s, in fact, the overly central role of the state?

2. Given the artificial nature of Africa's borders, should we be surprised at the eruption of ethnic conflict—or surprised that there wasn't more?

Lecture Twenty-Nine—Transcript
The Taste Turns Sour

Independence was an achievement—a genuine achievement. The first taste of freedom in Africa was sweet, but it didn't last. The taste turned sour. The honeymoon ended. The *kwacha* (the "dawn") clouded over. Although the degree of decline certainly varied widely and in some places never occurred at all, there's no avoiding the conclusion that in much of Africa, the hope and promise of independence changed to disillusionment.

In this lecture, we focus on the political and social aspects of this story, and in the next lecture on the economic. We've seen repeatedly in recent lectures that state power was central—or more than central—maybe all important—in the overall political economies constructed in the colonial period and carried over into the independent countries. Important implications flow from this fact.

In more developed and diversified societies, there are, to put it bluntly, many ways, many avenues, and many paths to do rather well financially. A politician or a bureaucrat in such places who loses his or her position or job through elections or otherwise can turn to a host of other occupations. You can go back to the law firm—to the law practice—where so many seem to come from, of course. You can become a lobbyist. We all know what the revolving door between Congress and the lobbying organizations is like in a town like Washington, D.C. You can turn to business.

This was far less the case in the new African nations. Getting access to the state machinery—at high stations or at low—was, in a sense, the name of the game. It often seemed to be the only game; and that in turn meant that it was a game likely to be played with considerable seriousness, if not indeed with deadly ferocity.

As is so often the case, I think we can get a better feel for this by turning to an artist and, in fact, we'll do that by turning to one we've turned to before, none other than Chinua Achebe, the legendary writer out of Nigeria. In this case, I want to turn to his novel entitled *A Man of the People.*

I will just mention in passing that this book was published in the United States in 1967, and the copyright held by Achebe is 1966. I assume that he was writing it in 1965 and 1966. In that sense, it is an incredible forecast of what his home country, Nigeria, was about to experience. We'll come back to that story in a moment, but I'll just say that in some respects, it bears a comparison with a book like *The Quiet American* by Graham Greene, published in 1955 and yet extremely prescient about what the future might bring in the history between Vietnam and the United States.

Let's set the scene here for this excerpt from *A Man of the People*. Our protagonist—who is a bright, young man—has gone and he has spent an evening with a member of parliament in the newly independent African nation—in fact a minister—and he's sort of dazzled by it. His host, whose name is Nanga, is known for his ebullient personality and his generosity. He's also known—increasingly suspected—to be engaging in illegal activities and in corruption.

So, the protagonist, after dinner and after the after-dinner drinks, goes back to his well-appointed room, and I'll pick it up at that point:

> I was simply hypnotized by the luxury of the great suite assigned to me. When I lay down in that double bed that seemed to ride on a cushion of air and switched on the reading lamp and saw all the beautiful furniture anew from the lying-down position and looked beyond the door to the gleaming bathroom and the towels as large as a lappa, I had to confess that if I were at that moment made a minister, I would be most anxious to remain one forever.

> We ignore man's basic nature if we say, as some critics do, that because a man like Nanga had risen overnight from poverty and insignificance to his present opulence, he could be persuaded without much trouble to give it up again and return to his original state. A man who has just come in from the rain, and dried his body, and put on dried clothes is more reluctant to go out again than another who has been indoors all the time.

> The trouble with our new nation, as I saw it then, lying on that bed, was that none of us had been indoors long enough

to be able to say, "To hell with it!" We had all been in the rain together until yesterday. Then a handful of us—the smart, and the lucky, and hardly ever the best—had scrambled for the one shelter our former rulers left and had taken it over and barricaded themselves in.

From within, they sought to persuade the rest through numerous loud speakers that the first phase of the struggle had been won and that the next phase, the extension of our house, was even more important and called for new and original tactics. It required that all argument should cease, and the whole people speak with one voice, and that any more dissent and argument outside the door of the shelter would subvert and bring down the whole house.

So, if I can paraphrase here some of the highlights from that passage from Achebe, if you were inside what he called the "one shelter our former rulers left," as Achebe described it—he's talking, of course, about the state—formerly colonial, now independent. If you were inside, you wanted and intended to stay inside. To those outside, you said, "Stop your clamoring; though you are there, and I am here, we must think of ourselves as one; we're doing everything we can and will pass you morsels through the window."

Or, to change the metaphor, "Our challenges are great; our enemies [often erstwhile imperialists] are many; don't rock the boat, else we all shall sink.

So, Opposition—dissent—competition—came increasingly to be seen as threat, and depending on the case, as treacherous threat, even indeed treasonous threat.

The upshot of all of this was the move almost everywhere in Africa to greater authoritarianism. The open, multiparty parliamentary systems left behind by the departing colonialists began to be abandoned. But remember that these had begun life very late in the colonial day, in a sort of deathbed conversion to the virtues of dispensing democracy. The colonies, after all, had been quite autocratic institutions themselves until late in the day.

The late historian Michael Crowder once wrote an article whose title was a play on the title of a play in the 1980s. The title of the article was "Whose Dream Was It Anyway?" He sort of challenges the notion—this dream—and concludes that it was a bit of a pipe dream to have expected that these plants of Western-style parliamentary democracy with such shallow roots would thrive. Instead, they were rather easily stunted.

One option, chosen by a great many rulers, was the declaration of the one-party state. It's an important term for much of recent African history. As so often, positively or negatively, Nkrumah of Ghana led the way, but all the "great ones"—Kenyatta, Nyerere, Kaunda, Banda, Houphouët-Boigny, Senghor—all of them followed suit. In all of those countries led by the legendary nationalists of the nationalist generation, the one-party state became the legal reality a decade or so after independence.

At its best and most sophisticated, the one-party state was posited—was put forward—as a more authentically African political model than the imported one. Indeed, I often hear people say—especially people who are sympathetic to Africa in this country (in the United States)—"Well, you know what's needed here is something more authentic—something rooted in African. Maybe they can find or return to something that is a more authentic form of governing."

But I think it's important to recognize that it's not like this has never been tried. The one-party state—again at its best—was an attempt in precisely that direction. The arguments went something like this: that rather than this constant negative competition—this dragging each other down—we should look for or search for consensus. The imagery drawn here—and this is why I say they harkened back to something they argued was more authentic—rather like the village gathering of old. You don't take a vote. You stay there until a decision is reached by some sort of consensus.

So the notion of "first past the post, winner takes all" and that kind of thing was that it had negative ramifications. Again, the argument sometimes taken to be that, "Our challenges are so great—whether that challenge is to mobilize for development or increasingly to foil the lurking imperialists—we cannot afford the luxury [and that's how it was often put], and the wasted time, of disunity."

So, again, at its most positive in the formulations presented by some brilliant minds like Julius Nyerere in Tanzania or Kenneth Kaunda in

Zambia—they argued in this vain, that we can move to a one-party state and indeed, in their formulations of it, with considerable reality, they permitted within the single ruling party a fair amount of competition and dissent.

You can see this particularly perhaps in Tanzania, where I think this idea had perhaps the greatest reality. Even during the one-party era in Tanzania, it was relatively common for some prominent politicians—members of parliament and, indeed, quite often ministers—to be thrown out of office—to be defeated at the polls—by a challenger who, it was true, had to be vetted by the party leadership, and so on—but, nonetheless, was able to compete against someone in power and replace him.

It comes down to sometimes, "What are your measures for the vitality of democracy?" One measure that some would use is, "How frequently do you get the rascals being thrown out?" In Tanzania, at least, that was with some frequency. Voter turnout in Tanzania's one-party era was often in the 70–80% range, and 90% occasionally. That was under a one-party system and with, the evidence suggests, relatively little compulsion. That's certainly a considerably higher portion than one gets in the elections in the United States, for instance, particularly off-year congressional elections.

I have said repeatedly here the one-party state at its best. The fact is the one-party state operated at its worst in quite a number of other cases. In these instances, the one-party state was simply a quite transparent cloak, if you will, for iron dictatorship. The new emperors, in many cases, had no genuine ideological clothes. They had naked power.

So, the one-party state was one aspect of what Ali Mazrui, the East African scholar, calls "the search for stability." Indeed, if you measure stability by longevity in office, several of the rulers mentioned above found it by turning to the one-party state: Senghor, in power for 20 years in Senegal; Houphouët, something close to 30 in Cote d'Ivoire (Ivory Coast); Kenyatta for 15 years in Kenya, and only ended with his death; Nyerere for 24 years in Tanzania; Kaunda, 27 years in Zambia; and Mobutu, 32 in the Congo, or Zaïre as he called it.

In many cases, longevity was papering over growing instability, but even stability as a measure strictly by longevity in office was not the case—was illusive—in a great many other places.

So, what were the threats to stability? One of them certainly was ethnic conflict. As we know, almost all the African countries contained numerous "nations," if you will—ethnic groups, so-called "tribes"—and faced a rather daunting task, before and after independence, of building a new and larger sense of national identity based on the externally imposed units. Why did Kaunda start every rally with "One Zambia!" and have the crowd shout back to him, "One Nation!"? Trying to build that new form of national identity.

In my view, there's nothing "natural"—it's often assumed to be—or inevitable—it's often assumed to be—about ethnic conflict or ethnic difference. Tolerance and coexistence are just as common historically between ethnic groups as conflict, but it's also not surprising that in a struggle in an arena—the state arena—over quite limited resources in these new nations and with these greatly heightened expectations and hopes, it's not surprising—shouldn't be surprising to us—that people often mobilized around ethnic lines.

As we stressed early on, and I always stress when I talk about ethnicity or so-called "tribe" or nation in Africa, ethnicity is fluid. It's changeable. It's expandable, contractible, etc. You can see this in the history of previously quite separate communities coming together to mobilize as an ethnic bloc. I've seen this in southern Zambia, where you find that peoples who often had conceived of themselves as separate "tribes," if you like—separate ethnic groups—begin to discover, or at the very least begin to emphasize, cultural affinities, cultural similarities, common identities…Why? I suggest partly to mobilize for power for resources—for a piece of the pie.

In its more benign form, this is common to politics in very many places. The situation I'm describing could lead, for instance, in Africa as it has elsewhere to "ethnic balancing acts"—taking the cabinet and making sure that there are enough from the east and from the west and enough Bemba, enough Lozi, enough Nyanja, enough Tonga so that indeed everybody gets a piece of the pie and keeps the lid of satisfaction on.

This is quite familiar to any student, I think, of, say, American politics. Again, it's something quite common, so the benign form there.

But in certain circumstances in these African nations (to use Crowder's term) "cobbled together" at one point—he's talking about the borders and the artificiality of the borders constructed during the Scramble—in certain circumstances, this ethnic reality was dynamite. The most obvious example here was Achebe's home country, Nigeria, the most populous country in all of Africa. Something like one out of every five or six Africans on the continent today is a Nigerian.

In Nigeria, we find three large ethnic blocs—there are many smaller ones—coexisting in the past and in the present uneasily: the Hausa and Fulani in the north, heavily Islamic area there; the Yoruba in the southwest, who probably had the greatest prosperity in the middle, at least, of the colonial period because of cocoa production; and the Ibo peoples in the southeast.

The Ibo in particular—and this, in fact, is Achebe's home ethnic group—had taken to Western education with alacrity and often wound up in relatively elevated positions all through the country of Nigeria. In other words, they would get a position of bureaucracy and be posted to the north, or the west, or to the capital, or what have you. To some extent, this is echoed in commercial life as well.

Ibo people, then, increasingly found themselves to be the targets, frankly, of resentment.

All of this exploded in 1966 on the occasion of Nigeria's first military coup. It erupted in the north. What can only be called *pogroms*—systematic attacks resulting in thousands of deaths of Ibo—were carried out in northern Nigeria in 1966. A great number of Ibo from there and from elsewhere in Nigeria retreated, if you like, to their home area in the southeast, and leaders led by Colonel Ojukwu in the southeast essentially declared independence. They attempted to secede from Nigeria, and the name that they gave their fledgling or would-be potential new nation was Biafra.

This all took off in 1967. Nigeria's rulers had other ideas, as you might expect. A bloody civil war raged from 1967 to 1970. This was the first time that I personally can remember the images that have become so distressingly familiar of essentially hungry or starving children, in this case the results of food cordons or prevention of food getting through into southeastern Nigeria.

At the war's end, the military ruler of Nigeria, Yakubu Gowon, adopted a very Lincolnesque posture and asserted that there would be no victors, no vanquished, and so on. So Nigerian "unity" prevailed, but anyone can see 35 years later that it remains precarious.

Another threat to stability was the military coup that I mentioned in passing a moment ago. As no less than Mao Zedong said famously: "Power comes from the barrel of a gun." It is true that any leader, anywhere, without a loyal army is vulnerable. There's a paradox here, at least on the surface, because coups were often launched precisely in the name of restoring stability, of combating "indiscipline" and corruption. We'll come to corruption in a moment.

The officers involved—often young ones—the notion was, "We'll set things right, and then after we've righted the ship, we'll return to the barracks." Frankly, that rarely happened, although it was not unknown. The problem was that once the precedent was set, a new group of officers would get the same idea.

Yet again, Nkrumah in the lead: the shock of his overthrow in 1966—Nkrumah, the "Father of African Nationalism," overthrown, leaves the country as part of his grander and grander international ambitions—actually, he left the country to pursue diplomatic matters related to Vietnam in 1966. He was overthrown and not permitted to come back. The image of people pulling down the statue of himself, which Nkrumah had put up in the capital city, and smashing it to bits was shocking.

But the shock diminished as coup after coup—over 150 of them in all—became a dismally familiar bit of news out of Africa.

Finally and obviously, we must mention corruption. We looked briefly at the Congo's (or Zaïre's) Mobutu, who has to be considered the all-time champion, but many, many others found it impossible to resist the temptation, as Achebe put it, once they were inside the "shelter," albeit on a vastly diminished scale from Mobutu.

Some saw themselves as deserving after all those years of struggle—again, Achebe's image: after all those years of being out there in the rain. Others, as the fine political scientist Peter Ekeh suggests, saw the state arena as an alien trough. He suggests that this was seen as an alien implantation and, therefore, not subject to traditional African mores about accountability and honesty. Again, it echoes Michael Crowder's notion of whose dream was this anyway? If this is an alien thing, then it doesn't pack the same moral punch (or immoral punch) to feed at that trough.

Eventually, as the Ghanaian novelist Ayi Kwei Armah in his book *The Beautyful Ones Are Not Yet Born*, which is a thinly disguised parable, really, about the overthrow of Nkrumah—he showed brilliantly in that novel that at some point, to many people, it simply seemed stupid rather than courageous not to join in this free-for-all.

The larger problem in a way was that it was often what I'll call "dead-end corruption." After all, I take it that corruption of various types and to various degrees is a universal. I simply think that there is no such thing as a political system or a society that is free of corruption. It's a question of degree. It's a question of whether ordinary people can get on with their lives without running into roadblock, after roadblock, after roadblock.

It's a question of whether what corruption does take place is simply a pay-off—in other words, you pay off somebody so that you don't get in bigger trouble—you pay off the police commissioner, or the cop at the roadblock, or what have you. Dead-end corruption like straightforward rip-offs of foreign aid money, such as Mobutu unquestionably carried out—in other words, dead-end corruption like that; not, unfortunately, a sort of "commission" on a project that might otherwise be genuinely productive.

I'm going to paraphrase a story that comes from the book written by Keith Richburg, the African-American journalist who reported for *The Washington Post* for quite a number of years from Africa. It's a story that he was told in Africa. It goes something like this:

There are two quite brilliant, outstanding, young men students: one from an African nation and one from an East Asian nation or southeast Asian nation—one of those economies called the "Asian tigers" eventually. They both earn scholarships, and they both go to

Britain and study at a place like Cambridge or Oxford and study finance. They both come back and become prominent in their home countries and occupy positions like ministers of finance, and so on.

Finally, 20 years later or so, they visit each other. First the African man goes to visit his Asian friend, finds him in a very luxurious home with a swimming pool. They're out there on the deck and overlooking the city, and he sees the freeways, and the skyscrapers, and the apartment blocks, waving palm trees, and so on, and the African asks his Asian friend: "How did you do so well here? How did you get into such good circumstances?"

The Asian friend waves his hand at the city below and says: "Ten percent."

Then the next year, according to Richburg, the visit is reversed. The Asian gentleman visits his African friend and finds him in an equally sumptuous domestic palace with a beautiful home and a swimming pool on a hill, elevated, overlooking the city. But they're looking at streets with potholes with bridges that haven't been repaired, with crumbling skyscrapers and falling down apartment blocks, and so forth.

According to Richburg, the Asian friend asks his African friend: "How did you do so well?" The African friend waves his hand at the city and says: "One hundred percent."

That's what I'm getting at here in terms of corruption, which is, I assume, going to happen, but the degree and what it also accompanies, whether productive or not, is clearly an additional issue.

"Coups, Conflict, and Corruption": That's the title of a *Time Magazine* cover story from the mid-1980s. It's a picture that was/is exaggerated in the West, for sure, but it was real enough, and it wasn't Westerners who were paying the price. Thank you.

Lecture Thirty
The World Turns Down—The "Permanent Crisis"

Scope:

As many African nations seemed to veer between dictatorship on one hand and chaos on the other, world economic conditions turned against them as well. In hindsight, one can see the mid-1970s as a turning point, marked by the international oil shocks and falling prices for exported African commodities. One response was to borrow ever more furiously—and Africa's debt crisis, still with us today, was born. By the 1980s, in such places as Zambia, development seemed to many a bitterly forgotten dream; day-to-day survival seemed a more relevant objective. Add to this South Africa's turmoil and ongoing wars in several hotspots, and more than a few asked: Can it get any worse than this? Then, a funny thing happened: Something like a democratic renaissance began to emerge.

Outline

I. Historians are always trying to "periodize," that is, divide the unbroken stream of time into eras, break points, watersheds, turning points, and so on. The most obvious break point in recent African history is the break between colonial and independent Africa.

   A. For most of the continent, that point was around 1960.

   B. But as Frederick Cooper, professor at Yale, articulates brilliantly, it is possible to make a persuasive argument for the mid-1970s as an equally, perhaps more, important dividing line. As Cooper puts it, this is when "modest progress turned into prolonged crisis."

   1. The modest progress, as we have seen, took place in the late colonial and, especially, the early independent years. By almost any measure—health, mortality, literacy, education, overall growth and development, or political and social participation—ordinary peoples' lives got better.

   2. One context for this was an expansionary world economy, which among other things, created demand for

exports from Africa's still-not-fundamentally-altered economies.

C. Both of these situations changed—dramatically—beginning in the mid-1970s.

    1. The initial stimulus was external. We can start with the oil shocks—major price rises—related ostensibly to Middle East conflict.

    2. Partly because of these shocks, Western economies began to contract, with the dire consequence of reducing the demand and price for the primary products, the agricultural and mineral products, coming out of Africa.

    3. Meanwhile, some Western nations, notably the United States, responded to the problems by raising interest rates to levels hard to imagine today.

    4. Rather suddenly, then, African countries and their leaders confronted conditions in which the value of their exports was falling; the price of their most vital import, oil, was rising; and the cost of funds to make up the difference, let alone invest in future productivity, was rising as well.

D. Given the deteriorating terms of trade—that is, what you can bring in in return for what you send out—even the best leaders would have been presiding over places where they "must run faster and faster to stay in the same place." And, as many Africans would point out, their leaders were often not the best.

    1. Most countries began to see a decline in all the realms that had so recently seen improvement: GNP, industrialization, education, health, and infrastructure.

    2. Understandably, this decline generated discontent. Those in power, who had already moved to one-party states or military rule, reacted defensively by clamping down even further and making sure that feathering their own nests remained a priority, or they were replaced by new rulers through military coups, who then did much the same.

II. Allow me to illustrate from Zambia, as I did in the last lecture and will again in the next.

A. Zambia's principal export, indeed only real export, was copper. And demand for copper began to fall almost exactly at the critical juncture of the mid-1970s. It has never quite recovered. Think of telecommunications: Quite apart from the wireless revolution, even the wires changed over to fiber optics, as opposed to metals, some time ago.

B. Zambia produces no oil, yet of course, oil is absolutely critical for all manner of transportation and energy.

C. With a fall in the crucial export commodity and a rise in the crucial import commodity, Zambia needed to produce much more copper just to stay even. It didn't.

D. In addition, in much of the 1970s, the country was surrounded by wars on three sides: those in Angola, Rhodesia, and Mozambique.

   1. The wars produced direct strains: Tens of thousands of refugees and attacks by Rhodesian forces since President Kaunda's personal commitment to the liberation of Southern Africa led him to allow bases in Zambia for Zimbabwean guerilla forces.

   2. Zambia is a landlocked country; movement of exports and imports has always been lengthy and expensive. With the wars, two of the three main routes were closed.

E. Though Zambia was never a place where persons disappeared in the night, Kaunda's rule became steadily more authoritarian, and the dead hand of state (mis)management created all kinds of shortages. Meanwhile, those at the corrupt top continued to get rich. All this exacerbated public anger and inspired attempted coups.

III. Many countries, Zambia included, borrowed furiously, despite the rise in interest rates, in attempts to keep going what they could of the economy and social services. They were encouraged to do so in some lending sectors from the First World. These were bad business decisions all around. Debt rose exponentially.

A. As the ability to make payment faltered, many turned to lenders of last resort—the International Monetary Fund (IMF) or the World Bank.

B. What help they got came with the considerable strings of Structural Adjustment Programs (SAPs), which called for a reversal of the large state role and a turn to market solutions, including lowering tariffs, reducing social expenditure, devaluing currency to make exports more competitive, and so forth.

C. The jury is still out on SAPs in terms of macro-level improvement; certainly some reforms were necessary. But there is little doubt that for ordinary people, life got harder in terms of declining standards of health care and education and rising costs.

D. The debt crisis is still with us and has recently been the target of campaigns for reduction or forgiveness. The argument is that today's population had nothing to do with the bad decisions (many were not alive) and should not be saddled with insuperable debt-service burdens.

IV. On the face of it, Africa's oil-producing countries should have been in a very different boat. A country such as Nigeria—a member of OPEC—should have benefited from the oil shocks.

A. Yet Nigeria, Angola, and Gabon were what Cooper calls "spigot economies"—the oil was produced by foreign companies for foreign consumers. There was very little linkage to the rest of the economy.

B. And what revenue there was was wasted by astounding levels of mismanagement and corruption. It prompted Achebe to write his blistering jeremiad, *The Trouble with Nigeria.*

V. If all this were not enough, let us add wars. We mentioned Angola, Rhodesia, and Mozambique; add Sudan, Sierra Leone, Liberia, and Somalia. People in these places suffered the worst of the worst.

VI. And add, finally, South Africa, mired in the 1980s in a low-level war of its own. Could things get any worse? Then…phoenix-like, something like a democratic renaissance began to gather steam—the subject of our next lecture.

Suggested Reading:

Chinua Achebe, *Anthills of the Savannah.*

George Ayittey, *Africa Betrayed.*

Frederick Cooper, *Africa since 1940: The Past of the Present*, interlude and chapters 5, 7.

Questions to Consider:

1. Which was the greater "watershed"—independence, coming for most countries around 1960, or Frederick Cooper's alternative date of the mid-1970s?

2. Do IMF/World Bank SAPs represent "the new imperialism," as some critics charge, or commonsense prescriptions for improvement?

Lecture Thirty—Transcript
The World Turns Down—The "Permanent Crisis"

We saw in the last lecture that as the euphoria of independence faded, many African nations seemed to veer somewhere between dictatorship on one hand and instability, if not chaos, on the other. At a certain juncture, world economic conditions turned against them as well.

Historians are always trying to "periodize." We're always trying to divide the unbroken stream of time into eras, epochs, ages, break points, watersheds, turning points, and so on. That's what we do. That's how we argue and find the debates that keep us stimulated. The most obvious break point in recent African history is, of course, the break between colonial and independent Africa, for most of the continent coming, as we've seen, around 1960. I've argued that that is, indeed, an important break point.

On the other hand, as Frederick Cooper articulates brilliantly in his book, *Africa since 1940: The Past of the Present*, a volume that I strongly recommend and have put on the essential reading list for this course—Cooper argues that it's possible to make a persuasive argument for the mid-1970s as an equally, perhaps even more, important dividing line.

As Cooper puts it, this is when "modest progress turns into prolonged crisis." The modest progress, as we have seen, took place in the late colonial period—there certainly was some—and especially in the early independent years. By almost any measure—health, mortality, literacy, education, overall economic growth and development, political and social participation—ordinary lives got better. I've argued also that Africa's leaders in that era deserve some credit for this.

But it's also true that one context for that was an expansionary world economy, which among other things created demand for exports from Africa's still-not-fundamentally-altered or restructured economies. I think it's fair to say that many, if not most, of the independent African territories remained what I called a few lectures back essentially "monoeconomies," dependent upon the export of one to three basic products.

Both of these situations—that is, the modest progress and the hospitable international climate—change, and they change dramatically beginning in the mid-1970s. The initial stimulus was external. We can start with the so-called "oil shocks"—that is, the major price rises of that period related ostensibly, at least, to conflict in the Middle East. Those of you who were around in the U.S., for instance, in 1973, 1974, 1975 can recall the first of these so-called "oil shocks." We've certainly seen some since. I need hardly to make the case, I think, for the centrality of oil in modern economic life everywhere.

So, partly due to these "shocks," Western economies began to contract in the mid-1970s. This had the dire consequence for Africa of reducing the demand and the price for many of the primary products—the agricultural and mineral products—coming out of the continent.

Meanwhile, some Western nations, notably the U.S., responded to the problems they were encountering by raising interest rates to levels hard to imagine more recently. I was fortunate enough to be able to purchase my first home in the late 1970s. Assistant professors normally are purchasing modest homes, but mine had to be particularly modest because the interest rates, of course, that I had to sign on to (in terms of the mortgage) were well into the teens.

Rather suddenly, then, African countries and their leaders confronted conditions in which the value of their exports was falling, on which they were so dependent. The price of—in many instances—their most vital import, oil, was rising. The cost of borrowed funds to make up the difference, let alone to invest in future productivity, was rising as well.

What we have been discussing at one level is captured in a simple but useful concept—a simple term—and that term is the "terms of trade." Essentially, how much can you bring in of a particular commodity in return for what you send out? It is a useful concept, and it doesn't necessarily have to be related only to, for instance, a country's international trade context. I've seen it applied in a place like Zambia, for instance, to terms of trade between the urban and rural sectors. Many African leaders and governments did things such as subsidize food supplies in the urban areas precisely because their judgment, which has turned out to be correct, is that urban areas are where popular protest and disruption are most likely to be carried out. So, terms of trade can be applied in many contexts.

Let's bring it back to the notion of how much can you bring in in terms of how much you are sending out. If the terms of trade are deteriorating—that is, from your perspective, from where you sit, if you can bring in less and less for what you send out—in a situation like that, and that was the situation for much of Africa beginning in the mid-1970s, even the best leaders would have been presiding over places where, as one of the ones put it: "We must run faster and faster to stay in the same place." As many Africans would not be hesitant to point out, their leaders were often not the best.

So, from about this juncture, most countries began to see a decline in all the realms that had so recently seen improvement: in overall GNP, product, economic growth becomes negative; in industrialization; in education; health; and infrastructure. Understandably, this in turn, generated discontent. Those in power, who in very many cases had already moved to one-party states or military rule, as we traced in the last lecture, reacted defensively by clamping down even further and making sure that feathering their nests in this declining situation remained a priority—or, in some cases, they were replaced by new rulers through a military coup, who then did much the same thing.

Allow me, once again, as I did in the last lecture and will in the next lecture, to illustrate from the place I think I know best—and that is Zambia. As we've seen, Zambia's principal export—indeed, its only real export—was copper. From the time copper is discovered in Zambia in the 1930s along its so-called "copper belt," the figure for copper as a percentage of Zambia's (even Northern Rhodesia's, during the colonial period) exports was consistently over 90%—and, in some cases, over 95%.

As Kenneth Kaunda, the country's first president put it—again, someone whom I described some in the last lecture—"We were born with a copper spoon in our mouth." It's a rather striking way to say that, "We had some things going for us. We had some blessings at independence." He was referring to this long-run boom, if you like—there were certainly slumps in it, but it was essentially consistently expansionary world demand for the one thing that Zambia had in abundance: that, of course, was copper.

Demand from the outside world for copper, though, begins to fall almost exactly at Cooper's critical juncture of the mid-1970s. It has never quite recovered. I don't mean to say that it's disappeared, obviously, but it's never gotten back to the buoyant phases that we saw in the late 1940s, in the 1950s, and much of the 1960s.

There are numerous reasons for this, but even a moment's reflection, I think, would tell us one. If you think of telecommunications, quite apart from the whole wireless revolution that we're all witnessing, of course, even if we think of the wired kinds of communications, quite some time ago, metals, including copper, began to be replaced in wires in this critical industry with things like fiber optics, and so on.

Zambia produces no oil. It doesn't produce any petroleum whatsoever—not one drop comes out of this landlocked country. Yet, of course, oil is absolutely critical, as it is everywhere, for the matters of transportation and applications of energy to all kinds of projects, including running the machinery to operate the copper mines.

With the fall, then, in the crucial export commodity and a rise in the crucial imported commodity, Zambia needed to produce much more copper just to stay even. It produced somewhat more copper, but it certainly did not stay even. We start a downward slide from which, in a number of respects, the country has yet to escape.

Just to add a few more straws to the camel's back in the case of Zambia, during the 1970s, the country is surrounded on three sides by war: in Angola to the west, Mozambique to the east (we looked at those so-called late decolonization cases a couple of lectures back), and of course, its old partner in the federation days, Rhodesia.

The wars produced direct strains on Zambia in the 1970s quite apart from the kinds of terms-of-trade troubles that I've been outlining: tens of thousands of refugees from these wars, flowing into western Zambia from Angola, flowing into eastern Zambia from Mozambique, and so on.

From Rhodesia, there were certainly refugees, but it went a bit further in that case. Zambian President Kaunda's personal commitment—and it was a personal commitment, and he paid for it—to the liberation of southern Africa, if you like, led him to allow bases in Zambia initially for both guerilla movements in Zimbabwe, but eventually for one. He allowed the bases for the ZAPU movement (Zimbabwe African People's Union) in various places in Zambia.

Of course, Rhodesia was directly next door, and many places in Zambia were very quickly reached by the aircraft controlled by Ian Smith's Rhodesian air force. In my visit to Zambia in 1979, just as the Zimbabwean war was coming finally to a close, but it certainly was not there yet, this came home very vividly. There were two or three occasions in the capital, when I would walk out of the archives, and someone would say, "Look that way. Look to the west." You could see the smoke rising from fighter bomber attacks essentially launched from Rhodesia and hitting ZAPU bases, which everybody knew were located some miles to the west of the capital.

Indeed, Joshua Nkomo, the leader of ZAPU, at that time, his headquarters was in a house in a residential area in the capital of Zambia Lusaka. I remember being taken by friends of mine in a car around to see this house after it had been attacked in a lightning helicopter raid of Smith's forces across the border and right into, in a sort of daylight boldness, the center of Lusaka. The attack on that house had left it a burned-out shell. They actually drove, and you could see barely and literally the bathroom window on the back. In this case, he came out threw the bathroom window. Given that Nkomo is a very large man, or was—he's no longer with us—that's how he escaped. It might have been a quite comic scene had it not been so deadly serious.

I can remember being in Livingstone, which is near Victoria Falls and therefore, of course, right near the border with Rhodesia at that point, and going to the local office of the Ministry of Education and using their phones, finally making telephone contact with a rural school about 20 miles outside of Livingstone, where an old friend of mine from my earlier dissertation research days was a teacher—an assistant principal—and finally getting him on the line and saying, "Well, gee, I'm ready to come and visit you. I'll hire a taxi here in town," and having Nelson Seminagle my friend, saying, "No. Don't come. Forget that. I will come in to see you. I'll explain why."

When he got there, the reason was that that school was right next door to a ZAPU base. Had I rolled into that particular region and rolled past some of those ZAPU guerilla soldiers, they, of course, might have mistaken me for an agent of Mr. Smith, and you can guess the possible outcome at that point.

These wars also had indirect consequences for Zambia. Zambia, after all, is a landlocked country. The movement of exports—its copper—and the imports—the oil, for instance—has always been lengthy and expensive. With the wars on these various sides, two of the three principal routes out of Zambia were, in fact, closed: the one through Angola, and the one through Rhodesia and from there on out to Mozambique. So, this left one of the very few exceptions to the rule we enunciated a few lectures back: that most of railway lines in Africa were built during the colonial period. One great exception to that was the Tanzam Railroad, which connects Tanzania and Zambia. That became the only way to get what copper Zambia could produce out. Okay, but it's a much longer, more expensive route. Again, this adds to the overall declining viability of the industry on which Zambia was most dependent.

Zambia was never a place where people disappeared in the night—where bodies were found as a result of government's kidnapping and murdering them, and so on. It was never like that. Still, it's true to say and it's fair to say that Kaunda's rule became steadily more authoritarian. It's true also that the dead hand in this case of state (mis)management—I'll say it—we know the central role of the state and whatever successes it had earlier, it became increasingly unresponsive to the citizenry's needs and, frankly, less and less efficient.

You could see some very real manifestations of this by the 1970s and into the 1980s. The lines for commodities, when things were not being distributed on basically market models, and so on, you'd see people who got the word, "Well, they're going to bring in cooking oil tomorrow. Let's send a child down there and get in the queue—get in the line." Often these lines would stretch for many blocks, waiting to get an essential or basic commodity. People would send different family members to take each other's places in the lines. You can imagine that tempers flare in a situation like this. This is starting to take on a social and cultural series of manifestations.

Sometimes the (mis)managements and downturn here took on an almost comical kind of appearance. I was raised in Northern Virginia and spent a lot of time in the mountains of Virginia and West Virginia, and I have seen on occasions that young good ol' boys and good ol' girls who want to have a party on a Friday or Saturday night will find somebody's field and bring around the cars or, in many cases, the pickup trucks and assemble them sort of in a circle, and people will shine their headlights (Are there any missing words here? Sounds like maybe a skip in the audio)—a nice little spectacle and a good place to have a party.

I mention that because in 1989, as this crisis goes on and on, I was in Zambia, and I wanted to attend a commemoration of the 50th anniversary of what is the Institute for Social and Economic Research. It started life in 1939 as the Rhodes Livingstone Institute, and it's one of the great research institutions anywhere in Africa. I was an affiliate of it. I still am an affiliate of it. I wanted to be there to be part of the celebration. It was to be held at the Institute's own headquarters.

The reason I mention the headlights, and so on, is because by this time, Zambia's electricity supply was hopelessly erratic. In a place like the capital city, you'd have it on for a few hours, and it would go out; you'd have it on a few hours, it'd go out; and so on. It might be a few hours; it might be a few days, but it was extremely undependable.

All of these dignitaries—some of the great anthropologists and social scientists of the world well beyond my station in life—are assembled for an evening ceremony—well, there's no power. Incredibly, what happened was that they brought a number of government Land Rovers around, assembled them in the old West Virginia-style circle, and that's how we carried out the ceremony.

I remember at a time in the 1980s, there were no matches to be found. When you're in a country where a lot of people still cook over fires, matches are pretty important. They'd bring on the manager of the state-run match factory, and he'd say, "Well, we put 500 cases out there. I don't know where…" You're getting black marketeering, of course, that's going on and extortion that way from these heavy hands of state (mis)management, again.

At the same time that you couldn't get any matches, for instance, though, you could go down the road to the local service station, and you could find hundreds of Zippo lighters. How does that happen? You can imagine if I'm asking that question, what kinds of questions Zambians are asking.

Meanwhile they see that those at least at the very top are continuing to get rich. All of this exacerbated public anger. It inspired attempted coups eventually against Kenneth Kaunda.

What do you do? Many countries, Zambia included, began to borrow furiously despite the rise in the interest rates, which eventually did fall again, of course. They begin to borrow furiously in attempts to keep going what they could of the economy and of the social services that they had built up in the first period after independence.

They were encouraged to do so in some lending sectors from the first world. These were bad business decisions all around, and debt rose exponentially. As the ability to make payments on those debts faltered, many African countries turn to lenders of the last resort—the International Monetary Fund, the World Bank. What help they got came with considerable strings. These are usually referred to as "Structural Adjustment Programs," which called for a reversal of the large state role in these economies and a turn to "market solutions," so-called, including lowering tariffs; most importantly, perhaps, reducing government budgets, including expenditure on social services; devaluing currency to make exports more competitive; and so on.

The supporters of Structural Adjustment Programs essentially argue that these are prescriptions of short-term belt-tightening in order to make long-term growth possible. The critics of the IMF and the World Bank call it long-term belt-tightening in order to facilitate debt repayment.

The jury is still out on SAPs (the Structural Adjustment Programs) in terms of macro-level improvement. There's no doubt that some reforms were certainly necessary—and the dead hand of state (mis)management in Zambia was a good example of that. On the other hand, there's little doubt that for ordinary people, life got harder in terms of declining standards of healthcare and education, or rising costs, to put it differently, as these are privatized and subject to market solutions.

Of course, the debt crisis in Africa is very much still with us and has recently been a target of campaigns for reduction, or restructuring, or forgiveness. A movement organization called Jubilee 2000, which included Archbishop Tutu from South Africa, a Nobel Peace Prize winner, and so on, which took its model from passages in the Old Testament where every 40 or 50 years, or what have you, there was a jubilee, and people were forgiven, and debts were forgiven, and so forth.

In the summer of 2005, a number of great rock stars, and actors, and so forth participated in a series of concerts called "Live 8." The eight there, of course, was a reference to the eight richest countries on earth whose leaders were meeting at the time that these concerts went forth. It made the case—they were trying to get the ear of those governments to restructure, reduce, or forgive debts from the world's poorest countries, most of which are in Africa.

The argument for debt restructuring and forgiveness is essentially that today's population had nothing to do with the bad decisions that were made a generation or two ago, often by leaders that aren't there anymore—and that, therefore, they shouldn't be saddled with it. In other words, if it had been an individual who took on all this credit card debt, or what have you, unwisely, the person might be able to declare bankruptcy and get a fresh start, but that option is not available for countries who continue to bear these burdens.

Maybe at some point in listening or watching this, you said to yourself, "Now wait a minute. Aren't there some oil-*producing* countries in Africa?" On the face of it, shouldn't they have been in a very different boat from the cases like Zambia that I was just discussing? Of course, there's a lot to that. A country like Nigeria, a member of OPEC, for instance, certainly in theory—I would say in reality—should very definitely have *benefited* from the so-called "oil shocks" that did, indeed, shock many countries lying elsewhere on the continent.

Yet Nigeria, Angola, Gabon—they amount to what Cooper calls "spigot" economies. The oil was turned on, as it was. The oil was produced by foreign companies (often by foreign technicians) for foreign consumers. There was very little linkage to the rest of the economy. In a place like Angola, you get some very bizarre scenes in the 1970s and 1980s. Remember that Angola has this ongoing civil war, and you have companies like Gulf producing oil just offshore, and the Marxist government of Angola using its own and Cuban troops to protect the oil production against opponents in Angola's civil war supported by the U.S. government. Talk about strange bedfellows there.

But again, extremely little linkage, and what revenue that the Angolan government got out of oil production often went into the costs of fighting the war. What linkage there was—what revenue did accumulate from oil production in a place like Nigeria—it was an enormous amount of money in terms of raw figures—often it was wasted by astounding levels of (mis)management and corruption.

This prompted our old friend, Chinua Achebe, to write a book that was *not* a novel, and that was a non-fiction essay, essentially, called *The Trouble with Nigeria* (his home country, of course). Achebe in the first couple of pages of that book says, "You know, I don't want to hear it. There's nothing wrong with Nigeria's climate. There's nothing wrong with our culture, nothing wrong with our people, etc. We've been given this great blessing of this oil beneath the surface, and look what's happening to it, and how the rest of us are getting nothing out of it."

He pointed his finger right at the authorities and said the trouble with Nigeria—his terms: "Simply and squarely, a failure of leadership."

If all this were not enough, we can add more wars. We mentioned Angola, Rhodesia, and Mozambique—but, unfortunately, you could add Sierra Leone, Liberia, Somalia, and Sudan; people in those places suffered the worst of the worst. You could finally add South Africa, mired in the 1980s in a low-level war of its own. It's not surprising that many people could ask, "Can things get any worse at this point?"

Then a funny thing happened: Phoenix-like, something like a democratic renaissance began to gather steam—and we turn to that in our next lecture. Thank you.

Lecture Thirty-One
A New Dawn? The Democratic Revival

Scope:

If the "winds of change" were sweeping across Africa in the early 1960s, in the late 1980s and early 1990s, they seemed to affect the whole globe. As the Soviet Bloc and the Berlin Wall fell, authoritarian regimes in many parts of Africa faced unprecedented challenges to open up, to permit opposition organizing and free speech, and to loosen the state's grip on economic life. There has been considerable debate over whether the impetus for this change came from below, from frustrated citizens, or from outside, from frustrated donors. There is room for both in our analysis. In any case, in country after country, civilian replaced military rule, and/or one-party states gave way to multiparty competition. Of course, as in the heady days of independence, disappointment resurfaced. Nonetheless, certain "lessons learned"—about popular participation, about transparency—seem unlikely to be reversed.

Outline

I. It's still a bit breathtaking to think back to the years of the late 1980s and early 1990s.

  A. To Americans raised on the Cold War, the collapse of the Soviet Union and the satellite regimes of East Europe—symbolized by the Berlin Wall—were almost unbelievable and certainly unpredicted.

  B. But other parts of the world—Latin America and most definitely our focus, sub-Saharan Africa—were equally part of a rising tide of democracy and freedom.

II. The international context is indeed important for the African case, in two ways.

  A. On one hand, we have the inspirational power of example—if they can do it, why can't we?

  B. On the other, we see the much more mundane form of pressure from international donors, upon which many African regimes had become dependent.

III. But let's begin with the more exciting stuff, the internal pressures generated by African citizens themselves against their authoritarian rulers. I will rely heavily here on the masterful synthesis of *Democratic Experiments in Africa* by Michael Bratton and Nick van de Walle, who developed a prototypical succession of steps seen in country after country between 1989 and 1994.

    A. The preconditions are the economic crisis surveyed in our last lecture and the generalized, deepening crisis of legitimacy facing African rulers as the 1980s progressed. People had simply lost faith that their leaders could solve their problems or offer them a better life or were even much trying: *They* are living high on the hog while *we* suffer.

    B. Widespread popular protests broke out, mainly over economic grievances, above all, the erosion of purchasing power.

        1. Students shut down universities over bursaries that left them literally hungry; trade unions and civil servants struck over pay holdups and freezes; market women demonstrated over imposed price freezes.

        2. Almost entirely, the protests were urban rather than rural in base.

    C. Authoritarian rulers responded in the usual fashion, which I would characterize as *crack down* and/or *buy off.* But the critical difference this time around was that the constricted economy limited the resources with which they could do either. The protests did not abate.

    D. Instead, they took on an increasingly political character. People—again, often inspired by the sense of possibility that the international context offered—began to fashion genuine visions of alternatives. At a minimum, and most importantly, this meant an end to political monopolies, either one-party or military rule.

    E. The next step in the developing dialectic was political liberalization by the rulers: End the government monopoly of all media and allow the discussion of a return to multiparty competition. We can control and limit the process and palliate the dissension.

F. The opposition took due advantage of the opening, often by organizing the ubiquitous national conference. Often presided over by unassailable figures—religious leaders, for instance—these conferences actually drafted alternative constitutions and sometimes even declared themselves sovereign!

IV. At this point, we should step back and return to the international context.

   A. With the end of the Cold War, African leaders could no longer proclaim their Marxism-Leninism or their anticommunism and expect aid from one side or the other.

   B. With the collapse of the Soviet Bloc, assistance from the West became, essentially, the only game in town. Thus, the SAPs of the IMF/World Bank, which we encountered in the last lecture, loomed that much larger.

   C. On the surface, it's slightly hard to believe that the policymakers of the IMF and World Bank, on the one hand, and struggling urban Africans, on the other, would share an agenda, but in some respects, they did. The donors were concerned about the sheer inefficiency of corrupt, closed regimes, a concern that meshed with the yearnings of "the people."

   D. Thus, various degrees of political conditionality were increasingly a part of SAP packages—hold multiparty elections, allow independent media, and so on.

   E. That said, Bratton and van de Walle conclude, and I agree, that these international pressures, though important, were secondary to the domestic ones.

V. In any case, all over Africa, one-party and military regimes conceded the inevitability of multiparty elections, which were duly held. This period was the high tide of the democratization movements; after this period, things become less clear.

VI. I will again illustrate from my first love, Zambia.

   A. By the late 1980s, Zambia was, to be blunt, a mess, an economic basket case. People were fed up with Kaunda's regime; a nice man, perhaps, but they had had it.

B. True to the model, protests erupted, especially food riots when subsidies were removed on staples. Kaunda was able to repulse a coup attempt.

C. Heavily dependent on foreign assistance at this point, Kaunda had little choice but to listen to Western encouragement of liberalization—including that from his friend Jimmy Carter.

D. The opposition coalesced around the perfectly named Movement for Multiparty Democracy (MMD), led by the diminutive trade unionist Frederick Chiluba.

E. In 1991, elections were held. Kaunda, rather like Mugabe in Zimbabwe a decade later (about which we will hear more in Lecture Thirty-Five), was shocked when the people rejected him after 27 years, electing Chiluba president by a margin of four to one.

F. To his everlasting credit, Kaunda accepted the verdict and went gracefully. In fact, his stock has resurged more recently, as the replacement proved far more corrupt than the incumbent.

VII. Some might say that the "democratic moment" came—and went.

    A. To be sure, this "revolution of rising expectations," like the first one at independence, has met much disappointment.

        1. Some leaders held on to power, manipulating the very reforms they permitted.

        2. In other cases, once in power, the new leaders, like Chiluba, proved worse than the old.

    B. Still, there is virtually not a single official one-party state or military government in Africa. In such places as Zambia, people and parties compete for power with a tolerance unthinkable a short time ago. People are less likely to acquiesce in corruption and misrule, and I doubt they will go back.

Suggested Reading:

Michael Bratton and Nick van de Walle, *Democratic Experiments in Africa: Regime Transitions in Comparative Perspective.*

Questions to Consider:

1. Do you think the democratic resurgence of the late 1980s/early 1990s in Africa would have occurred, could have occurred, without the equally dramatic democratizations elsewhere, such as the collapse of the Soviet bloc?

2. Has there been a paradigm shift in Africa's political culture, or have the basic problems merely been papered over? Are we likely to see one-party states or military regimes again?

Lecture Thirty-One—Transcript
A New Dawn? The Democratic Revival

Welcome. It's still a bit breathtaking to think back to the years of the late 1980s and early 1990s. If the "winds of change" were sweeping across Africa in the early 1960s or even earlier in the 1950s, in the late 1980s and early 1990s, they seemed to affect the whole globe.

To Americans raised on the Cold War, the collapse of the Soviet Union and the satellite regimes of East Europe—symbolized, perhaps above all, by the literal collapse of the Berlin Wall—was almost unbelievable, and certainly unpredicted. It's true. It was not predicted in virtually any quarter. Liberals thought that for better or worse, the Soviet Union was here to stay and you better learn to coexist with it or else we'll blow up the whole world. Conservatives considered it the "evil empire," constantly expanding its strength and perhaps installing new bases in the New World and the Western Hemisphere like Nicaragua. It's actually only on the far intellectual right, people like Milton Friedman, who predicted that the Soviet experiment would collapse of its own weight. It's food for thought.

In any case, the other parts of the world involved in this rising tide of democracy and (let's call it what it was) freedom certainly included Latin America and, not least, our own focus, sub-Saharan Africa. The international context of the late 1980s and 1990s is important for our African case in two main ways: first, through the inspirational power of example. "If they can do it," people asked, "Why can't we?" Just as India in the late 1940s—becoming independent in 1947 and 1948—served as a model of inspiration for the aspirations for independence in Africa, we see something similar in the dynamic at this point.

Secondly, the international context was important in the more mundane form of pressure from international donors upon which many African regimes had become dependent.

Let's begin, though, with the more exciting stuff: the internal pressures generated by African citizens themselves against their authoritarian rulers. I will rely substantially here on the masterful synthesis of the whole process in a book called *Democratic Experiments in Africa* by Michael Bratton and Nick van de Walle.

Michael Bratton grew up in Southern Rhodesia, which became Rhodesia. He left that country rather than be drafted to be a soldier in Ian Smith's army and began his research at the same time I was next door in Zambia. Since then, he's conducted ongoing political science research in many countries in Africa. I don't know anybody with a better grip, a better understanding, and a more encyclopedic knowledge, and I'm going to depend on him.

They develop in this book a prototypical succession of steps seen in country after country between about 1989 and 1994. I'd like to summarize them for you.

The precondition is the economic crisis surveyed in our last lecture, as well as the generalized, deepening crisis of legitimacy facing African rulers as the 1980s progressed. People had simply lost faith that their leaders could deliver any more, could solve their problems or offer them a better life—or even worse, that they were very much trying. "They are living high on the hog while we suffer."

The second step, then, follows from the first: Widespread popular protests broke out, again, in country after country, some of the very first in the West African country of Benin, formerly known as Dahomey. Protests break out mainly over economic grievances, above all the erosion of purchasing power. It's another way, I suppose, of looking at the terms of trade: What do I have to pay to get a loaf of bread?

Students shut down universities over bursaries that left them literally hungry; trade unions and civil servants struck over pay hold-ups and freezes; market women demonstrated over imposed price freezes. Almost entirely, the protests were urban rather than rural in base. That probably shouldn't surprise us. Cities, after all, since the wave of strikes that we looked at a few lectures back in the 1930s and 1940s and that very much preconditioned the rise of nationalism—cities have been where the action was.

The third step, then, is that the authoritarian rulers responded in the usual fashion, which I would characterize as crack down and/or buy off—that is, use a lot of stick but also some carrot. But the critical difference this time around was that the constricted economy limited the resources with which the authoritarian rulers could do either of these things (either crack down or, especially, buy off). The protests, therefore, did not abate.

Instead—and here's our fourth step—they took on an increasingly politicized and aggressive character. People (again often inspired by the sense of possibility that the international context offered) began to fashion genuine visions of alternatives: "Maybe it doesn't have to be this way." At a minimum, and most importantly, in many people's minds, this called for an end to political monopolies, whether those took the form of the one-party states or they took the form of the military governments usually created by military coups.

The next step in the developing dialectic was political liberalization by the rulers: "Okay, we'll end the government monopoly of all the media. We'll allow the discussion of a return—just talk about it, at least—of a return to multiparty competition. We can control still and limit the process. We can palliate the dissension. Again, we can let the steam off a bit."

It rarely seems to work that way, as we've seen before when the British and French reformed their empires. Soon enough, they lost them. When the Soviet Union began its process of reform, it was the beginning of the end.

The opposition took due advantage of the openings, often by organizing the ubiquitous national conference. You see a form of this happening again in country after country. It's usually a gathering of all manner of representatives from what a lot of people call "civil society"—that is, from women's organizations, cooperatives, the Boy Scouts, certainly churches, trade unions, and so on. They're usually presided over by figures with a sort of an above-it-all kind of status—a sort of unassailable status—quite often religious figures—a bishop, for instance—who by virtue of their own virtue and by virtue of their position are less likely to wind up being arrested, for instance.

So, these conferences actually drafted—in many cases—alternative constitutions, and sometimes they even declared themselves to be sovereign! Again, like some of the things that took place in the 1950s, these were enormously exciting gatherings, assemblies of people by their participants. I think of a scholar like Georges Nzongola-Ntalaja, based at Howard University but originally from the Congo and the author of a number of works on Congolese history, and his own excitement in taking part in the early 1990s in a national convention in—where else?—Mobutu's Zaïre at that time.

Even though subsequent history has certainly not turned in terribly positive directions, Nzongola certainly will make the case that this was a permanent contribution to what must eventually come in his home country. He'll argue, for instance, that merely the testimony that they gathered day, after day, after day of how the Mobutu regime actually worked will in the long run prove valuable.

At this point, we should step back and again return to the international context. With the collapse of the Soviet Union came, of course, the effective end of the Cold War. We've seen in previous lectures just how important the Cold War context could be in a place like the Belgian Congo and in a place like Angola. African leaders, with the disappearance of this Cold War context, could no longer simply proclaim their Marxism-Leninism, for instance, and expect aid from the Soviet Union, as Agostinho Neto and the MPLA government in Angola, for instance, could.

They could no longer proclaim their adherence to capitalism and anti-communism as Mobutu in Zaïre did or as Jonas Savimbi, the would-be president—the rebel leader in the UNITA movement—in Angola did. They couldn't simply proclaim their anti-communism and automatically expect aid from the West. So, this definitely reduces the options available to Africa's leaders.

With the collapse of the Soviet bloc, assistance from the West became, essentially, the only game in town. We go from what they would have called a "bipolar world" to, essentially, a "monopolar world." There's one superpower, the United States, very much alive with the economic union—the European union—in Europe, obviously. Essentially that's where one has to turn.

In this respect, the "Structural Adjustment Programs" (the "SAPs") of the institutions like the International Monetary Fund and the World Bank, and which we looked at at the close of the last lecture, in this new context, the SAP option, with it being or becoming essentially the only game in town, looms that much larger.

On the surface, it's slightly hard to believe that the policymakers of the IMF and the World Bank on one hand and struggling urban Africans on the other would share an agenda. But, in some respects, they did. The donors were interested in—were concerned mainly about—the sheer inefficiency in basic economic performance measurement—the sheer inefficiency of corrupt and closed regimes.

The "people," on the other hand, if I can say that, said, "Damn right! Open 'em up! We agree. These closed and corrupt regimes can no longer deliver. Let's get something in their place."

So, various degrees of political conditionality were increasingly a part of the SAP packages—these Structural Adjustment Programs. In other words, it isn't simply, "Lower the tariff barriers," or, "Balance your budget," or, "Devalue your currency." Now the lenders of last resort are multiparty elections. They're insisting on removing the curbs on media and allowing publication of independent newspapers, in some cases even broadcasting being opened up as well.

So, these features—the end of the Cold War, the political accountability criteria beginning to be added to the Structural Adjustment Programs—are aspects of this international context, which certainly made a difference in the democratization movements that we are discussing.

That said, Bratton and van de Walle conclude—and I agree—that these international pressures, though important, were secondary to the domestic one—secondary to the ones generated from the populations themselves.

In any case, all over Africa—and I do mean all over Africa—one-party and military regimes eventually conceded the inevitability of multiparty elections, which were duly held. In a lot of respects, that moment coming in the early 1990s (in most cases) was the moment of the high tide—the peak tide—of these democratization movements. After them, things become less clear. The water muddies again. We shouldn't expect a fairy tale, and we don't get one.

Yet again, let me illustrate from my first love, and that is Zambia. By the late 1980s, Zambia was, to be blunt, a mess—an economic basket case. You might say that it was on life support, except there was very little support coming through the tubes—the IV. People had lost their patience with Kenneth Kaunda's regime—a nice man maybe, but we have had it.

I can give you two illustrations of this, one urban and one rural. I was in Zambia in 1989 conducting research, and for a time I lived in a hostel attached across the road from the University of Zambia, which by that time, I'm sad to say, had become a shadow of that gleaming new citadel of learning that represented the hopes of the whole generation and the whole country when it was built in the 1960s. In any case, I'm living amongst a group, essentially, of graduate students at the university, of young lecturers—very bright people, indeed. Most of us took our rather humble meals in the hostel's dining hall each evening, and most people—there wasn't a whole lot to do—retired to the lounge to watch a little bit of TV on the one black-and-white television that we had at this hostel.

On most evenings, the news, which, of course, was controlled by the government—controlled by the one party allowed to be legally in existence and to control the government—the news usually included and turned to President Kaunda's message for the day, or his activities of the day, or what have you. Time after time, when that stage came, these young people simply got up and left. They didn't throw things at the television. They didn't curse it or curse him, I suspect because, on the one hand, of some lingering respect that they still had for a guy who did retain a fundamental sense of decency throughout, and secondly because it had, perhaps, become increasingly dangerous to take aggressive anti-Kaunda stances.

Let me give you a royal example, though. Down in southern Zambia amongst the village folk that I have been visiting for 30 years or so, if you're visiting down there and you take a nice meal produced usually, it has to be said, by the women of a particular household—a meal of *nshima*, let's say, that thick porridge based on ground cornmeal, and some nice *gishu*, some sauce perhaps it's made from *nyama* (meat), *madede* (tomatoes), or *nkuku* (chicken). After you've finished a meal like that, the proper thing to say—the polite thing to say—is to say, "*Twakuta.*" In fact, you might even sort of rub your belly a bit. *Twakuta* means "satisfying—I'm full. Thank you." It's a form of courtesy. It's a form of etiquette. *Twakuta*: I'm full.

People by 1989 were muttering *"Twakuta"* in a very different context. The closest translation would be: "We're fed up. We've had a bellyful of Kaunda. We've had a bellyful of one-party rule," and so on. So, true to the model proposed by Bratton and van de Walle, protests begin to erupt, again particularly in the cities, especially what were usually called "food riots" when the subsidies were removed on staples, particularly (again) the staple at this point in Zambia's history, obviously maize meal or maize cornmeal.

Bear in mind that the removal of the subsidies on this is often in response to the prescriptions of the Structural Adjustment Programs, which call for allowing the price of cornmeal to rise to its economic level, and so forth. The notion of subsidizing urban consumption is often lifted as one of the conditions of obtaining assistance from external donors—but, of course, perhaps predictably, this turns around and has consequences in terms of discontent and the eruption of protests.

Indeed, by the late 1980s, we have a couple of instances where Kaunda is able to stay in power by repelling or repulsing attempts at military coup.

Heavily dependent on foreign assistance at this point, Kaunda had little choice but to listen to Western encouragement of liberalization, including the encouragement that came from his friend Jimmy Carter, who as we know has remained quite active in international affairs since his retirement from the presidency. Indeed they are friends. They share some things. They both have lost the presidency, although Kaunda had a considerably longer run at it than Carter. But I think the real basis for their friendship, frankly, is very simple: It's a shared quite deep and sincere Christianity.

Now the opposition in Zambia coalesced around the perfectly named Movement for Multiparty Democracy (the MMD), which was led by the diminutive trade unionist, Frederick Chiluba. Chiluba occupied, then, the head of what had always been—from the 1930s on—a strategic point of power, and that is the apex of workers' organizations. After all, in the critical industries like copper, organized workers obviously wield a very considerable measure of influence and power. Chiluba had used that trade union position to gradually expand his own agenda and his own visions and was supported by many for doing so.

I said "diminutive." Chiluba is quite the opposite from figures like Joshua Nkomo in Zimbabwe or Jonas Savimbi in Angola. He stands barely five feet tall, but believe me, he loomed large at that moment, articulating again and again the necessity for change—and change now. Somebody gave me a tee shirt from the early 1990s in Zambia that is an MMD tee shirt, and it has a picture of Chiluba on one side, and on the other side, it has a picture of a clock. The minute hand is up there at about :58 or :59, and it says: "The hour has come." That was their mantra, repeated again and again. Now is the time to open this system up—the Movement for Multiparty Democracy.

Finally, in 1991, elections were held. Kaunda, and this is a precursor to a phenomenon we'll see in our 35th lecture on Zimbabwe and Robert Mugabe—Kaunda actually believed that he'd prevail. He was the father of the nation. We sometimes lose sight of the fact of how isolated from reality leaders can become. Sometimes people talk about, you know, the isolation of the Oval Office in the case of American politics, or what have you, but it's true that leaders can often be surrounded by people who tell them the good news—and tell them that the people are still behind them, and so forth.

Kaunda, in a lot of respects, was genuinely shocked when the results of this election, which international observers by and large pronounced to be free and fair, came in. The electorate had rejected Kaunda after 27 years in power and elected none other than Frederick Chiluba by a margin—and it is a staggering margin—of four to one: 80% to 20% against Kaunda, the father of the nation, and replacing him with Frederick Chiluba.

To his everlasting credit, Kaunda accepted the verdict. He didn't cancel the election after it's gone on for several hours or after the returns are coming in. That certainly has happened in other places. He didn't decide that it had been fraudulent, which would have been hard to do since his own government organized it in many respects. He accepted it, and he went gracefully. He offered his successor the best.

Like Carter, Kaunda has remained active and, in fact, his stock has risen again in Zambia. In the decade and a half, or something like that, since he was thrown out of office, many people, precisely because his incumbent proved more corrupt than anybody in Kaunda's regime, have taken to reminiscing a bit about the good ol' days under Kaunda—something that would have been unthinkable in the late 1980s.

It is sad to say that Chiluba began a very hopeful moment in Zambia's history and allowed it or turned it himself quite sour. He has, in fact, in the last couple of years actually been arrested and charged with corruption. He is out on what we would call "bail." At this point, it remains to be seen whether those charges will materialize or not.

Some might say, looking at Zambia or elsewhere in Africa, that the "democratic moment" came and that it went—that we had a sort of return to the status quo ante. To be sure, this "revolution of rising expectations"—or maybe we should call it "revolution of rising expectations II"—it's the second democratic revolution in recent African history. Like the first one—the one that, of course, revolved around the gaining of independence—this revolution has met with much disappointment. Some leaders held onto power, manipulating the very reforms they permitted. In other cases, as I've just mentioned, a figure like Chiluba proved worse than the old, once in power.

Also, we might pause here to say that freedom can mean many things. As in the Soviet Union, freedom from the old regime of the Communist Party dictatorship certainly opened up a lot of things that we recognize as democratic, or libertarian, or what have you. But freedom has also resulted in the former Soviet Union—in a place like Russia—as I think a lot of Russians could tell you, in the freedom to swindle, the freedom to hustle, and the freedom to cheat. You have a greater scope to sort of act the part of the confidence man once the party monopoly on things is no longer in place.

People in southern Zambia, for instance, the farmers I've been talking about, they used to curse at the inefficiency, and the slowness, and so forth of the government-owned marketing boards who would collect the maize from them, or the cotton, or what have you—but, you know, they'd get there late, and some of it would spoil, or the checks that they were promised didn't come, and so forth and so on.

At first, this seemed like a great alternative. Those boards are gone. The marketing operations are now in private hands, but they then found, of course, that they'd have guys who would show up in trucks, take the maize, promise payment of one sort or another, and issue them counterfeit stuff or simply disappear—you know, come in and spirit it off in the middle of the night, and so forth. Freedom is great stuff, but it can take a lot of unpredicted—and not always positive—turns.

We can be as disappointed as we like, but it's almost true to say that today, there is not a single official one-party state or military government left in Africa. In places like Zambia, people and parties compete for power with a tolerance that was unthinkable even a little while ago. People are less likely to acquiesce in corruption. There's a lively free and critical press. They're less likely to accept misrule. I doubt that they will go back.

No, it wasn't a fairy tale, but the democratization movements were a courageous step forward and should be recognized as such. Thank you.

Lecture Thirty-Two
The South African Miracle

Scope:

If any country, anywhere, saw a democratic breakthrough stunning enough to rival the Soviet Union's, it was South Africa. In the 1960s–1980s, even with African nationalist movements outlawed, their leaders imprisoned or exiled, and the white Afrikaner leadership exuding confidence, the cracks in apartheid's foundation gradually widened. We examine the martyred Steve Biko's Black Consciousness movement, the Soweto schoolchildren's revolt of 1976, a halting guerilla war, and the growing international pressure in the form of sanctions. In the mid-1980s, South Africa seemed destined for a future of unending low-level turmoil, à la Israel/Palestine. Then, no less than Nelson Mandela, from behind bars, began to find common ground with a new generation of realists within the ruling camp. The end result has rightly been termed a miracle—a negotiated transition to genuine majority rule, with stability and economic growth.

Outline

I. There were many remarkable stories of democratic transition in the late 1980s and early 1990s—the Soviet Union, Eastern Europe, in Latin America, in several countries in Africa—but it's hard to top South Africa. In 1990, Nelson Mandela was in prison, and no black South African could vote. Four years later, he was elected president of the nation.

II. When last we focused on South Africa, we ended by noting that in the late 1960s and early 1970s, apartheid appeared to be in the saddle.

   A. The active opposition had been silenced, with Mandela jailed for life and his and other movements banned, operating in exile if at all.

   B. The government was pursuing its grand apartheid scheme of separate development, and the white population was prospering.

   C. But beneath the surface, trouble was brewing for the rulers.

III. A number of key factors and a number of key steps led to South Africa's transformation. Let us examine them in turn.

    A. The quiet of the late 1960s and early 1970s was deceptive. Black anger never diminished but needed channeling in place of resignation.

        1. A crucial development, especially among the younger black population, was the movement usually called *Black Consciousness.*

        2. In many respects, it was, first and foremost, a psychological movement: It called on black South Africans to "free their minds first"—to utterly reject the notions of inferiority the system handed them and to respect and take pride in themselves and their capacity to change things.

        3. The preeminent spokesman for the movement was a brilliant and charismatic medical student, Steve Biko. Constantly harassed by the authorities, Biko, with his biting, incisive analyses and steadfast humor, struck a chord with many, particularly the young.

    B. In 1976, the cocksure government made a classic blunder: It ordered that certain subjects be taught in Afrikaans in secondary schools.

        1. Many objected on many grounds, but to the black students, this order was tantamount to having the "language of the oppressor" crammed down their throats.

        2. The outrage led students in Soweto, South Africa's biggest township, to organize a rally and march—large but peaceful.

        3. The police responded, as they had at Sharpeville in 1960, with gunfire. But this time, it was not a one-off affair: In the days, weeks, and months to come, the conflagration spread throughout South Africa. Police battled defiant students, hundreds if not thousands were killed, and townships were in flames.

        4. Something like order returned, but a bit more than a year later, Steve Biko was arrested at a roadblock. In the next several days, he was essentially murdered by the security forces. South Africa erupted again.

5. We have spoken before of watersheds and turning points and periods. For my money, 1976 marks a watershed: From that date, it was a matter of when, not if, the apartheid system would fall.

C. Meanwhile, the African National Congress had been intensifying its military campaign against the regime, directed from abroad from bases in Zambia, Angola, and Tanzania.

1. Many young people from the "generation of '76" slipped across the borders and revitalized the guerilla forces. And they began to slip back, organizing attacks on police stations, the Air Force headquarters, and other targets.

2. This was important; however, at no time did the ANC have the strictly military capacity to, say, ride into Pretoria in tanks as the North Vietnamese/Viet Cong did in Vietnam.

D. More important, in my view, was a state of civil insurrection, driven by young comrades, youth activists. "Make the townships ungovernable," the ANC had called for from abroad, and indeed, this is what happened, though hardly at the ANC's specific direction. The comrades had developed a momentum of their own.

E. The 1980s can be viewed as the decade of "neo-apartheid," symbolized by the country's penultimate white leader, P. W. Botha.

1. Botha initiated a series of cautious reforms, including elimination of passes (identity booklets).

2. His constitutional reforms of 1983 ended the exclusively white parliaments but replaced them with a plan that still excluded 75% of the population.

F. South Africa had always depended on black labor.

1. Another reform initiated by Botha included legalizing black labor unions in the hope of controlling them.

2. The plan backfired, and the labor movement increasingly added its enormous weight to the tide of dissent.

G. Finally, the international community stepped up the pressure on South Africa. "Sanctions"—boycotts, withdrawal of investment, denial of capital—all began to take a toll.

H. In summary, four factors coalesced in the 1980s and brought about the changes that began to unfold in South Africa:

    1. A low-level guerilla war.

    2. A state of civil insurrection in and around the townships.

    3. Increasing exhibition of the power of trade unionists.

    4. International sanctions.

IV. All this turmoil began to convince certain figures in the inner circle of South African power—rather like it had in the old Soviet Union—that the system could not go on like this. They began to advocate reaching out and forging some sort of compromise. And who better to seek out than the symbol of the opposition, Mandela?

    A. For his part, Mandela was thinking along the same lines: better gain without war than war without gain. He cultivated several reformist figures inside the power structure from inside his different and more conducive prison environs.

    B. Botha, shortly after inviting Mandela to tea in 1989, had a stroke and was replaced by F. W. de Klerk, precisely one of the reformists we mentioned.

    C. In his unforgettable speech of February 1990, de Klerk freed Mandela, legalized all political parties, and forever changed South African politics.

    D. It is important to realize that Mandela took a very considerable risk by initiating and responding to possibilities of negotiation. Many in the ANC opposed this course, and it is quite conceivable that Mandela might have wound up marginalized in the whole story.

V. South Africa was hardly out of the woods. There ensued an incredibly tense and, indeed, very violent period preceding general elections in April 1994. As the whole world knows, with most South Africans voting for the first time, Mandela and his party, the ANC, came to power.

VI. Since then, though beset by numerous and significant problems, South Africa has, among other things, enjoyed basic stability, more open and peaceful elections, and positive economic growth. There are those who scoff at the term "South African miracle." I don't. If you want an alternative possibility, consider Israel and Palestine.

Suggested Reading:

Nelson Mandela, *Long Walk to Freedom: The Autobiography of Nelson Mandela*, parts 8–11.

Allister Sparks. *Beyond the Miracle: Inside the New South Africa.*

Allister Sparks, *Tomorrow Is Another Country: The Inside Story of South Africa's Road to Change.*

Questions to Consider:

1. How would you compare the ending of apartheid in South Africa with the ending of segregation in the United States?

2. Was South Africa's transition bound to happen anyway, or were the roles played by Mandela and de Klerk absolutely crucial?

Lecture Thirty-Two—Transcript
The South African Miracle

Hello again. There were many remarkable stories of democratic transition in the late 1980s and 1990s: certainly the Soviet Union, Eastern Europe, in Latin America, and in several countries in Africa, as we saw in our last lecture. But it's hard to top South Africa.

In 1990, Nelson Mandela was in prison, and no black South African could vote. Four years later, he was elected president of the nation.

When we last focused on South Africa, we ended by noting that in the late 1960s and early 1970s, apartheid appeared to be in the saddle. The active opposition had been silenced, Mandela and a great number of his peers and cohorts jailed for life, and his and other movements banned, operating in exile—if operating at all. The government was pursuing its grand apartheid scheme of separate development based in the so-called homelands. The white population was prospering.

But beneath the surface, trouble was brewing for the rulers. A number of key factors and key steps led to South Africa's transformation. Let us examine them in turn. We can start with that period of the late 1960s and early 1970s, perhaps through the mid-1970s, and observe that the quiet on the surface was deceptive. Black anger certainly was not diminishing—had not diminished—but it needed channeling in the place of resignation.

A crucial development in this regard, especially among the younger black population, was the movement usually called "Black Consciousness." It bears some comparison with the "Black Power" movement of the 1960s and 1970s in the United States, though bear in mind always, not just in this case, but in looking at history and politics in these countries in general, that we're talking, of course, about a black minority in one case and a majority in South Africa.

"Black Consciousness" in many respects was first and foremost a psychological movement: It called on black South Africans to "free their minds first"—to utterly reject the notions of inferiority the system handed them, to respect themselves, and take pride in themselves and pride in their capacity to change things themselves.

There's a way in which there's an eerie echo in the "Black Consciousness" movement with certain features of Afrikaner nationalism in, say, the 1920s, 1930s, 1940s. Afrikaner nationalists in those days had looked to their population—of course, I'm referring to the Dutch-descended white settlers in South Africa—and again said, "Have some respect for yourself. Don't let the stereotypes of, you know, the bumpkin (created by the British in this case) saddle you with a perceived self-hatred or sense of inferiority. Stand up. Be men and women. Realize your pride in your capacity to change things." Of course, change things they did, particularly symbolized by the 1948 election.

So, "Black Consciousness" and Afrikaner nationalism, in some respects, are at completely opposite ends of the spectrum, and yet in this emphasis on psychological self-strengthening, they do bear certain similarities.

The preeminent spokesman of the "Black Consciousness" movement was a brilliant and charismatic medical student named Bantu Stephen Biko—Steve Biko. It was Biko who looked at the average black South African around him and called him a "hollow shell." He called upon people to change that—to not allow the system to fill that hollowness with these senses of self-hatred and self-accepted versions of inferiority.

Constantly harassed by the authorities, Biko, with his biting and incisive analyses and his, not least, steadfast humor, struck a chord with many, particularly the young. Let me give you an example of this. I'm going to paraphrase a scene that occurred in a courtroom during one of Biko's numerous trials on a variety of offenses. It was later brilliantly reenacted by Denzel Washington, no less, in the film *Cry Freedom* based on the book by Donald Woods entitled *Biko*— and obviously about him. The screenplay was taken directly from the court transcript. Again, I'm going to paraphrase it a bit.

Biko was on the stand, and the white South African judge at one point addresses him and says: "Mr. Biko, why do you people refer to yourselves as black? You're not black. You're brown." Biko quite calmly replies: "Why do you people refer to yourselves as white? You're not white. You're a sort of off-pink."

His point was that, of course, people distort and manipulate reality to construct so-called "races." But his further point was if you can proclaim white supremacy, don't tell me that I can't proclaim "Black Consciousness."

In 1976, the cocksure government of South Africa made a classic blunder. It ordered that certain subjects be taught in Afrikaans in the secondary schools. Many objected to this proclamation on many grounds, but to the students themselves in the high schools, this was having the so-called "language of the oppressor" crammed down their throats.

The outrage over the new policy led students in Soweto, South Africa's biggest township, to organize a rally and march—large but peaceful. You may recall the dichotomy, which I put forward in Lecture Eighteen, born really at the diamond mining town of Kimberley, between the mine and the compound initially—in other words, the point of production, if you like, and the place over there set apart and easily controlled representing the black workforce.

I suggested at that point in that lecture that that dichotomy really was enlarged and transposed and becomes a feature of virtually every urban place in South Africa, large or small. The town, town center, the city, and then over there, some distance away, easily surrounded if not anymore actually fenced, was the township. The largest township in South Africa then was Soweto (which was actually an acronym and stood for southwest townships), lying about 6 to 10 miles southwest of downtown Johannesburg.

This was June 16, 1976, when the rally against the new policy of classes being conducted in Afrikaans was held. The police responded to the students' gathering, as they had in Sharpeville in 1960, with gunfire. But this time it was not a one-off affair: In the days, the weeks, the months to come, the conflagration that began at Soweto spread throughout South Africa. Police battled defiant students; hundreds if not thousands were killed; townships were in flames.

Something like "order" eventually returned, but a bit more than a year later, Steve Biko himself was arrested at a roadblock. In the next several days he was beaten unconscious, thrown in the back of a police Land Rover, and transported in the night over 600 miles up to Pretoria, where he died of brain damage. He'd been, essentially, murdered by the security forces. As you can imagine, his martyrdom had the result that South Africa erupted once again.

We've spoken before at several junctures in this course of watersheds, turning points, periods—again, this is one of the great games that historians play. For my money, 1976 marks a watershed: From that date forward, I think, it is a matter of when, and not if, the apartheid system will fall.

Meanwhile, the African National Congress (ANC) had been intensifying its military campaign against the regime, directed from exile from bases abroad in Zambia, Angola, and Tanzania above all. Many young people from the so-called "generation of '76" (a reference to Soweto and the accompanying demonstrations)—the "generation of '76," showing a "spirit of '76," if you like—many of them slipped across the borders, and this had the effect of greatly revitalizing the guerilla forces. We recall that Mandela in 1960 and 1961, in the wake of the bannings of the ANC, the Sharpeville Massacre, etc., had, of course, led the turn of the oldest nationalist organization, the African National Congress, towards an embrace of armed warfare. The organization *Umkhonto we Sizwe* (or "Spear of the Nation") was the military arm that I'm referring to when I talk about these attacks from exile.

The ANC forces, again, bolstered by these new recruits, if you like, created by the events of 1976—an increasing number of them slip back into South Africa, organizing attacks on police stations, on the Air Force headquarters (most dramatically in 1983), and on other targets like very posh, high-end shopping centers along the lush Florida-like Natal coastline.

This armed-struggle aspect, if you like, was important in the South African transition. However, I think it's accurate to state, and I think it's important to state, that at no time did the ANC, let alone any other organization, have the strictly military capacity to say, ride into Pretoria on tanks the way that, as we all know, in 1975 the North Vietnamese/Viet Cong did in Vietnam. So, this is certainly an aspect—the military aspect—but it would have to be accompanied by a number of others to produce the change that eventually would come.

Much more important than this low-level guerilla conflict, in my view, was a state of, I would call it, "civil insurrection" that eventually enveloped most of the townships and, indeed, more than occasionally slipped over into the legally "whites only" town centers or city centers of South Africa—a state of civil insurrection driven by the so-called young "comrades." That was their word for themselves—the youth activists who in name might be attached to the ANC, but often operated completely independently of it.

The ANC from its exile bases had called for the comrades to make South Africa ungovernable, and in a lot of respects they did, but that doesn't mean that they did so at the direct instigation of, let alone the direction of, the ANC itself. Indeed, they operated largely on their own and developed a momentum on their own.

Let me say that the comrades' activities in creating civil insurrection were not always positive. They set up, for instance, so-called "people's courts" on their own, and in more than a few cases, what happened was that they hauled people whom they wanted to settle a score with—someone suspected on the slightest evidence of being a sellout, or a stooge, or what have you—vendettas, in other words. They particularly enraged some of their elders. Middle-class people or elderly people were shocked at the notion that people who, in many cases, were teenagers were bringing them in and charging them with this or that violation.

For a moment, as I continue to put together some of these forces that lead to the dramatic transition, let me look back to the government policy unfolding in the 1980s. In a lot of respects, the 1980s can be referred to in South Africa, I would say, as the decade of neo-apartheid (of new apartheid). It was symbolized by the premiership of South Africa's penultimate (next to last) white leader, and that was Peter Botha—P.W. Botha—who when he was elected president (he was actually prime minister at that point)—when he was elected the leader of South Africa in 1978, one of his first pronouncements was that South Africa, in his words: "Must adapt or die."

So Botha initiated a series of cautious reforms, some of them a bit more significant than others. He, in essence, did eliminate the hated passes—these identity booklets—that, of course, black South Africans had to carry to prove their right to be in a particular area, particularly an urban area, at any time.

But the hollowness of Botha's attempts at reform and the ridicule with which they were greeted by a great number of the majority of the country is seen perhaps in his constitutional reforms of 1983. He put forth a new constitution with great fanfare and campaigned vigorously for it to obtain its passage in a whites-only referendum. Eventually it was passed by a margin of something like 60%.

His constitutional revision of 1983 would end the exclusively white parliaments that South Africa had had since 1910 and the creation of the country. Botha's new parliament would have three wings. It would have a white house of parliament. It would have a so-called coloured house of parliament (remember that coloured has a different meaning in South African history from black). This applied to approximately 9% of the population at that time. It would have a third house for the Asian or predominantly Indian population in South Africa, which constituted about 3% of the total.

In other words, you now have a tripartite still-segregated parliament, open for the first time to people of colour, if you like, but still excluding 75% of the population, which was comprised, of course, by the Bantu-descended black South Africans. They, as before, were to find their political destiny in the so-called "homelands."

One of Botha's reforms was to legalize black labor unions. This was probably undertaken in the hope of ending what were increasing numbers of wildcat strikes, and unannounced walk-offs, and so forth—the notion of legalizing them in the hope, perhaps, of obtaining some greater structure and control over them.

Like so many reforms we've seen in other contexts in this course, it backfired. The labor movement increasingly flexed its muscle. Of course, this was an enormous amount of power, precisely because South Africa at no time had ever ended its great dependency upon black labor.

Finally, the international community increasingly stepped up the pressure on South Africa. The 1980s was the time of popular songs like "Biko" by Peter Gabriel, or "We Don't Do Sun City," a reference to the casinos located in one of the so-called homelands, and so on. All over the world, there were "Free Mandela" festivals, often employing music and performance as well as a variety of high-profile participants.

More seriously, perhaps, or at least more substantively, this was the "age of sanctions." By sanctions, I mean the application of economic pressure above all. In other words, sanctions can take many, many forms, but the notion of the boycott, either voluntary or imposed and required by government laws—for instance, the notion that krugerrands, the one-ounce coins made of pure gold—it would become illegal to purchase those, and so forth.

So, again, sanctions could take a whole variety of forms. This was the time when students in American universities often called upon their boards of trustees to withdraw the universities' endowments from companies that did business in South Africa. It was the time when banks, quite on their own, would often begin to withdraw capital because of their fears of an impending blow-up and a loss of order in South Africa.

The sanctions began to take a toll. One crucial turning point came in 1985 and 1986, when the United States Congress overrode President Reagan's veto, and the United States added its muscle, then, to a whole variety of countries around the globe applying these sanctions—which, again, began to actually be felt inside South Africa itself.

So, I've isolated four basic factors that I think coalesce in the 1980s and propel us toward the enormous changes that begin to unfold at the end of that decade: a low-level guerilla war; a state of civil insurrection in and around the townships; a rapidly increasing exhibition of power and application of power on the part of trade unionists and black labor unions; and finally, an international application of pressure in the form of sanctions. All of these factors together began to convince certain figures in the inner circle of South African power—rather like it had in the old Soviet Union—that the system could not go on like this. They began to advocate reaching out and forging some sort of compromise, and who better to seek out than the symbol of the opposition residing in one of their prisons, of course, and that was Mandela.

For his part, Mandela had been thinking along similar lines: you might say—better gain without war than more war without gain. He began to accept the notion of negotiation and compromise more than his colleagues, at least publicly, embraced from their exile bases. He cultivated several reformist figures in the inside of the power structure, and he did so from inside his different and steadily more conducive prison environs. He was actually shifted from Robin Island to a second and eventually to a third prison under far better conditions. It was from there that he began these negotiations.

P.W. Botha, the president in 1989, invited him that year to have tea at Town House, the place where the president stays when he's in the city of Cape Town, just next to the parliament there. I was in South Africa when this occurred, and it was an electrifying moment. The notion that the president of South Africa would sit down for a talk with Nelson Mandela was, indeed, a very substantial and hugely symbolic departure.

Shortly later, Botha suffered a stroke. He was replaced by F.W. de Klerk (Frederik de Klerk)—precisely one of the inner-circle reformists that we mentioned a moment ago. De Klerk, I think, actually can be compared in a number of places or points with Mikhail Gorbachev of the old Soviet Union. After all, both of them had been sort of loyal party members, and party servants, and party officials. They had worked themselves up by showing competence within the older structures of the state and party. But both were exceptionally perceptive men, and again, as I put it before, they realized that the system could not go on the way that it had.

In his unforgettable speech of February 1990, de Klerk, in his opening of parliament at that point, freed Mandela and legalized all political parties, including the ANC, the Pan Africanist Congress, the Communist Party, and so forth. With that speech, he forever changed South African politics.

I think it's important to realize that Mandela took a very considerable risk in doing what he did from prison with only sporadic and incomplete communication with the exiled leadership of the ANC. Many of the ANC opposed this course. They wanted to continue and step up the pressures that we mentioned before. It's quite conceivable that Mandela could have wound up marginalized in this whole transitional story as opposed to occupying a place at its very center.

South Africa was hardly out of the woods after the legalization of political parties and the freeing of Mandela and other political prisoners. There ensued an incredibly tense and indeed very violent period preceding the general elections of April 1994. It seemed at various stages like this whole process of transition was a bit like a very old train on a very old set of tracks, in that it wobbled from side to side and at any moment might indeed tip over and produce a complete stop to the whole process. There were rumors and possibilities of military coups on the part of the white South African military. There was a huge conflict between, essentially, the followers of the ANC and the followers of what I would call a "Zulu nationalist movement," the Inkatha, later known as the "Inkatha Freedom Party." This resulted in a tremendous amount of carnage, particularly in what is now KwaZulu-Natal, the areas around Durban, South Africa, and so forth.

There were a lot of ways in which this thing could have been derailed and which would have raised a whole different kind of future and reality in South Africa.

As the whole world knows, though, the elections did come in April of 1994. The images of it are still striking: the lines snaking around many blocks, where you see whites and blacks standing next to each other in a line to vote; the old women and men showing up in wheel chairs who are 80 or 90 years of age and voting for the first time in their lives. It's still a moment that packs a great deal of emotive power.

As we know, Mandela and his party won that election and became the ruling party—the government of the new South Africa. Since that time, South Africa has certainly been beset by its share of problems. Millions of its people suffer from the HIV/AIDS virus. It has a very serious problem with violent crime. Some suggest that South Africa's old racial structure has simply been replaced with a class structure. Nonetheless, among other things, South Africa has enjoyed essential and basic stability. It has conducted more open and peaceful elections. It has experienced positive economic growth.

There are those who scoff at the term "South African miracle." I don't. If you want an alternative possibility, consider that represented by Israel/Palestine. Is it conceivable that we could have seen in South Africa a seemingly endless cycle of rocket attacks, draconian government sweeps and crackdowns, and suicide bombings? From the perspective of the 1980s, that was entirely conceivable. What did happen was something very different. That still strikes me as miraculous.

Lecture Thirty-Three
The Unthinkable—The Rwanda Genocide

Scope:

In the same year, the same *month*, that Mandela's election marked a triumph for freedom and justice everywhere, a nightmare unfolded in the East African country of Rwanda. After the president was killed in an unexplained plane crash, Hutu radicals initiated a furious attempt at a "final solution": the extermination of the minority Tutsi ethnic group. At least 500,000 Tutsi were murdered—along with a number of moderate Hutu—in a wave of hand-to-hand, neighbor-to-neighbor killings that redefine the word *horror*. In this lecture, we step back to review Rwanda's precolonial and colonial history in an attempt to grope toward an "explanation" of an event that remains, essentially, inexplicable.

Outline

I. In April 1994, exactly three weeks before Nelson Mandela was elected president of South Africa, a plane carrying the president of Rwanda was shot down, killing him; within hours began the biggest genocide the world has seen since the Jewish Holocaust. As the Nigerian writer and Nobel Prize winner Wole Soyinka said a bit later, "South Africa is our dream; Rwanda our nightmare."

II. Media coverage of Rwanda in 1994 vividly pronounced it a "tribal bloodbath," a bursting forth of the "ancient hatreds" between the majority Hutu and minority Tutsi.

   A. There is some truth in this—it was certainly a bloodbath, and ethnicity was certainly a crucial aspect.

   B. But the media reaction is a classic example of oversimplification based on flawed assumptions. Several more recent media productions, including some feature-length films, provide far richer understanding.

III. Historically, who *are* the Hutu and Tutsi?

   A. Hutu refers to the original Iron Age Bantu farming and herding peoples of the mountainous region of today's Rwanda, Burundi, and eastern Congo.

B. And what about the Tutsi? Beginning several centuries ago, migrants began to enter the region as well, mostly from the north and east. There was not a single "great migration" of "Hamitic" or even "Semitic" peoples (read: less "Negro") from far to the north, as many accounts have it, but a number of migrant streams over a considerable period, interacting in complex ways with the original population.

C. Still, it is fair to say that the term *Tutsi* originates with these newcomers who, in some cases, were able to establish power over the older indigenes and who tended to hold substantial wealth in cattle. The nearest translation of *Tutsi* in English turns out to be "aristocracy," suggesting a class rather than a narrowly ethnic status.

D. In my early lecture on ethnicity, I emphasized that ethnic identity is fluid, changeable, a matter of self-perception and perception by others. I stated that language difference is probably the best single criterion for determining "ethnic difference" in Africa but hastened to add that no single criterion is 100 percent reliable. And here is your proof: Hutu and Tutsi, parties to the deadliest ethnic violence in Africa's history, speak the same language, Kinyarwanda.

E. Several kingdoms emerged in this region, and the rulers were Tutsi.
   1. And there was inequality, though it tended to be a linked rather than strict caste inequality; cattle-holders (mostly Tutsi) had clients (mostly Hutu).
   2. But there was also considerable intermarriage, including with royalty. Some people whose ancestry was at least partly Hutu "became," and were accepted as, Tutsi.
   3. And there was conflict, not between Tutsi and Hutu but between kingdoms composed of both.

F. Eventually, two principal kingdoms emerged, each with very similar ethnic makeups: Rwanda to the north and neighboring Burundi, to the south.

G. Physically, the stereotype (held also by many Rwandans) has been tall, slender Tutsi and shorter, squat Hutu. But reality confounds this as often as it confirms it: Even the Hutu murderers of 1994 often had to look at identification cards before deciding whom to kill.

IV. Rwanda and Burundi were originally colonized by Germany, but Belgium took them over after World War I. Both, but especially the Belgians, found it useful to view the Tutsi as "natural aristocrats," and both favored and depended upon them.

  A. Almost all the officially recognized chiefs were Tutsi.

  B. The Catholic Church, which dominated the education system, similarly favored Tutsi, who became the principal members of a new kind of literate, Western-educated elite.

  C. The Belgian bureaucracy also "froze" ethnic identity in a sense, symbolized by the issuing of identity cards bearing a Hutu or Tutsi designation.

  D. Inequality, then, was greatly sharpened, as was, not surprisingly, Hutu resentment.

V. In the 1950s, as in most colonies, it was the educated elite, largely Tutsi, that began to clamor for self-government.

  A. But some Hutu—seizing the moment of colonial twilight, perhaps—issued their own Hutu Manifesto in 1957. Anti-Tutsi riots, called the Hutu Social Revolution, broke out in 1959.

  B. The Belgians did something of an about-face at this last minute (see Lecture Twenty-Five on the Belgian Congo) and began favoring the Hutu. In elections leading to independence in 1962, a Hutu-dominated government came to power.

  C. All of this is not to "blame" the Belgian colonialists for 1994, which is a gross reach, but this context cannot be ignored.

VI. Uncertainties over what independence would bring exacerbated tensions, and as the postcolonial era progressed, these tensions did not diminish.

  A. From 1959–1963, early anti-Tutsi moves and smaller-scale pogroms propelled the first waves of Tutsi going into exile, mainly in Uganda, where some eventually organized militarily, forming the Rwandan Patriotic Front (RPF).

  B. By the 1970s, Rwanda was in the sort of tailspin we described in Lectures Twenty-Nine and Thirty: declining terms of trade, unfulfilled expectations. In Burundi, there were mass killings of Hutu by Tutsi, sending great numbers of Hutu refugees into Rwanda. President Habyarimana seized power in Rwanda in a coup in 1973 and held it for 21 years.

C. Within Hutu inner circles, there developed moderate and extremist factions with regard to the Tutsi "problem."

D. In October 1990, northern Rwanda was invaded by Tutsi-led RPF exiles. Indeed, from that time until 1994, Rwanda was in a state of civil war.

E. In October 1993, the first Hutu president of Burundi was assassinated, apparently by the Tutsi-dominated army.

F. In Rwanda, President Habyarimana had been somewhat on the fence between the moderates and extremists but was returning from a peace conference with Tutsi exiles on April 6, 1994, when he was killed. No one is sure who assassinated him.

    1. Some say he was killed by RPF forces.

    2. Others believe he was killed by Hutu extremists, who had settled on plans quite different from peace initiatives.

VII.   Claiming Tutsi had murdered President Habyarimana, the Hutu extremists seized power and launched what we now know was a well-prepared and coordinated plan for a "final solution"—the elimination of the Tutsi population once and for all.

A. Some of their earliest targets, however, were not Tutsi but Hutu moderates—and there were many of them—who refused to countenance such a slaughter.

B. The army carried out many operations, but in the "swamps"—as the killing grounds were called—it was usually the Interahamwe, the ragtag Hutu militias, who took care of the "cockroaches," as the Tutsi came to be called.

C. And some neighbors, it is true, killed neighbors; others courageously protected them.

D. The world, despite considerable intelligence before and after April 6, essentially did nothing.

    1. The UN force, which was *reduced* as the crisis deepened, was pathetically inadequate.

2. In hindsight, the inaction is unforgivable. At the time, an intervention might have been labeled "imperialism" in some quarters, including those most critical of the inaction.

E. Rather incredibly, the genocide ended—after 700,000 deaths—with an invasion in July 1994 by Tutsi-led RPF exiles.

F. But some 2 million Hutu refugees, including many *génocidaires*, fled into eastern Congo. The ensuing destabilization there contributed to Mobutu's downfall and is part of the ongoing greater-Great-Lakes conflagration that has devastated the region.

VIII. In Rwanda, some sort of basic stability has been restored, which is remarkable enough. And there have been serious efforts to deal with the genocide and its aftermath.

A. A UN-sponsored International Criminal Tribunal operating in Tanzania has brought and is bringing criminal cases against the chief organizers of the killings.

B. Internally, there have also been prosecutions. But there remain today tens of thousands of suspects held in facilities like stadiums. This is a source of tension in itself.

C. Perhaps most promising have been grassroots initiatives in local communities, efforts to reach some sort of accounting and tolerance, if not reconciliation.

IX. A confession: I cannot explain the Rwanda genocide. I can barely comprehend it. But I hope this background helps build a clearer view.

Suggested Reading:

Alison Des Forges, *"Leave None to Tell the Story": Genocide in Rwanda.*

Philip Gourevitch, *We Wish to Inform You that Tomorrow We Will Be Killed with Our Families: Stories from Rwanda.*

Mahmood Mamdani, *When Victims Become Killers: Colonialism, Nativism, and the Genocide in Rwanda.*

André Sibomana, *Hope for Rwanda: Conversations with Laure Guilbert and Hervé Deguine.*

Questions to Consider:

1. How and why did the Hutu/Tutsi divide sharpen during the colonial period?

2. What explains the outside world's inaction, even as the scale of the Rwanda genocide became known?

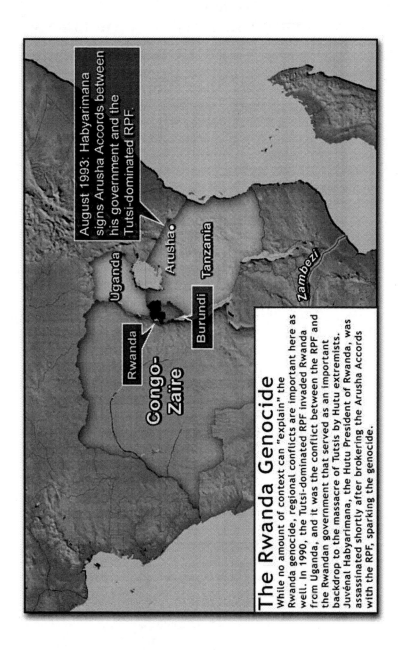

The Rwanda Genocide

While no amount of context can "explain" the Rwanda genocide, regional conflicts are important here as well. In 1990, the Tutsi-dominated RPF invaded Rwanda from Uganda, and it was the conflict between the RPF and the Rwandan government that served as an important backdrop to the massacre of Tutsis by Hutu extremists. Juvénal Habyarimana, the Hutu President of Rwanda, was assassinated shortly after brokering the Arusha Accords with the RPF, sparking the genocide.

August 1993: Habyarimana signs Arusha Accords between his government and the Tutsi-dominated RPF.

Uganda

Arusha

Tanzania

Burundi

Zambezi

Rwanda

Congo-Zaïre

Lecture Thirty-Three—Transcript
The Unthinkable—The Rwanda Genocide

Welcome. Rwanda, 1994—a Rwandan remembers:

> On the 7th of April, in the morning, they started burning
> houses over there and moving towards here. Only a few were
> killed. The burning pushed us to this place. Our group
> decided to run to this place. We thought this was God's
> house; no one would attack us here. On the 7th, 8th, up to the
> 10th, we were fighting them. We were using stones. They had
> *pangas*, [That is, machetes] spears, hammers, grenades. On
> the 10th, their numbers were increased. On the 14th, we were
> being pushed inside the church. The church was attacked on
> the 14th and the 15th. The actual killing was on the 15th. On
> the 15th, they brought the Presidential Guards [This was a
> unit of the Rwandan army]. They were supporting the
> Interahamwe [Who were the civilian militia death squads]
> brought in from neighboring communes. I was not in the
> group up here. Here, there were women, children, and old
> men. The men had formed defense units outside. I was
> outside. Most men died fighting. When our defense was
> broken through, they came and killed everyone. After that,
> they started hunting for those hiding in the hills. I, and
> others, ran to the swamp.

Another Rwandan remembers:

> The club is more crushing, but the machete is more natural.
> The Rwandan is accustomed to the machete from childhood.
> Grab a machete—that is what we do every morning. We cut
> sorghum. We prune banana trees. We hack out vines. We kill
> chickens. Even women and little girls borrow the machete
> for small tasks, like chopping firewood.

> In the end, a man is like an animal. You give him a whack on
> the head or the neck—and down he goes. In the first days,
> someone who had already slaughtered chickens and
> especially goats had an advantage, understandably. Later,
> everybody grew accustomed to the new activity, and the
> laggards caught up.

April 1994 was the month that saw South Africa's first democratic election—the election that brought Nelson Mandela to power. Exactly three weeks (21 days) before that election, on April 6, 1994, a plane carrying the president of Rwanda was shot down, killing him. Within hours began the largest genocide the world has seen since the Jewish Holocaust. As the Nigerian writer and Nobel Prize winner for literature, Wole Soyinka, said a bit later: "South Africa is our dream; Rwanda our nightmare."

The contemporary media coverage of Rwanda in 1994 vividly pronounced it to be a "tribal bloodbath," a bursting forth of the "ancient hatreds" between the majority Hutu and the minority Tutsi. There was certainly some truth in this. It was certainly a bloodbath. Ethnicity was certainly a crucial aspect, as was hatred. But it's a classic example, I believe, of oversimplification based on flawed assumption. Let us try in this lecture to develop a firmer understanding, though I will state at the outset that for me, there will probably never be such a thing as an "explanation" for the Rwanda genocide.

There have been many fine works on this episode already, and I have listed a number of those in the suggested reading. Today, I'll refer particularly to the work by Columbia University historian Mahmood Mamdani and by the remarkable book by the only Rwandan I know who has given an account, really a series of interviews: the late Andre Sibomana, a Rwandan, a Hutu, a Catholic priest, and a distinguished journalist.

One point that will emerge repeatedly, I think, is that we must take a regional perspective towards this history and this particular episode. It will not do to confine ourselves strictly to the boundaries of what is, after all, a quite small country—and that is Rwanda.

Historically, who are the Hutu and the Tutsi? Hutu (in general) refers, ancestrally speaking, to the original Iron-Age Bantu farming peoples of the hilly, mountainous regions of today's Rwanda, Burundi, and the eastern Congo. But they were of varied political and ethnic communities and, in fact, they became Hutu only when incorporated into the states that we will mention and that included the historical kingdom of Rwanda.

By mentioning those states, we beg the second question, then, about who are the Tutsi? Beginning several centuries ago, probably especially after the 15th century, migrants began to move into this region as well, mostly from the north and the east. This was not a single "great migration," but rather a whole series of migrant streams over a very considerable period of time, interacting in complex ways with the original population.

In the 20th century, this whole process was greatly oversimplified and distorted. This gave birth to what I will refer to as the "Hamitic hypothesis," which in a nutshell suggested that peoples of very different origin from the original Iron-Age Bantu peoples, from far to the north in today's Ethiopia or the Horn of Africa, who were Hamitic—the word comes from the biblical character of Ham—or even Semitic peoples came, rather suddenly imposed their dominance in a short time, and created the kingdoms that we're talking about.

By "Semitic" or "Hamitic," the strong suggestion in the colonial period was that they were, if you will forgive the term, "less Negro." They were, as Mahmood Mamdani puts it, "Caucasians of a lesser breed."

Despite its simplifications, it is fair to say that the term *Tutsi* originates with these more recent arrivals, who in some cases indeed were able to establish power over the older indigenes and who tended to hold substantial wealth in cattle. The nearest translation of *Tutsi* in English turns out to be something like the word "aristocracy," suggesting a class, perhaps, rather than a narrowly ethnic status.

In my early lecture on ethnicity, Lecture Six, I emphasized that ethnic identity is fluid. It's changeable. It's a matter of self-perception and a matter of perception by others. Nonetheless, in an attempt to give us something to go by in order to determine "ethnic difference," I did suggest that probably the best-bet criterion would be difference in language. I also hastened to add to that that no single criterion, including language, works 100% of the time.

Well, here's your proof. Hutu and Tutsi, parties to the deadliest ethnic violence in Africa's history, speak the same language, Kinyarwanda.

Over time, several kingdoms emerged in this region, and at the top—in the royal families—the kings were all Tutsi. At the lower levels, however, there were quite a number of regional chiefs, sub-rulers, governors, if you like, who were Hutu.

There was certainly inequality, although it tended to be a linked relationship of inequality as opposed to a strict caste inequality; cattle-holders (mostly Tutsi) had clients (mostly Hutu). There were some poor Tutsi (later the Belgians called them the *"petite Tutsi"*) and some well-off Hutu, but in general, you see a picture here of Tutsi association with power and greater wealth, and Hutu otherwise.

But there was also considerable intermarriage between the two, including some intermarriage into the royalty. Some people whose ancestry was at least partly Hutu "became," if you like, and were accepted as Tutsi.

Still, it seemed to emerge as the rule and remains the case today that everyone appears to fall into one category or the other following the patrilineal rules that we also saw in Lecture Six: If your father was a Tutsi, you were Tutsi; if your father were Hutu, you were Hutu.

There was conflict in the long-ago, pre-colonial period, but the conflict was usually not between Tutsi and Hutu, but between rival political states (kingdoms) composed of both. Eventually, through consolidation, two principal kingdoms emerged: one was Rwanda to the north; the other, with a very similar ethnic makeup, Burundi, just next door to the south.

Physically, the stereotype—and this is an important part of this entire history and story—the stereotype of Hutu and Tutsi—and I rush to add here, it's a stereotype held by many Rwandans; this is not merely something imposed or believed by outsiders—has been essentially this: Tutsi are taller. They're slender. They have narrow facial features. Hutu tend to be shorter—squatter, if you like—with broader facial features.

But these stereotypes, like so many stereotypes, including stereotypes about physical appearance—consider the stereotypes of Swedes versus Spanish, for instance—there are so many exceptions to these that one wonders where the rule really winds up.

Let me show how reality confounds these stereotypes as often as it confirms them. I'll go to a short account given by the distinguished Sudanese scholar, Frances Deng, who, before the genocide—he's writing this in 1995 afterwards, but he delivered a presentation before it next door in Burundi to a quite high-level group. I'll give you his own encounter here as he spoke, much as I'm speaking, to a group in that region:

> I had come to know, more or less, the stereotypical description of the short, Negroid Hutu and the tall, fine-featured Hamitic Tutsis. As I looked at my audience, I saw a few who were clearly Tutsis and a few who were clearly Hutus, but most were somewhere in between, and I could not identify them.
>
> I later asked the Burundis, including senior government officials and ministers, whether they could tell a Tutsi from a Hutu. The response from the foreign minister, which represented the general tone, was a confident, "Yes, but with a margin of error of 35%." [Deng comments:] A remarkable margin given the confidence of the affirmative answer.

Indeed, even the Hutu murderers of 1994 often had to look at identification cards before deciding whom to kill.

Rwanda and Burundi were originally colonized by Germany, but when Germany lost the First World War, Belgium took them over. When we considered the colonial period and its possible relationship to the history that we're talking about here, you might assume that I'm going to reiterate a point that I've made at several junctures in this course, and that is that colonial boundaries tended to be artificial. They tended to throw together ethnic communities that were not in the same political unit prior to colonialism and, therefore, perhaps sowed the seeds in some ways for civil war between rival ethnic groupings.

That is not the case with Rwanda. Just as in the case of language difference here, we have an exceptional situation rather than a typical one for Africa. Rwanda is one of the few cases where a colonial country and today's independent Rwanda actually bears some realistic relationship to the pre-colonial boundaries of the kingdom known as Rwanda. So, we have to look beyond the mere question of borders and boundaries to examine the colonial impact and what legacy it may have had for independent Rwanda.

It mainly boils down to this: Both the Germans and the Belgians, but especially the Belgians, found it useful—found it quite convenient—to view the Tutsi as "natural aristocrats," so-called. They both favored Tutsi and depended upon them. There was a sort of sub-imperialism or sub-colonialism that developed in Rwanda. As one Tutsi put it in describing his relationship with the Belgian colonial officials, he said that they told him: "You whip the Hutu, or we will whip you."

It's equally true, however, that many Tutsi took advantage of the opportunities—the favoritism—that they were granted under Belgian rule and were able to do quite well out of the same relationship. This was the real heyday of the Hamitic hypothesis, this notion that there was an original indigenous population here, the Hutu, and this alien, aristocratic, and more Caucasian and less Negro aristocracy that had come centuries before and that were the natural choices for both favoritism and assistance in the colonial enterprise.

Almost all the officially recognized "chiefs" in colonial times were indeed Tutsi. The Catholic Church, which dominated the education system, similarly favored the Tutsi, who became the principal members of a new kind of literate, Western-educated elite. There were exceptions (Hutu who became educated as well), but they were relatively few.

The Belgian bureaucracy "froze" this ethnic identity, in a sense, and this was indeed symbolized several decades before the end of colonialism by the starting of the issuing of identity cards bearing a Hutu or Tutsi designation. Inequality, then, in the colonial period was greatly sharpened—it emerged as something much closer to a true caste relationship. In Mamdani's analysis, what were ethnic differences became indeed racialized, reflected in the Hamitic hypothesis and greatly deepened.

In the 1950s, as in most colonies, as we've seen before, it was the educated elite—and in this case that was largely Tutsi—which began to clamor for self-government. But there were some Hutu—a budding counter-elite, if you like—who seized the moment of the colonial twilight and issued their own "Hutu Manifesto" in 1957. It's worth quoting from that document a little bit to see how this Hamitic hypothesis is, in fact, seized for their own purposes by both Hutu and Tutsi.

According to the Hutu Manifesto, the heart of the matter is "the conflict between the Hutu and Hamitic [i.e., foreign] Tutsi." They sought a double liberation "both from the Hamites and the *Bazungu*" [that's the reference to the whites' colonization], that the "indigenous racial problem" (their term) was the "monopoly which is held by one race: the Tutsi."

This was followed in 1959 by what is usually called the Hutu Social Revolution. Indeed, it was just that. It resulted in the ending of the Rwandan kingship and the replacement of almost all chiefs by Hutu. The Belgians did an incredible about-face, as, of course, they did next door in the Congo, at the last minute of their colonial legacy and indeed, not only allowed but promoted this sudden reversal at the twilight of their own power there. In elections leading to independence in 1962, a Hutu-dominated government came to power.

I review this colonial history not to "blame" the Belgians. That seems like a gross reach to me for a colonial power that departed over four decades ago. I think that Andre Sibomana captures actually the importance and the limitations of the colonial period as an explanation rather well. Listen to him:

> If the settlers [He means the Belgians there.] had taken into account the realities of the country—if they had refrained from imposing their simplified vision—no doubt Rwanda's history would have been very different. If power had not been given in its entirety to one group, the Tutsi, to the detriment of other groups and if subsequently had not been taken away in its entirety from that group and handed over in its entirety to another group, the Hutu, we might have been able to avoid a genocide.

> If colonization were to be put on trial that is where the accusations would be leveled. The Belgian settlers implanted racist stereotypes which we were not able to shake off, but the responsibility of these settlers should not obscure the responsibility of Hutu and Tutsi extremists who, one after

the other and each in their own way, exploited these stereotypes and served the purposes of their struggle to conquer to hold onto power.

A bit later: I don't believe anything "necessarily brought on the genocide in Rwanda," said Sibomana. "Men are products, but not prisoners, of their history. They decide themselves what to do."

Uncertainties over what independence would bring exacerbated tensions, and as the post-colonial era progressed, these did not diminish. The early anti-Tutsi moves in 1959—particularly between 1959 and 1963—smaller-scale killings of Tutsi—"pogroms," if you like, to use the old Eastern European term—propelled the first waves of Tutsi going into exile, mainly to Uganda. Eventually, some 600,000 Tutsi would wind up in Uganda, where they not only sought to mobilize and organize themselves politically, but eventually militarily in a movement known as the Rwandan Patriotic Front (RPF).

By the 1970s, Rwanda was in the sort of tailspin that we observed in Lectures Twenty-Nine and Thirty affecting so much of independent Africa: declining terms of trade and unfulfilled expectations. As if more problems were needed, next door in Burundi, there were mass killings of Hutu by Tutsi in 1972, which propelled large numbers of Hutu refugees northward into Rwanda.

In 1973, a coup d'état—which we've seen in other countries, of course—occurred, and President Juvénal Habyarimana seized power, which he held for 21 years.

Within Hutu inner circles, there developed moderate and extremist factions with regard to the so-called "Tutsi problem." These divisions between the radical Hutu power advocates within the Hutu community and those seeking some sort of accommodation with the Tutsi, especially the exiled Tutsi, were brought to a head by a critical event in the explanation of this whole episode. That is the invasion of northern Rwanda by the Tutsi-led RPF, the exiles coming from Uganda, beginning in October of 1990.

Indeed, between 1990 and 1994 (when the genocide occurred), this country was in a state of what amounted to civil war. It was the fear, utilized and exploited by Hutu extremists—through powerful propaganda instruments—day after day, that the Tutsi are on the march; they are coming; you must do to them first what they will do to you. This sort of message, broadcast on radio, seen in the extremist newspapers, again, a product of fear generated in a civil war in which the deteriorating Rwandan army was, in fact, losing ground month after month to the invading RPF.

Again, the external factors: In October 1993, the first Hutu president of Burundi, where you had not had a Hutu revolution before, was assassinated by apparently members of a Tutsi-dominated army. New waves of Hutu, fearing again that the Tutsi are going to re-impose the Hamitic hypothesis sort of domination—these sorts of fears begin to emerge and grow almost day by day.

President Habyarimana had sort of been on the fence between the moderate Hutu and the extremists, who began to call, in not very veiled terms, for something like an extermination. Habyarimana, though, eventually moved towards the possibility of tolerance—or at least reconciliation—and, in fact, he signed Arusha Accords (Arusha is the town in northern Tanzania where negotiations between his government and the Tutsi-dominated RPF took place). He signed agreements in August of 1993.

In fact, he was returning from a further negotiating session in Arusha on April 6, 1994, when his plane was brought down by a missile attack over the airport. It is still not clear who carried out that attack. It was certainly well planned. It's possible and many people believed at the time—and, of course, this fanned the flames of fear that the RPF had carried out the attack, and that therefore you can see what they have in mind for Tutsi domination in Rwanda. Many believe now that, in fact, it was extremist Hutu who brought down the plane in order to forestall Habyarimana's efforts at some kind of negotiated accommodation.

Within hours, the extremists seized power after the assassination of the president and launched what we now know was a well prepared and coordinated plan for a "final solution." I mean a "final solution" in the same sense that Hitler and the Nazis meant it: the elimination of the Tutsi population once and for all.

Some of their earliest targets, however, were not Tutsi at all, but Hutu moderates. There were quite a number of them. Some 50,000 of them eventually were killed. The army carried out some operations of the genocide, but in the "swamps"—as the killing fields were called (and as you saw in my opening quote, sometimes in the churches)—it was usually the Interahamwe, the ragtag Hutu militias drawn from the impoverished youth—male youth, mainly, around the cities—who took care of the *inyenzi* (the "cockroaches" as the Tutsi came to be called—the vermin, the filth).

It must be said that there were large numbers of ordinary people who took part. Fewer of the Hutu courageously shielded Tutsi or moderate Hutu from the killers. But they were fewer, and it is this that is, perhaps, the most troubling aspect of the entire genocide. When they asked Sibomana to explain that, he said:

> I don't explain it. You can't explain everything or understand all forms of human behavior. It's a fact: During the genocide, not only were hundreds of thousands of people killed, but many were victims of cruelty, torture, and forms of ill treatment, which defy imagination.

> Where did it come from, this hatred of others? I can only explain it by an insurmountable hatred of oneself. Indeed, some killers committed suicide after they had killed. They were many, especially among young people from poor districts of the capital, whose lives were completely empty, who had no family, no religion, no work, no hope. They saw no future for themselves in the world. They turned upside down the value system to which they no longer had access. Instead of taking advantage of their youth to build themselves a life, they used their energy to destroy the lives of others.

The world, despite considerable intelligence before and after April 6, essentially did nothing. The United Nations force of peacekeepers was actually reduced as the crisis deepened and was pathetically inadequate in any case. In hindsight, the inaction seems unforgivable. Even President Clinton, who was in power at that time, actually went to Rwanda later and apologized, essentially, for his own inaction. It's still worth saying, though, that an intervention at the time might have been labeled in some quarters as Western "imperialism," indeed from some of the same quarters who later condemned the inaction.

The genocide ended in July 1994 with the successful taking of Kigali by the RPF (by the Tutsi-led exiles). By that time, some two million Hutu refugees were on their way, and these included many of the so-called *génocidaires* (those who had carried it out) on their way into the eastern Congo. There they were part of the ensuing destabilization that contributed to the downfall of President Mobutu in Congo, which we saw in an earlier lecture. This is part of the ongoing greater-Great-Lakes conflagration that has devastated that region.

In Rwanda, some sort of basic stability has been restored, which is remarkable enough. There have been serious efforts to deal with the genocide and its aftermath. A UN-sponsored International Criminal Tribunal, operating in Tanzania, has brought and is bringing criminal cases and has obtained convictions for some of the organizers of the killings, who will serve their lives in prison.

Internally, there have also been prosecutions, but the RPF government certainly has its own bases for criticism. There remain today tens of thousands of suspects held in facilities like stadiums; this is a source of tension in itself.

Perhaps most promising have been the efforts to commemorate and remember at the grass-roots initiative—the so-called *gacaca* process of local-level investigations conducted in the old African way, if I can put it that way, of getting at what happened in a particular community and trying to promote some sort of accounting, and at least tolerance, if not reconciliation.

Andre Sibomana's book is entitled *Hope for Rwanda*, which seems almost incredible. He himself died in 1998 of a rare allergenic disease. It's a sad thing to say, but his friends were almost relieved to find that he had died of that cause, given the alternatives in Rwanda and the fact that he continued his criticism of injustice wherever he found it.

I'll, nonetheless, end with words from Andre Sibomana:

> We don't have the right to give up hope. Life has been given to us. It is a gift from God. As a believer and especially as a priest who must help others find the way, I don't have the right not to hope.

We must learn to live together again. Some diplomats who presumably thought we would never be able to live together again have suggested creating a Hutu land or a Tutsi land. This idea is not only stupid but very harmful. Apart from the fact that a division of Rwandans along these lines would be a magnificent victory for advocates of racism, I don't think that problems are solved by shifting them or pushing them to one side—quite the contrary.

Finally, the last words of his book:

Just before leaving Kigali, one of my journalists asked me this question: "So when will Rwandans ever be able to hope to die of old age?" That is my wish now. Let us give Rwandans time to live, and let us give children time to bury their parents—bury their parents dead of old age.

Thank you.

Lecture Thirty-Four
The New Plague—HIV/AIDS in Africa

Scope:

Disease has, of course, played a major role in human history, from bubonic plague in medieval Europe to the post-Columbian catastrophe that befell Native American populations. In the late 20th century, a new disaster developed—AIDS. It emerged first in Central Africa, and we investigate the quite different theses about its origins, including the possibility that Western-sponsored vaccine testing went horrifically awry. Although AIDS threatens populations all over the world, Africa suffers most, by several orders of magnitude. We examine the social and economic impact of a malady that mostly affects people in their prime, including the orphaning of multitudes of children. We look at the curious, some say bizarre, reaction of South Africa's President Thabo Mbeki, which has surely cost his country time—and lives. But we counter with the cases of Senegal and Uganda, where determined and effective efforts have rolled back the pandemic.

Outline

I. Disease has been a major factor in human history, and we know a lot more about this than we used to. We have encountered it at several junctures already in this course, as a partial explanation for the turn to African labor in the Americas or as a further blow to Khoisan populations already reeling from Dutch pressure in the Cape Colony.

II. The diseases common in Africa for a long time, such as malaria, yellow fever, and river blindness, are factors that have plausibly contributed to Africa's relatively low population growth and lack of economic development. More recently discovered diseases, such as Ebola or Marburg fever, are horrifying in their effects but, thus far, have had little widespread effect.

III. Not so, unfortunately, for another recent arrival, HIV/AIDS (*HIV* stands for human immunodeficiency virus, which leads to *AIDS*—acquired immune deficiency syndrome).

A. AIDS is a global phenomenon—a pandemic—but it has already had an incomparably greater impact on Africa than anywhere else, and even if today, everything that *could* be done to counteract it *were* to be done, it would still have major effects for decades to come.

B. The statistics are staggering.

  1. In 2005, the total was approaching 30 million deaths from AIDS worldwide, and something like 80 percent of those have occurred in Africa.

  2. In every region of Africa, the percentage of adults who are HIV-positive is at least 5 percent (compare with a U.S. rate of less than 1 percent). The lowest rates in Africa are in West and North Africa; they are higher in Central and East Africa.

  3. The epicenter of the pandemic is Southern Africa, with the highest rates by far in the world. Botswana's is more than 30 percent; Zimbabwe's, not much less. The country with the largest absolute number of HIV-positive adults is the Republic of South Africa.

IV. AIDS was first identified in the United States in the early 1980s, but almost certainly it originated in Central Africa. Almost all authorities agree that HIV "jumped" from simians—especially chimpanzees—to humans, but how the jump occurred is not clear.

  A. One possibility, caricatured as the "cut African" or "bushmeat" theory, suggests that there was an accidental blood transfer to humans from simians in Central Africa, where indeed, these animals are occasionally slaughtered for food. (In other parts of Africa, they are quite taboo.)

  B. In 1999, Edward Hooper published a massive book, *The River*, that suggested but did not prove (nor did Hooper claim that it proved) that HIV may have been introduced to humans when some 1 million people in the Belgian Congo were given trial doses of oral polio vaccine in the late 1950s.

  1. The vaccine used in the trials, sponsored by Western scientists, was developed using chimpanzee tissue.

  2. Hooper is not a crackpot; he is a former UN official and BBC reporter. His theory remains unproven but continues to provoke controversy. At the very least, quite apart from AIDS, it raises troubling questions about drug trials in African and other Third World populations.

V. Why has HIV/AIDS spread so much faster in Africa? What are the manifestations—social, economic, even political—of its impact?

    A. AIDS almost surely was around in Africa well before it was identified in the early 1980s. Thus, it had a kind of "rolling start," making it more difficult to reverse.

    B. One reason for the delay in identifying AIDS, of course, is that it is a secondary infection, like pneumonia, which sickens and finally kills. This fact can still lead people to avoid accepting that AIDS is/was the key problem.

    C. HIV/AIDS is spread through sexual contact and/or exchange of bodily fluids, especially blood. In the United States, AIDS was concentrated, at first, in the homosexual community and among intravenous drug users. In Africa, on the other hand, it has spread almost entirely through heterosexual activity, which obviously involves a far greater number of people.

        1. Some quickly assume that promiscuity, especially of African males, is the problem. I personally have great doubt that a tendency toward promiscuity is any more pronounced in Africa than elsewhere (though it is fair to add that some articulate African women have had harsh words for men).

        2. Better explanations have to do with labor migration and poverty.

            a. When one spouse, usually the male, goes away to work for a substantial time, it doesn't take notions of "natural" or "cultural" predispositions toward promiscuity to posit that this creates an atmosphere that facilitates multiple sexual partners. Labor migration is a deeply ingrained pattern, especially in Southern Africa, as we have seen.

    b. Poverty, limiting access to health care and health education, can result in higher rates of other sexually transmitted diseases—and this raises the likelihood of transmission of HIV. Poverty can also make condom use prohibitively expensive, though there is evidence of cultural resistance to their use as well.

   3. In addition, women are unlikely to have as much access to education or the means to negotiate safe sexual relationships with men. Likewise, poor young girls sometimes see a relationship with an older man as a way to escape poverty.

D. The AIDS pandemic can be deceptive. The visitor to Southern Africa is not going to encounter writhing, hemorrhaging bodies on the streets. The sad truth is that people withdraw to back rooms and dark huts and waste away.

E. The impact of their withdrawal, and eventual loss, affects almost everything.

   1. A great many of the victims are in their most productive years—20s, 30s, and 40s. The cost of their loss to the workforce—and AIDS strikes the skilled and educated workforce as well as the impoverished—is obvious. Institutions such as those involved in education are directly affected by the loss of teachers.

   2. Food security is a subject not to be taken lightly in Africa. Sick people cannot work fields.

   3. When adults in the age groups mentioned die, they often leave children. AIDS orphans are a real, huge, and growing problem; some say there are now 15 million. These may be the AIDS victims you'll see sleeping in the street, leaping out to "watch your car" when you park.

VI. What hope is there?

A. Antiretroviral drugs (ARVs) can radically improve and extend an AIDS patient's life; indeed, the disease is no longer necessarily fatal at all. In Africa, the problem is cost; however, there have recently been breakthroughs here, with drug companies permitting generics with a far lower price.

B. But the key, obviously, is public education. It is popularizing knowledge of the causes of HIV/AIDS and how to prevent it; it is overcoming the stigma of AIDS, which still leads many people to avoid the subject.

C. The role of leadership—*public* leadership—by those at the top, seems to be critical.

    1. This is what has made the statements and policies of South African President Thabo Mbeki so troubling. Mbeki, a gifted and intelligent man, was openly skeptical that HIV causes AIDS. Though he has rather reluctantly changed course, precious time has been lost.

    2. His predecessor, the living legend Mandela, on the other hand, has increasingly used his "retirement" to tirelessly publicize AIDS awareness.

    3. The most successful cases of rolling back the pandemic have occurred in Senegal and Uganda, again through aggressive and clever public education. The positive personal role of Ugandan President Museveni, for instance, has been critical.

Suggested Reading:

Susan Hunter, *Black Death: AIDS in Africa.*

Questions to Consider:

1. What factors explain why Africa has become the epicenter of the world HIV/AIDS pandemic?

2. What are the *indirect* effects of HIV/AIDS in Africa—the effects on people who are *not* infected, on society as a whole?

Lecture Thirty-Four—Transcript
The New Plague—HIV/AIDS in Africa

Hello. In our last lecture, we looked at a catastrophe: the Rwandan genocide of 1994. We had to. There's no way to avoid it. It would be a disservice to do so in a course such as this one. I, nonetheless, attempted to end with some hope even in that situation by looking at the remarkable life and words of the Rwandan priest and journalist Andre Sibomana.

Today, alas, we examine another catastrophe of an entirely different sort—but indeed with a much deeper and wider impact. I refer, of course, to the plague represented by the spread of HIV/AIDS in Africa. After detailing its horrors, I will again attempt to end with a note of hope by looking at a couple of places—Senegal and Uganda—where HIV/AIDS has been contained or indeed rolled back.

Disease has been a major factor in human history. We know a lot more about this than we used to. We've encountered it at several junctures already in this course. We looked at it as a partial explanation for why there was a turn toward labor from West Africa to serve in the plantations of the Americas. We looked at it as a further blow to the Khoisan peoples in the old Cape Colony, already reeling from Dutch pressure and then undergoing a smallpox epidemic in 1713.

We know that the year-round warmth in tropical Africa has provided a hospitable clime for the microbes causing diseases for many, many, many thousands of years. The diseases common in Africa for a long time, like malaria, yellow fever, and river blindness—the legendary African diseases, if you like—are factors that have quite plausibly contributed to Africa's relatively low population growth and lack of economic development. More recently discovered diseases like Ebola or Marburg fever are horrifying in their symptoms, but—thus far—have had little widespread impact.

That is not true—not remotely true, unfortunately—for another relatively recent arrival, HIV/AIDS. By the way, "HIV" stands for human immunodeficiency virus, and it is that virus that leads to "AIDS," which is acquired immune deficiency syndrome.

AIDS is a global phenomenon—it's a pandemic, not just an epidemic. It's already had incomparably greater impact on Africa than anywhere else on the globe, so much so that even if today—if we could imagine that everything that could be done to counteract HIV/AIDS in Africa *were* to be done, we would still be reeling from the effects for decades to come. Remarkably, by the way, this is the first epidemic of a totally new human disease in the world since the 1400s.

The statistics both in the world but most especially in Africa are staggering, but they bear review. In 2005, the world was approaching 30 million deaths from AIDS. It was exceeding 40 million people worldwide who are positive with the HIV infection. Let's try to put that into perspective. This means that something on the order of 3 million people are dying as we move into the late part of the first decade of the 21st century—three million people dying per year. That's an average of something like 8,200 persons per day, approximately three times as many as died, for instance, in the attack on the World Trade Center on September 11, 2001.

By 2010, the deaths from HIV/AIDS will have surpassed the "Black Death," so called, of the 14th century, which began in Asia and, of course, swept through Europe, leaving one quarter to one half of the population dead. It will exceed by 2010 the second greatest population catastrophe of all time after the bubonic plague or the Black Death, and that was the depopulation of the Americas in the aftermath of the Columbian and other voyages. Of course, that was part of the reason why I referred to the turn to West African labor in the history of the Atlantic slave trade. By 2010, the total death toll will approach the total death tolls of World War I and World War II combined.

Something on the order of three-quarters—75–80%—of this entire burden of HIV-positive infections—of deaths from AIDS—will fall on Africa. In every major sub-region of Africa, the percentage of adults who are HIV-positive is at least 5%. That's compared with the U.S. rate of less than 1%. The lowest rates in Africa are in West and North Africa. They are higher in Central and East Africa.

But the epicenter of the pandemic is southern Africa, with the highest rates by far in the world. The landlocked country of Botswana's rate is over 30%. Zimbabwe is not far behind. The country in the world with the absolute largest number of HIV-positive adults is the critical country of the Republic of South Africa.

AIDS was first identified in the United States, in the early 1980s, usually said to be 1982, but almost certainly originated in Central Africa. Almost all authorities agree that HIV "jumped," if you will, from simians—that is, from monkeys, chimpanzees, etc.—to humans; but exactly how this trans-species "jump" occurred is not completely clear.

One quite realistic possibility, and indeed the prevailing theory for the origins of this trans-species "jump," is sometimes caricatured as the so-called "cut African" or so-called "bushmeat" theory. It suggests that there was a blood transfer from simians to humans in Central Africa, where indeed these animals are sometimes hunted and slaughtered for food. I should add that in many other parts of Africa, even next door in Zambia, these are considered quite taboo, and people are quite shocked that in the former Belgian Congo, for instance, that people would have slaughtered chimpanzees or monkeys for food.

In 1999, Edward Hooper published a massive book entitled *The River*, which suggested, though it did not prove (nor did Hooper claim that it proved) that HIV may have been introduced to humans in a very different—a radically different—way. He theorized that this could have occurred when some one million people in the former Belgian Congo, now the Democratic Republic of the Congo, were given trial doses of oral polio vaccine, in the late 1950s. The vaccine used in the trials, sponsored by Western scientists, was developed using chimpanzee tissue.

Hooper is not a crackpot; he's a former UN official and a former BBC reporter. His theory certainly remains unproven but continues to provoke controversy.

At the very least, quite apart from AIDS, it does raise troubling questions about drug trials in African and other Third World populations—about conducting trials of drugs in poor populations—often desperately poor populations—and populations desperate for medications of any kind in order to develop drugs that would—eventually, of course—be marketed for profit. If you would like to read a most engrossing novelization of this subject, I would suggest the noted espionage writer John le Carré's book, *The Constant Gardner*, much of which takes place in Africa, now made into a motion picture.

Why has HIV/AIDS spread so much faster in Africa? What are the manifestations—social, economic, even political—of its impact? First of all, AIDS was almost surely around in Africa well before it was even identified—before anyone had even heard of it—in the early 1980s. It was growing and being spread before there were any tests to detect HIV—indeed, before the link between HIV and AIDS was confirmed; before epidemic-tracking systems emerged; before anti-retroviral drugs (ARV drugs that I'll refer to later), which treat the symptoms, were discovered.

Thus in Africa, there was very much of a "rolling start" for this entire epidemic, making it that much more difficult to reverse. Again, the momentum that an epidemic develops often plays itself out years after the most energetic efforts to put it into reverse.

One reason for the delay in identifying AIDS, of course, is that it weakens the immune system, and that means in turn that it is secondary infection, like pneumonia, for instance, that actually sickens and finally kills an AIDS victim. In addition, remember that the HIV virus can be inside the human body for 7 to 10 years before there are any symptoms at all. These factors can still lead today to people avoiding the acceptance that HIV or AIDS was—or is—the key problem.

HIV/AIDS is spread essentially five ways: through heterosexual contact; through homosexual contact; through intravenous drug use (the so-called "dirty needle syndrome"); through the distribution of tainted blood supplies (it was probably that that led to the death of the great American tennis player, Arthur Ashe); and finally through the transmission of the virus from an HIV-positive mother to her child.

In the United States, AIDS was concentrated, at first, in the homosexual community and amongst intravenous drug users. In Africa, on the other hand, it has spread almost entirely through heterosexual activity, although the last method I mentioned—transmission from positive mother to child—is gaining on that, although it's obviously a product of heterosexual activity.

It has been predominantly heterosexual activity, then, and almost by definition this involves a far greater number of people. After all, this is part of the universality of human experience. So, some people quickly assume, therefore, that promiscuity, especially of African males, is the problem. Indeed, the whole notion of AIDS being one more thing that afflicts Africa and that it is this sexual promiscuity that explains its prevalence there really falls into a whole kind of "Africa is lost, the sad realities of Africa" kind of dismissal of the place, which I brought up in my very first lecture in this series.

The notion would go something like this, as the South African Karen Yockelson has put it: the notion of seeing Africa as "a sick and dying continent, harboring deadly disease and inhabited by an essentially promiscuous people who are part of a dangerous, wild, natural world and bound by primitive traditions and superstitions."

I personally have great doubt and I know of no reliable evidence that a tendency toward promiscuity is anymore pronounced in Africa than elsewhere. In fact, part of the stigma and stigmatization of HIV-positive people—of people with AIDS—is one of the real problems in addressing the identification and, therefore, the prevention of further spread. Part of the stigmatization is precisely because one will be suspected of promiscuity, if that is the case.

I might just say a word about this stigma. In 1989, I was working in Zambia, and I read the national newspaper there, a sort of feature column. There was a style column, if you like, written by a quite hip, university-educated, young Zambian woman. The message in her column was essentially this: that she had stopped jogging. The reason she had stopped jogging was because it had assisted her to lose weight, which was her original objective. It made her slender, but remember that in many parts of Africa the nickname for AIDS is, in fact, "slims," from the wasting away that people sometimes go through. She didn't want to raise the slightest possibility of that to avoid that conceivable stigmatization.

I mentioned that I find it unconvincing: a higher overall rate of any sort of promiscuity (although I think it is only fair to add that there are some very articulate African women, perhaps of the sort I just mentioned, who have had harsh words on this score for men). I will return to gender inequality in a moment.

I think better explanations have to do with labor migration and poverty. We know that these have enormous histories and enormous realities in Africa's past and in its present. When one spouse—usually the male—goes away to work for a substantial time, it doesn't take notions of "natural" or "cultural" predispositions toward promiscuity to posit that this creates an atmosphere that facilitates—almost invites—the possibility (at least) of multiple sexual partners. Labor migration is a deeply ingrained pattern, as we have seen in this course, and above all in southern Africa, the epicenter of this epidemic in Africa.

The relationship between overall poverty and disease is, of course, clear and affects many other diseases beyond HIV and AIDS. Limited access to healthcare or to health education can result in higher rates of other sexually transmitted diseases, such as herpes, genital ulcers, and so forth. These are shown quite clearly to increase the rate of transmission from an HIV-positive person to a sexual partner.

Poverty can also make condom use prohibitively expensive, although as we'll see, there's also evidence of cultural resistance to this as well.

I mentioned gender inequality—inequality between men and women. It's a reality—and not just in Africa, of course. Women are unlikely to have as much access to education or to resources. They are less likely to have the knowledge or resources to either be independent or to negotiate safe sexual relationships with men. There is a cultural expectation, for instance, that wives are not to resist the sexual advances from husbands.

Young girls, in particular, find themselves in situations mired in poverty, tempted into sexual relationships from older men precisely because of that poverty. In Uganda, they say, in fact: "Sex is the poor girl's food."

The AIDS pandemic can be deceptive. If you visit southern Africa, you're not going to see writhing, hemorrhaging bodies on the sidewalk—on the streets. The sad truth is that people withdraw to back rooms. They withdraw to dark huts and waste away. The impact of their withdrawal—their eventual loss if they die—affects just about everything—almost every aspect you can think of—in what makes a society go. It affects everybody.

It has affected me personally, though obviously indirectly. I've mentioned my first love, Zambia, many times. It's a southern African country, and one out of every six adults in Zambia is HIV-positive. My longtime—three-decade-long—best friend and research partner in Zambia has lost his second-born son in 2003 and his third-born son in 2004. These were men that I knew well. They were men in their 30s, and that age is typical of those, for obvious reasons of sexual activity, who contract HIV or suffer the ultimate consequences of AIDS—people in their most productive years: their 20s, their 30s, their 40s—not just for themselves, but, of course, for their entire societies.

One report from Zambia, for instance, notes that the AIDS epidemic severely damages every sector of Zambia's economy. In the first place, employers bear the direct costs of absenteeism, medical care, funerals, and extra recruitment. What is even more significant is that as AIDS kills people in the prime of life, the workforce is stripped of valuable skills and experience. The situation becomes yet worse as there are fewer people to teach the next generation. All of this means that production costs rise while at the same time consumer spending falls because people affected by AIDS have less money to spare. Zambia has been one of the world's poorest countries since the late 1970s, and AIDS has made a bad situation even worse.

That paragraph mentioned the impact of teachers. Consider this: In the year 2002, Zambia lost 2,000 teachers to AIDS.

Food security is a subject, obviously enough, not to be taken lightly in Africa. Sick people cannot work fields. It is certainly not at all a difficult link to make between the HIV/AIDS epidemic and the food shortfalls that we've seen in a number of countries around the continent in the last decade.

When adults in the age groups I have just mentioned die, they, of course, often leave children. "AIDS orphans" are a real, huge, and growing problem; some say that we're approaching 15 million children orphaned by AIDS across the continent now. Zambia's estimate is something like 650,000 people.

As one, again, Zambian expert said: "In the days before the full impact of the HIV and AIDS pandemic, street children were a very rare sight in Zambian cities and towns. Now they are everywhere: sleeping under bridges, behind walls, and in shop corridors." *These* kids may be the AIDS victims that you will see if you visit southern Africa, sleeping in that street, in the park, leaping out to "watch your car" when you park. You agree to pay them the small amount, both because you want your car intact when you come back and out of simple compassion. You will see them. It doesn't take a stretch of the imagination to see that they can be an obvious target—that they could obviously be tempted into far less legitimate kinds of undertakings. AIDS presents security and crime issues as well.

So what hope is there? Anti-retroviral drugs (I mentioned this before) can radically improve and extend an AIDS patient's life. Perhaps the most famous American to contract AIDS might have been the basketball legend, Magic Johnson. The fact that he leads not just an active life but even a vigorous life nearly 15 years after announcing that he was HIV-positive shows the effect that anti-retrovirals can have. The disease is no longer necessarily fatal at all.

But the problem in Africa, of course, is cost. Recently, however, there have been breakthroughs here, with drug companies agreeing to provide drugs of greatly reduced price or permitting generic manufacturers. The companies, it has to be said, resisted that right through the late 1990s and were backed by the World Trade Organization and indeed by the American government. They brought lawsuits. For instance, in South Africa there was a very famous lawsuit that sought to prevent South Africa manufacturing its own generic versions of ARVs or purchasing them cheaper from places like India. The first defendant named in that lawsuit was President Nelson Mandela. As you can imagine, this was a public relations disaster for the pharmaceutical companies. Indeed, to their credit, they have withdrawn from that and, as I say, made the affordability of these drugs much greater.

But the key, obviously, at every stage is public education. It's popularizing the knowledge of the causes of HIV/AIDS and how to prevent it, it's overcoming the stigma of HIV/AIDS, which still leads many people to avoid the subject. There is misinformation out there. People have told me that they believe that it's witchcraft and not the

HIV virus. There is this need for well-informed people, including people who have the virus themselves and those who support them, to carry the message of how this thing can be reversed.

The role of leadership—of public leadership—by those at the top, seems to be critical. It is this that has made the statements and policies of South African President, the man who succeeded Mandela, that is, Thabo Mbeki, so troubling. Mbeki is a gifted and very intelligent man, but for a long period of time—it is that time that makes this so sad—he was openly skeptical that HIV causes AIDS. Although he never denied that link explicitly, he was connected with a small group of dissident scientists who have questioned that, despite the overwhelming evidence to the contrary. Though he has rather reluctantly changed course, precious time has been lost. Again, there's a way in which the momentum of this does not yield its deadly reward until years after the first steps are taken to reverse it.

His predecessor, of course, Mandela, although admittedly mostly after he left office, has increasingly used his "retirement" to tirelessly publicize AIDS awareness. You may have seen Mandela wearing a t-shirt on which it says: "HIV-positive." He's not, but he's casting his lot with those who are in order to lend his enormous prestige toward the erasure of that stigma that we've talked about before.

His old rival, Gatsha Buthelezi, leader of the Zulu nationalist organization, Inkatha, announced that his son had died just as Mandela's son had died from this disease. The former President of Zambia, Kenneth Kaunda, has launched the Kenneth Kaunda Foundation precisely to address the problem of AIDS orphans in cities like Lusaka, the capital.

Probably the most successful cases of rolling back the pandemic have occurred in Senegal and Uganda—one in far West Africa, one in East Africa—again through aggressive and clever public education utilizing music, drama, film, etc., to get the message out. Again, the personal role at the top has been critical. I'll come back to that in the case of Uganda in a second.

In Senegal, there's been a sort of liberal and conservative arm of this anti-AIDS attack, if you like. Senegal tolerates prostitution, for instance. The commercial sex industry is often an epicenter of these epidemics for understandable reasons. Senegal tolerates prostitution but insists that prostitutes (commercial sex workers) be registered, that they be given medical examinations, that they be supplied with condoms, etc.

The conservative arm would come from a quite conservative Islamic clergy, which has spoken openly of the dangers of HIV/AIDS from the Islamic equivalent of the pulpit. It's also an interesting correlation between the very high levels of male circumcision in the Islamic population, and this has been proven to be a retarding factor in the spread of AIDS.

In Uganda, when President Yoweri Museveni took power in 1986, one of the first things he did was to tour the country from east to west, top to bottom, talking about the danger of HIV/AIDS and, again, putting this on the public agenda. This was an enormous step and relatively early on. The message came to be in the education works in efforts in Uganda—the key phrase was: "zero grazing," which was a reference, of course, to the possibilities of more than one sex partner.

They adopted the so-called "ABCs" of education: A for "abstinence," B for "being faithful to one partner," and C for "condom use" if you stray from the first two prescriptions.

In Uganda, from the early 1990s to the early 2000s, the prevalence rate has fallen from some 14% to something on the order of 4–5%. This is a dramatic instance of a rollback and one that bears emulation from elsewhere.

In the shorter-run at least, the resources to combat this plague will need to come from outside. The contributions from the United States in the 1990s were the largest in the world, but the figure involved—about $70 million a year—was frankly rather paltry given the scale of the epidemic and the resources of the United States. In the first [G.W.] Bush administration that figure has been raised dramatically, at least in terms of what is promised, to something on the order of $15 billion over the coming years. We will see, of course, as we would with any promise, about the delivery. There's already some fear that some of those resources channeled through faith-based organizations are emphasizing only the A and the B (the abstinence and the fidelity to one partner), with a dropping of the third leg of the education campaign, and that is condom use.

As I've tried to do in these lectures on rather depressing topics, frankly, I've tried to end on a note of hope, and I'm going to do that by quoting a woman named Asunta Wagura. She's a member of an organization in Kenya known as the Network of Women with AIDS. This is what she says:

> So, here I am, an ordinary person with what is rapidly becoming a most ordinary virus. I've stopped feeling sorry for myself, and I've now learned to live, think, and even act positively. I've come out of my hideout, and I've found a stage where I can tell the world that I am not a victim, but rather I am a messenger—a messenger of hope. Tell me I am not a number—a statistic—but an equal partner in this struggle.

Thank you.

Lecture Thirty-Five
Zimbabwe—Background to Contemporary Crisis

Scope:

In recent years, no African country has received more attention in the West than Zimbabwe. President Robert Mugabe, the national hero of the independence struggle against white minority rule, has now been in power for a quarter-century. For much of that time, this beautiful land seemed a beacon of stability, relative prosperity—Zimbabwe regularly exported food to its needy neighbors—and racial reconciliation. Nonetheless, many Zimbabweans grew restive under Mugabe's lengthy tenure, increasing corruption, and authoritarian rule. When the populace rejected in referendum his proposed new constitution, and then nearly ended the ruling party's control of parliament, Mugabe reacted furiously. He seized remaining white-owned farms and cracked down ever more harshly on the opposition. The result—in the short run at least—has been economic decline, widespread hunger, and dispiriting conjecture about just where "the jewel of Africa" is headed.

Outline

I.   Since about the year 2000, no African country—not even South Africa—has received more attention than Zimbabwe in Western media. It may be worth pondering why this should be so. The word *crisis* is perhaps overly used with regard to Africa, but I have no hesitation in applying it to Zimbabwe today. In this lecture, we seek a fuller understanding of this situation.

II. Let's begin by reviewing briefly some aspects of Zimbabwe's history that we encountered in previous lectures.

   A. Named for magnificent stone ruins at the center of an old empire, modern Zimbabwe was originally, of course, the British colony of Southern Rhodesia, founded by and named for Cecil Rhodes.
      1. Southern Rhodesia was a settler colony. Though never more than 4 percent of the total population, whites were numerous enough to enjoy settler self-government within the British Empire.

2. The hallmark of settler colonies was expropriation of African land. In Southern Rhodesia, about half—the better half—of the total arable land was held by several thousand European farmers.

B. Shortly after the Central African Federation broke apart in 1963, the white settlers decided to buck the tide of African nationalism and, in 1965, unilaterally declared the country independent of Britain under the leadership of Ian Smith.

1. The Unilateral Declaration of Independence (UDI), in turn, led African nationalists to take up arms. A bloody war raged through the 1970s; eventually, negotiations led to an open election in 1980.

2. The election brought to power Robert Gabriel Mugabe and his party—formerly one of the liberation movements—the Zimbabwe African National Union-Patriotic Front (ZANU-PF).

III. Mugabe is, in many respects, a brilliant and remarkable character.

A. A devout Catholic, the idealistic young Mugabe went to Nkrumah's Ghana to teach school. He married a Ghanaian woman, who became independent Zimbabwe's first "mother of the nation."

B. Returning to Rhodesia (the "Southern" was dropped when Northern Rhodesia became Zambia), Mugabe became active with ZANU. He was imprisoned by the settler regime in the mid-1960s and spent the next decade there in one of Smith's prisons.

C. Mugabe's intelligence and intellectual bent are shown by his successful completion of graduate degrees through correspondence while in prison. He became an articulate advocate of Marxian revolution but never abandoned his pragmatism.

D. Released as part of an abortive peace initiative in 1975, Mugabe escaped to Mozambique, where he quickly rose to become director of ZANU's guerilla movement.

IV. Mugabe's first decade in power (the 1980s) saw some most impressive achievements and some ominous signs.

A. He had come to power fueled by popular resentment of white domination (some trace this to his bitter prison experience, including the denial of permission to attend the funeral of his deceased child) and, perhaps above all, resentment of the white control of so much land. On the other hand, the white farms, employing large numbers of black workers, were enormously productive, not only of foodstuffs but of Zimbabwe's leading export and earner of foreign exchange—tobacco.

    1. Mugabe chose neither radical redistribution of white-owned land nor preservation of the status quo but a middle course that saw some cautious resettlement of land-poor Africans, while maintaining the economic advantages generated by the large white commercial farms.

    2. He also extended many services to African peasant farmers who did not get more land—services largely denied to them under the old regime, such as extension advice, hybrid seed, fertilizer subsidy, improved transport, and full and prompt payment.

    3. The result was a nation that not only fed itself, with major input from both farming sectors, but regularly exported to its needful neighbors.

B. The country showed positive growth rates while achieving remarkable advances in health and, especially, education at all levels.

C. But Mugabe showed his iron fist by unleashing the notorious North Korean-trained Fifth Brigade to crush so-called "dissidents" in the ethnically Ndebele-dominated southwestern part of the country. Nonetheless, by decade's end, he had lured the predominantly Ndebele ZAPU party (his old rivals) into his government and muted his call for an official one-party state.

D. Most troubling to many was the increasingly brazen corruption of the elite, symbolized by the 1989 "Willowgate" scandal involving access to state-controlled cars. The hugely popular singer and musical hero of the liberation war, Thomas Mapfumo, hit a nerve with his English-language hit of 1989, "Corruption."

V. By the mid-1990s, Zimbabwe was still a place that largely *worked*—more than could be said for a number of places elsewhere. But the negative trends accelerated.

  A. Employment was shrinking, and prices were rising. In the urban areas, especially, there was increasingly open discontent.

  B. Corruption burgeoned. Mugabe funded the lavish lifestyle of his second wife, his former secretary, 40 years his junior, who was fond of flying on air force jets to Paris or Hong Kong for shopping sprees.

  C. Mugabe and his party's willingness to use heavy-handed intimidation continued unabated. In the late 1990s, he proposed a new constitution further entrenching the ruling party's power, confident he was still the hero of the people.

VI. The result of a referendum on the constitution, in early 2000, was a shock: 55 percent voted no. A few months later, despite every kind of intimidation and pro-ZANU saturation by the state-owned media, the opposition, crystallized as the Movement for Democratic Change, nearly won more seats in parliament than ZANU.

VII. Mugabe reacted with fury and played what can only be called the land card.

  A. Crowds of young men, so-called "war veterans," though most were barely born when the liberation war was fought, began to occupy white farms. Eventually, most of the white farmers were evicted; some were beaten, and a few killed. Physically, it was black farm workers who suffered most.

  B. The young men were largely party thugs, recruited from the desperate urban youth, and, through no fault of their own, not experienced farmers. Often, the re-expropriated farms did not even wind up in their

  hands—let alone those of land-hungry peasants—but in the possession of the well-connected elite.

  C. Predictably, at least for the short run, the economy crashed, by every measure. The former breadbasket of Africa became, by 2005, one of Africa's hungriest countries.

D. In 2005, the government launched a clearing operation against the squatter settlements, supposedly to clean up hotbeds of crime and disease. However, the targets were often hotbeds of opposition to the ZANU government. The plan was called "Operation Murumbatsvina"—"Operation Drive Out the Trash."

VIII. Mugabe seemed quite blasé about his nation's problems.

A. He attributed all opposition and criticism to whites and imperialists, especially Britain and the United States.

B. He and ZANU stay smugly in power, returned in highly dubious elections in 2002 and 2005.

C. Nonetheless, as my best Zimbabwean friend once put it, "There are a lot of brave people in this country," and they may yet prevail.

Suggested Reading:

Andrew Meldrum, *Where We Have Hope: A Memoir of Zimbabwe.*

Martin Meredith, *Our Votes, Our Guns: Robert Mugabe and the Tragedy of Zimbabwe.*

Questions to Consider:

1. What explains Mugabe's policies on land redistribution after independence in 1980, and what explains his abrupt shift from 2000 forward?

2. Historically, South Africa had an even more racially skewed land distribution than Zimbabwe; is it conceivable that South Africa will follow Zimbabwe's lead?

Lecture Thirty-Five—Transcript
Zimbabwe—Background to Contemporary Crisis

Welcome. Since the turn of the millennium (since about the year 2000), no African country—not even South Africa—has received more attention in the Western media than Zimbabwe. It may be worth pondering why this should be so. The word "crisis" is perhaps overly used with regard to Africa, but I have no hesitation in applying it to Zimbabwe today.

Part of the crisis is undoubtedly driven by very high prevalence rates of HIV and AIDS, the epidemic and pandemic that we surveyed in our previous lecture. In this lecture, I want to turn towards the political and economic aspects of this situation.

Let's begin by reviewing briefly some aspects of Zimbabwe and Zimbabwe's history encountered in previous lectures. Zimbabwe, of course, is named for the magnificent stone ruins, the largest in Africa south of the Nile Valley, which stood at the center of an old empire, Great Zimbabwe. Modern Zimbabwe, of course, originally was Southern Rhodesia. It was the British colony founded by, financed by, and named for Cecil Rhodes, whom we have certainly encountered before in this series.

In several earlier lectures, I made a distinction between settler colonies and non-settler colonies. In fact, I emphasized that, for my money, this was a more important distinction than the differences, for instance, between French versus British versus Portuguese colonialism, and so forth. A settler colony, again, is simply a place where substantial numbers of persons from the colonizing country, in this case Britain, come and intend to stay—set down roots.

Southern Rhodesia was a settler colony. Although never more—even at their peak—than 4% of the total population, whites here were numerous enough to enjoy, essentially, settler self-government within the British Empire from 1924 onwards.

The hallmark of settler colonies was the expropriation of African land. Again, colonialism happened all over the African continent, but in many colonies—non-settler colonies—whatever Africans may have lost, they did not lose the possession, in the direct sense, of their land. In Southern Rhodesia, however, about half—the better half, it will not surprise us—of the total arable land (cultivatable land) in the country was held by a relatively small number—still several thousand—European farming families.

It is that land division that is the absolutely critical starting point for understanding the unfolding of the Zimbabwean crisis in the 21st century.

Zimbabwe, when it was Southern Rhodesia, from 1953 to 1963, was part of the Central African Federation. We looked at the breakup of that federation, which at one point had bound together the countries now known as Zambia, Malawi, and Zimbabwe. It broke apart in 1963 precisely on the question of whether there would be a transition to majority-rule African government.

Britain by this time had accepted that for its colonies, but the white settlers of Southern Rhodesia had very different ideas. In 1965, under the leadership of the redoubtable Ian Smith, they declared unilaterally independence from Great Britain, and indeed the country was renamed Rhodesia. There was no need for the "Southern" after Northern Rhodesia had become Zambia.

The Unilateral Declaration of Independence (the UDI) was followed in turn rather quickly by the banning (prohibition) of essentially all of the African nationalist movements, which had emerged as they had all over the continent in the 1950s and early 1960s to challenge colonial rule.

As is typical of settler colonies, and a point we have made before, the path to decolonization and the path to independence was not peaceful at all. Following their banning—their "illegalization"—the African national movements launched a national war of liberation known still today in Zimbabwe as the Second Chimurenga (*chimurenga* being the Shona word for "struggle"). They launched this from neighboring countries as is typical of guerilla warfare anywhere.

All through the 1970s, this Second Chimurenga—this war—raged through the colony of Rhodesia. It led to some 30,000 people dead and a million refugees. As I said at a previous juncture, horrific things were done by all sides in this very bitter war.

Eventually, by the late 1970s, Smith had concluded that it was fruitless to try to continue to hold on forever, and that he would negotiate as best he could a post-independence deal. The Lancaster House negotiations took place, centered in London.

The results of that led to Zimbabwe's first national remotely democratic election in 1980, and at that moment, in 1980, the victory went to Robert Gabriel Mugabe and his party, formerly one of the two main liberation movements. Mugabe's party was known as the Zimbabwe African National Union, or ZANU. It had been allied on paper, though rarely in practice, with the other principal liberation organization, the Zimbabwe African Peoples Union. They had formed the Patriotic Front. ZANU-PF became the ruling party of independent Zimbabwe at independence on April 18, 1980.

Who is Robert Gabriel Mugabe? He was—he is—in many respects a brilliant and remarkable character. He's a devout Catholic. He was raised, in fact, on a Catholic mission in north-central Zimbabwe. He was part of that generation of the 1950s, youth that took very seriously the promises and hopes of decolonization and independence. It is not at all inaccurate, I think, to apply the word "idealistic" to Mugabe at this stage.

In fact, he left Rhodesia and went to the mecca of African independence in the late 1950s, and that, of course, was the country of Ghana in West Africa led by the "Father of African Nationalism," Kwame Nkrumah. Mugabe taught school in Ghana and, in fact, married a Ghanaian woman who later, when they returned to Zimbabwe, became Amai Mugabe, the "mother of the nation," despite the fact that her roots, in fact, came from a different part of the continent—a very highly respected figure I found in my experience in Zimbabwe.

When Mugabe returned to Rhodesia in the early 1960s, he became active with ZANU (with the Zimbabwe African National Union). Eventually, he was imprisoned by the settler regime of Ian Smith in the mid-1960s, and he spent approximately a decade (approximately 1965 to 1975) in one of Smith's prisons.

Mugabe's intelligence and indeed his intellectual bent are demonstrated by the fact that while he was in prison, he actually earned multiple graduate degrees through correspondence courses. It was in this period that his own ideology sort of crystallized, and he became an articulate advocate of Marxian revolution, on one level, but he never really abandoned a quite practical and pragmatic approach to politics and to power, on the other hand.

He was released as part of an aborted peace initiative that came in 1975 and quickly escaped to Mozambique. Mozambique, next door to the east of Rhodesia, at this time, of course, had just become independent of the Portuguese. The new rulers of Mozambique, anxious to show a kind of solidarity, if you like, across the African borders, allowed ZANU to establish numerous bases from Mozambique. This was truly one of the crucial turning points in the Second Chimurenga in the Zimbabwe War.

Mugabe in Mozambique quickly rose through the ranks and by the mid- to late 1970s certainly was the undisputed leader and spokesperson for ZANU.

In 1980, when Mugabe and his power were victorious in this first democratic national election in the new country, he was told by his old friend at the independence ceremonies, Julius Nyerere, President of Tanzania still at that point (president for almost two decades by that point and with considerable experience)—Nyerere told him: "You have inherited a jewel. Keep it that way."

For the first decade after 1980, in many respects, Mugabe and his party did keep it that way. There's a sort of echo in Zimbabwean history of the experience of many other African countries 20 years earlier. When we looked at the first decade after independence in country after country and saw indisputable achievements and gains that eventually turned very differently.

We saw some very impressive achievements indeed in the first decade of Zimbabwean independence, as well as some ominous signs. Mugabe, surprisingly to many inured to his revolutionary rhetoric, practiced and preached racial reconciliation at independence and not on a single occasion. He did so repeatedly and indeed for some time quite convincingly.

Let me give you an idea of a manifesto issued by the party in 1980:

> ZANU wishes to give the fullest assurance to the white community, the Asian and coloured communities [Again, "coloured" has a specific meaning in southern Africa] that as ZANU government can never in principle or in social or

governmental practice discriminate against them. Racism, whether practiced by whites or blacks, is anathema to the humanitarian philosophy of ZANU. It is as primitive a dogma as tribalism or regionalism. Zimbabwe cannot just be a country of blacks. It is and should remain our country: all of us together.

Impressive conciliatory rhetoric indeed. But remember, Mugabe had come to power behind, or at the head of, a guerilla movement. Participation in his movement was fueled, after all, by popular resentment of white domination and above all, probably, by resentment of the white control of so much land.

On the other hand, just to put ourselves, in a sense, of the shoes of Robert Mugabe and his power as they take the reigns of power, what are their options at that point? They come to power, I repeat, behind the popular pressure against white rule and resentment of white land domination.

On the other hand, these same white farms employed very large numbers of black workers. They were enormously productive. In many respects, they were mechanized examples of modern, high-input/high-output farming. They produced not only large amounts of foodstuffs, but were responsible for producing the bulk of Zimbabwe's leading export and earner of foreign exchange—earner of hard currency. That was the export commodity of tobacco, again, largely grown on these white farms. We've emphasized right through our look at 20th-century/21st-century African history that the reliance upon export commodities is something that was typical of the transformation of Africa in that century and certainly nothing to be taken lightly.

Mugabe, in the early going, chose neither radical redistribution of white-owned land nor the strict preservation of the status quo ante (in other words, he did not either accept the unequal division of land that he had inherited at independence). He pursued a middle course, which saw some cautious resettlement of land-poor Africans, while maintaining the economic advantages generated by large white commercial farms.

To some extent, his caution here—this middle course—was dictated by the terms and features of the constitution, which was hammered out at Lancaster House in the 1970s and which he inherited. In terms of land distribution, that constitution called for what is usually termed a "willing buyer/willing seller" mechanism. In other words, land could not simply be condemned. It could not simply be expropriated by the state and redistributed to land-poor African farmers. It had to come from paying, essentially, market prices for persons who were willing to sell.

That was the constitutional provision. Of course, he could have ignored that constitution; he did not. Again, that needs to be recognized.

I'll illustrate sort of both Mugabe's pursuit of this middle course, but also the sort of steel that lies beneath his personality from a personal anecdote. President Robert Mugabe came to my hometown now of Raleigh, North Carolina, where I teach history. He came as part of a visit that included visiting the United Nations, and so forth, and gave a speech at a neighboring institution to my own. He gave a speech at St. Augustine's University—St. Augustine's College, a traditionally African-American institution in downtown Raleigh, North Carolina.

I have to pause here and mention that the welcome for Mugabe's speech—after all, this was a sort of state occasion here—the welcoming address given by a pretty high-ranking North Carolina official created some acute embarrassment on the part of myself and others. In seeking to find commonalities between Zimbabwe and North Carolina, he mentioned a few. For instance, he mentioned tobacco, which has certainly been part of the history of both places.

He also stated that both the state of North Carolina and Zimbabwe had cities named Salisbury. It's quite true. There's a Piedmont, North Carolina, city named Salisbury. Salisbury, Rhodesia, had been the capital of that colony. It was named for Lord Salisbury, the British Prime Minister at the time that Rhodes had conquered and colonized the colony. The name had, in fact, been changed from Salisbury to Harare immediately after independence for the same sort of reasons that the country changed its name from Rhodesia to Zimbabwe. Our North Carolina official, alas, was apparently unaware of the change. Oh, dear.

My point in bringing up the speech is this: Mugabe talked about the land issue. He described the middle course that I've been talking about: you know, purchasing some farms, redistributing a substantial amount, although not an earth-shaking amount. Something like 35,000 families resettled in the first decade.

He described that process. He described the constitutional provisions that he was observing in obtaining that land on a "willing seller/willing buyer" basis. At one point he said: "We are required by the constitution [I'm paraphrasing] to purchase this land on the basis of willing buyer/willing seller. That is what we will do. The land that we need, we will pay for."

Then he paused and looked very seriously at the audience and said: "Though we were never paid for it," obviously making his political point despite the policy of moderation that he was enunciating.

In some respects, Mugabe attempted to compensate for relatively slow action on redistribution with some dramatic other measures. He extended many services to African peasant farmers who had *not* gotten more land—services that they had been denied under the old settler regime. I'm talking about high-level extension advice, hybrid seeds, subsidies for fertilizer, improved transport to get crops to market, payment promptly and in full, and so on.

In a lot of respects, on the old so-called native reserves there was a kind of agricultural revolution that took place in the 1980s. Food production multiplied out of those parts of the small-scale farming sector several times over. The result was a nation that not only fed itself with major input from both of these farming sectors, but regularly exported to its often needful neighbors. I certainly recall instances of being in Zambia, for instance, hearing of, and reading of, shipments of food coming from next door in the so-called "breadbasket of southern Africa" at that point.

The country in the 1980s showed positive overall macro-economic growth rates (GNP rates) while achieving remarkable advances in health and especially education, at all levels. Remember, this is taking place in the 1980s, when in many cases or in many ways, the terms of trade, which we surveyed in looking at Africa's downturn from about the mid-1970s onward—you know, he's carrying this out and making these kinds of advances in a far less hospitable international climate than the first generation of independence leaders had found themselves in.

On the other hand, Mugabe had already shown his iron fist, if you like, by unleashing the notorious, North-Korean-trained Fifth Brigade to crush the so-called "dissidents" in the ethnically Ndebele-dominated southwest of the country. This is still remembered as the *Gukurahundi*, in Shona. It's a reference to the fierce storms that sometimes emerge here and pound the ground. Anybody in Zimbabwe will recognize the terms like "Fifth Brigade," and to some it will bring a bit of a shudder.

Nonetheless, by the decade's end, he had lured the predominantly Ndebele ZAPU party (his old rivals) into his government. Joshua Nkomo, the leader of ZAPU, was made a vice president. He had muted his call for an official one-party state, which he had made earlier on.

But most troubling to all was the increasingly brazen corruption of the elite. This was symbolized by the 1989 so-called "Willowgate" scandal. The name, of course, is a play on "Watergate," which had already become famous by then. It involved access to, essentially, state-controlled cars. It was clear that ministers and other parts of the elite were getting fantastic deals on cars that were not being made available to the rest of the middle class.

The popular disgust with corruption that was growing around was captured by, arguably, Zimbabwe's most popular, and maybe most famous, artist. That is the singer Thomas Mapfumo. He released an album in 1989 with the title and a title song in English called "Corruption." It meant exactly what it said. The cover of that album showed a pair of right hands shaking hands and a pair of left hands with money being transferred one to the other. The chorus of that song, "Something for something, nothing for nothing, that's how it is in our country today" hit a raw nerve.

By the mid 1990s, Zimbabwe was still, however, a place that largely worked. I spent 1994 there as a visiting Fulbright lecturer at the University of Zimbabwe. "A place that largely worked" was more than could be said for a number of places elsewhere in the continent.

But the negative trends accelerated. Employment was shrinking, and prices rising. In the urban areas, especially, there was increasingly open discontent. Corruption burgeoned. Mugabe funded the lavish lifestyle of his second wife, his former secretary 40 years his junior, who was fond of flying on air force jets to Paris or Hong Kong for shopping sprees.

Mugabe and his party's willingness to use heavy-handed intimidation against any form of dissidence or opposition continued unabated. In the late 1990s, he proposed a new constitution further entrenching the ruling party's power, confident that he was still the hero of the people. He put it to a popular referendum. In early 2000, the results were shocking: 55% of the populace voted no on this referendum.

A few months later, despite every kind of intimidation and pro-ZANU saturation by the state-owned media, the opposition, now crystallized in an opposition party known—and still known—as the Movement for Democratic Change, very nearly displaced ZANU in the parliament and very nearly unseated this government.

Mugabe reacted with fury and played what can only be called the land card. Soon, by late 2000 and 2001, into 2002 and 2003, crowds of young men who were called "war veterans"—that is, veterans of the liberation war in the 1970s—began to occupy, take over, and invade the white-owned farms. They were called "war veterans," and certainly some were, particularly at the top. But if you look at the footage, do the math with me. Someone who is 20, or 25, or 30 years old in 1980 at the conclusion of that war, in 2000 would have been 40, or 45, or 50.

Not these people who carried out the farm invasions: Most of them were in their late teens. They were overwhelmingly male, late-teenage, and people in their 20s. They were drawn from the unemployed desperate youth of the cities, given a club—literally given a club—and given an occupation by the ruling party. Eventually, most of the white farmers were evicted; some were beaten, and a few were killed.

Physically, however, it was overwhelmingly the black farm workers who suffered the most. These young men who occupied the farms in the first instance, through no fault of their own—after all, they'd been raised in the city—were not experienced farmers. Often, the reexpropriated farms did not even wind up in their hands—let alone those of the land-hungry peasants—but in the possession of well-connected members of the elite (cabinet members, etc.).

Predictably, at least in the short run, the economy crashed by any measure. The former breadbasket of Africa became by 2005 one of Africa's hungriest countries. The indicators are many of the tailspin in Zimbabwe. Think of its currency. When I first went to Zimbabwe in 1983, a Zimbabwe dollar (that's the name of the currency) was worth U.S. $1.40. In 2005, the exchange rate was approximately 25,000 Zim dollars to one U.S. dollar. I never thought I'd see a day when the Zambian kwacha next door was worth more than the Zimbabwe dollar. Today, it's worth about five times as much.

I had a student from Zimbabwe who told me that by this time, people in Zimbabwe were leaving the smaller currency notes simply lying in the street.

In 2005, the government launched as well a clearing operation against the squatter settlements—the shanty towns—of thousands, probably tens or hundreds of thousands, of people around the capital city, in particular. It was justified as the clearing of hotbeds of crime and disease. Indeed, there is certainly some truth to that, but these were also hotbeds of opposition to the ZANU government. It had always been the urban areas from which most of the opposition came.

The operation was called (in Shona) Operation Murambatsvina ("Operation Drive Out Trash")—not exactly a flattering way to refer to your fellow citizens.

Mugabe seemed quite blasé about his nation's problems, attributing all opposition and criticism to whites and to imperialists, especially and above all Britain, with the U.S. not far behind. He and ZANU stayed smugly in power, returned in highly dubious elections in 2002 and 2005.

There's a tragedy about this. Had he retired in 1995 even, I think his place as the national hero in Zimbabwe would have been secure. I think, at this point he will be remembered by many very differently. I don't know of a clearer example of the old adage that, "Power corrupts."

Nonetheless, I'll close, again, with a personal incident. The last time I was in Zimbabwe, I was traveling in the capital city with my old supervisor in the economic history department. We were driving, and first a truckload of youth chanting songs, a few of them carrying sticks or clubs—he said: "That's the party youth." Indeed, these are the ones who are the enforcers—the intimidator—on the part of the party.

A little bit later, my friend saw a friend of his—a woman—a friend of the family. We stopped, got out, and she greeted us warmly with one of those Zimbabwean smiles that can light up a side street. We got back in the car, and my friend said that she was a high-ranking official in Zimbabwe's leading human rights organization, that she'd been arrested in the previous month, one of several such arrests, and that here she was greeting a friend, welcoming a stranger, and showing an absolute commitment to continuing her struggle—her speaking of truth to power.

My friend kind of shook his head, and he said: "There's a lot of brave people in this country."

I'm going to close this by paraphrasing William Faulkner. I think that those brave Zimbabweans will not only endure, they will prevail. Thank you.

Lecture Thirty-Six
Africa Found

Scope:

We conclude the course with a brief overview of some of the main themes: struggles with the environment, ethnic identity, statebuilding, and the constantly evolving interface between Africa and the outside world. We offer a sober assessment of contemporary Africa. Is the glass half-empty or half-full? Is talk of an "African Renaissance" empty rhetoric? With a very large dose of caution, we present some examples that may offer hope: ordinary (and some extraordinary) men and women showing courage, sacrifice, entrepreneurship, innovation, and vision.

Outline

I. So we come to the end of our journey. In this lecture we are going to do three things.

   A. First, we will review and summarize some of the critical themes of the course.

   B. We will then assess Africa in the first decade of the 21st century.

   C. We will conclude with some profiles of people who, in the recent past, have made some impressive contributions to progress in Africa.

II. So let's review briefly some of the main topics we've covered.

   A. Physically, Africa comprises numerous quite different environments. It can be an achingly beautiful place but has never been an easy place. Its soils are relatively weak, its rainfall is limited, and its disease environment is dangerous.

   B. Humankind emerged in Africa in several different stages; the rest of the world was populated out of Africa. The fundamental things that make us human developed here.

   C. People originally lived directly off the environment and transformed it but little. That changed dramatically as agriculture and iron resulted in much higher population and settled life.

D. African communities developed distinctive social relations, religious systems, and political institutions.
   1. We have been at some pains to gain a subtler understanding of ethnic identity and have examined its importance and its fluid nature at numerous junctures.
   2. We have looked at the emergence of major states, kingdoms, and empires—the fundamental units of the African political past—in many different settings.
E. Africa's "isolation" has frequently been exaggerated.
   1. Quite early on, we saw evidence of contact—especially commercial contact—for instance, across the Sahara or the Indian Ocean.
   2. We also studied religious contact, particularly the impact of Christianity and Islam in Africa, and we saw that there has always been a good deal of syncretism, the combination of these outside religions and much older spiritual ideas.
F. Still, we reached a turning point in Africa's relation to the outside world some 500 years ago, as Western European powers began to drive a global mercantile capitalist system.
   1. An important subdynamic of this phenomenon was West Africa's emergence as the primary source of slaves for the New World. This slave trade meant the loss of millions of persons to West Africa—either killed in the operation of the trade or exported across the Atlantic, where they were crucial in the transformation of the Americas.
   2. Another subdynamic was the origin of modern South Africa, the continent's most developed and powerful nation and one comparable at many historical points with the United States.
G. Eventually, Africa's relation with Europe took another dramatic turn with the scramble for Africa—the carving of the continent into European empires, a century or more ago.
   1. The basic national units of today's Africa—African countries—were created then and are still with us, the only exception being the creation of Eritrea in 1993 out of the country of Ethiopia.

2. Economically, African territories were made dependent on an export/import system, often monoeconomic, and this situation is still with us, too.

3. In some territories, significant numbers of European settlers came and took up land. They did not come only as missionaries or merchants or soldiers or government representatives.

H. With great energy, Africans organized nationalist movements against the colonial powers. Eventually, they gained independence: earlier and more peacefully in nonsettler territories, later and with arms in settler ones.

I. And with great hopes and expectations, Africans entered the independence period. By and large, those expectations were disappointed, for reasons both internal and external.

1. After impressive early gains in economic growth, education, and health care, the international economic climate turned inhospitable in the 1970s, and everything economic contracted.

2. Politically, the continent has been plagued with continuing wars, authoritarian rule, and corruption.

3. In the 1980s and 1990s, Africa's second period of democratization took place, with the conversion of South Africa to a democratic government being perhaps the most remarkable case of all.

III. Where does that leave us at this point in the 21st century?

A. I refuse to be, and will never be, Pollyanna. I can make a good case, I believe, for a quite dismal African future.

1. Where is the financial and social capital for genuine development going to come from? What is the realistic alternative to continued reliance on commodity exports—and what are the likely returns for those exports? Isn't Africa going to have to wait *another* epoch for its turn, as China and India bloom into developed powers?

2. As if this weren't enough, what about HIV/AIDS? And what else is out there? Just staying alive is going to be challenge enough.

3. As one corrupt leader shall be removed, so shall another be visited upon us. It's almost too easy to find examples.

B. As you have probably guessed, that is not where my heart is. But professors are supposed to use their heads—and I think there is plenty of evidence to suggest the possibility of something, not perhaps so grand as an "African Renaissance," but something like measurable progress.

    1. The ideas of fundamental political accountability and basic political freedoms—to speak, to write, to organize—have, I think, become entrenched. In this sense, the democratic revival of the late 1980s and early 1990s, despite setbacks, has made a lasting mark. There are virtually no one-party states or military regimes on the continent.

    2. This change, in turn, is the key to exposing corruption and bringing it within tolerable limits.

    3. The idea of taking Africa's farmers—perhaps, especially, Africa's *women* farmers—seriously has also gained ground. On it depends long-range food security, a subject not to be taken lightly.

    4. In Uganda and Senegal, vigorous public education has begun to reverse even a calamity such as HIV/AIDS.

    5. Debt restructuring and debt relief for a dozen or more African nations has meant a fresh start for these countries.

    6. In the digital age, a case such as Ireland—where heavy investment in education for a new era has sparked a boom—might offer a model. What if such education were offered to Africa's young, and very often enthusiastic, learners?

IV. I will end by offering some brief profiles of some people in Africa today who lead me to conclude the glass is half-full.

    A. Our first example is Hamilton Naki from South Africa.

        1. He worked at the University of Cape Town, first tending the grass around the tennis courts, then eventually assisting doctors in practicing surgery on animals. He became known for his ability to join tiny blood vessels with amazing delicacy and accuracy.

        2. In 1967, he worked with Christiaan Bernard, who performed the first heart transplant, even though at that time it was illegal for a black South African to be permitted in the surgical theater of a whites-only hospital.

  3. In 2003, he finally received a well-deserved honorary medical degree from the University of Cape Town. He died in May 2005.

B. Emmanuel Akyeampong, born in Ghana, earned a doctorate in African history.

  1. He is a professor of African history at Harvard. Akyeampong is not, however, symbolic of another phenomena taking place in poor countries: so-called "brain drain."

  2. His family still lives in Ghana, and he has worked to develop the African Public Broadcasting Foundation, similar to our Public Broadcasting Corporation, so that news, education, and information can be mixed with entertainment and reach the masses continent-wide.

C. Erik Charas from Mozambique graduated with a degree in electrical engineering from the University of Cape Town.

  1. He has developed an original and practical solution to a basic human health problem: the tragedy of 3 million children who die each year of vaccine-preventable diseases because the vaccines cannot be kept cold before they are injected.

  2. His propane-driven refrigerators keep vaccines cool in rural areas where no electricity is available.

D. Finally, we have Wangari Maathai from Kenya, who received her bachelor's and master's degrees in the United States and her Ph.D. in Veterinary Anatomy from the University of Nairobi, the first East African woman to gain a Ph.D. there.

  1. She worked on behalf of rural Kenyan women and started the Green Belt Movement to plant trees in Kenya and maintain the biodiversity of the land and conserve water. So far, 30 million trees have been planted in Kenya alone.

  2. She persevered despite conflict with plantation owners and Kenyan President Daniel arap Moi and is now the Assistant Minister for Environment, Natural Resources, and Wildlife in Kenya.

3. She has spoken out on the disproportionate number of women with HIV/AIDS and against female genital mutilation. In 2004, this remarkable Kenyan woman won the Nobel Peace Prize.

V. One final thought: Thirty years ago, I got hooked on Africa and its history after going there. I am not unique. Many of you have likely already made a trip there. If you are contemplating it, I leave you with this word: *Go.*

Suggested Reading:

Frederick Cooper, *Africa since 1940: The Past of the Present*, chapter 8.

Questions to Consider:

1. What has been the most surprising thing you have learned in this course?

2. What is *your* conclusion—is the glass half-full or half-empty? What are the prospects for Africa?

Lecture Thirty-Six—Transcript
Africa Found

So we come to the end. In this final lecture, I'd like to do three basic things. Firstly, I'd like to review and summarize some of the critical themes from our first 35 lectures—our look at the long run of Africa's history. Second, I'd like to offer as sober an assessment as I can of Africa in the first decade of the 21st century—in fact, alternative scenarios, if you'd like, a sort of glass half-full versus glass half-empty kind of analysis. Thirdly, I'd like to offer you some profiles—some looks at real people, individual lives—persons who in the recent past have been making some very impressive contributions indeed.

We started the course with geography, the way I start every course I do. Physically, Africa comprises a remarkable variety of physical and geographic environments. It can be an achingly beautiful place. If you stand at Victoria Falls or Mount Kilimanjaro, you can easily wonder if there's anything on earth to top this.

But it has never been an easy place. Its soils are old. They are leeched. They are, relative to some other parts of the world, weak. Its rainfall is limited. Its disease environment, partly because most of Africa lies in the tropics and receives year-round warmth, has been a dangerous one.

We looked at the emergence of humankind in Africa—why Africa—from a variety of evidences, including fossil evidence and DNA evidence in more recent times—can be shown quite conclusively to be the cradle of humankind—the birthplace of humankind. The rest of the world, in a quite literal sense, was populated "out of Africa." The fundamental things that make us human developed here, and developed here first.

It's worth just reading a line or two from a longer quotation I used from John Reeder in Lecture Four. He said that, "Humans dominate the earth and have been to the moon. We see visions of the future in the mind's eye and turn them to reality with aptitudes and talents which evolution bestowed in Africa."

People originally lived directly off the environment—extracted their livelihood directly from it as hunters and gatherers (as foragers)—

©2006 The Teaching Company Limited Partnership

and transformed it, therefore, rather little. That changed dramatically, as perhaps the greatest revolution in all of human history—the revolution of agriculture—aided, abetted, and reinforced in Africa by the revolution of the discovery and spread of iron use—changed Africa in numerous ways. Population increased. There was a much greater level of sedentary life, not just a village existence in a rural setting, but the emergence of Africa's first cities.

African communities developed—over centuries—distinctive social relations, religious systems, and political institutions. I've been at some pains to offer what I hope is a subtler understanding of ethnic identity, something that I find often misunderstood—in fact, often distorted—in the case of Africa. I've examined its importance and its fluid nature at numerous junctures.

We tried to develop an understanding of ethnic groups—of so-called "tribes," if we insist on usage of that term—that are identities not set in stone—not rigidly bound—which have always overlapped and which are not inevitably bound for conflict. There's just as much—in fact, for my money, far more—evidence of ethnic tolerance and coexistence as there is of conflict in Africa's history.

I simply asserted that this is a subject that we cannot ignore—that it is, on occasion, a life and death matter, as in Rwanda in 1994. But it is a category—a mode of analysis—that falls far short of explaining everything about Africa.

We've looked at the emergence of major states, kingdoms, empires—the fundamental units of the African political past, and we've done that in many different settings. In West Africa, we looked at legendary places of West Africa's so-called "Golden Age": the kingdoms of Ghana and Mali, which have lent their names to modern countries. We looked at Songhai. We looked at the legendary real place called Timbuktu, which played an important role in several of those kingdoms of the West African savanna.

On the East African coast, we looked at a variation on the theme of statebuilding, the emergence of Swahili city-states—that is, compact commercially oriented cities, 30 or 40 of them spread—going back at least 1,000, perhaps 2,000 years—along that East African coast.

We looked in southern Africa at another place that gave its name to a modern country. That was Great Zimbabwe, the greatest stone ruins in Africa south of the Nile Valley.

We've seen that Africa's vaunted "isolation" has frequently been exaggerated. Quite early on, we see evidence of contact—perhaps, especially, commercial contact—for instance, across the Sahara and across the Indian Ocean.

There was also religious contact. We tried to extract some of the fundamental principles of Africa's spiritual life in the indigenous religions found around the continent, but we looked over the long run at the impact of two of the world's great religions, Christianity and Islam, and emphasized that even though these have become major parts of contemporary Africa's scene, there has always been a large element of syncretism—of the combination—of the hybridization, if you like—between these religions coming into Africa and much older spiritual ideas that are far from gone.

Still, in terms of this question of isolation in the global context for Africa's history, we reach a turning point if we go back about 500 years ago. Of course, that's true for many parts of the world, not least the New World (the Americas). At that juncture, around the turn of the 16th century, symbolized probably still rather well by Columbus's voyage of 1492 and those undertaken thereafter, we begin to see that Western European powers drive a global mercantile capitalist system—a system wherein the pursuit of wealth is largely an enterprise driven by the effort to get things, and sometimes persons defined as things, and take them elsewhere for resale in the expectation or calculation, not always realized, of profit.

An important subdynamic of this post-1500 world and its impact on Africa was, of course, the emergence of the so-called "Atlantic System." Perhaps its single most important component was the development of the Atlantic slave trade. West Africa's emergence as the primary source of enslaved persons to labor in the New World had profound implications for the history of three continents. It meant the loss of millions of persons to West Africa, either killed in the operation of the trade or exported, of course, across the Atlantic, where they were crucial in the transformation of the Americas.

Another subdynamic of this world emerging about 500 years ago we found at the other corner—at the other end—of the continent in the origins of what today has emerged as one of the continent's most important countries—and that, of course, is the Republic of South Africa. South Africa has a colonial past stretching back to a considerably earlier date than much of the rest of Africa, and we looked at that in the case of the Cape Colony.

We've also emphasized at many places in this course the comparability between the histories of southern Africa, especially South Africa, and the history of North America, especially the United States. Both of them saw indigenous populations faced with incursions by European colonial immigrants. Both of them saw histories of slavery. Both of them saw frontier histories. Both of them saw the emergence of rigid, legalized racial domination and white supremacy called, in the first half of the 20th century, "segregation." Both, of course, have seen the efforts to change that system.

Eventually, Africa's relationship with Europe took another dramatic turn about 100 to 120 years back or so with the so-called "Scramble for Africa." The Scramble represented, of course, the carving of the continent—which King Leopold at the time called "this magnificent African cake"—into several European empires.

It was at that time during the "Scramble for Africa" that the basic national units of today's Africa—today's African nations—the 50 or so countries on the continent—the borders of those countries were created at the time of the Scramble. It may be remarkable to say they are very much still with us. There is one and only one case of legal formalized border change in Africa since the Scramble, and that was the creation of a separate Eritrea out of the country of Ethiopia.

Economically, African territories in the colonial period were made dependent upon an export/import system. The name of the game became the export of a single or perhaps two or three commodities (I call them monoeconomies) forged during the colonial system and symbolized in many respects by what was genuine investment in the infrastructure of railways, but leading invariably from the points of production of primary materials (crops out of the ground or minerals out of the earth) to the ports, and from those ports to the colonial mother countries and the world economic system. That export orientation—that monoeconomy situation—is still with us as well.

In some territories in colonial Africa, significant numbers of Europeans came not just as missionaries, or merchants, or governors, or soldiers. They came intending to stay. They were settlers, and I've emphasized at many points the importance of the difference between settler and non-settler colonies. This has affected a number of things, most obviously the question of whether Africans—whatever else they lost in the colonial period—would, in fact, directly lose their land.

Eventually, by the middle parts of the 20th century, with great energy, Africans all over the continent organized nationalist movements against the colonial powers. Eventually they gained independence, but here, again, we see the crucial difference in timing and means of decolonization represented by the distinction between settler and non-settler colonies.

To put it simply, in places where there had been little settlement, independence was likely to be achieved far more peacefully, and it was likely to come much earlier, in and around the year 1960—not a bad symbolic stopping-off point. In settler colonies, concentrated in the southern part of the continent—in Zimbabwe, Angola, Mozambique, and certainly in South Africa—majority rule was likely to come later, and it was likely to come only after often very bloody wars of liberation.

With great hopes, with great expectations then, ordinary Africans all over the continent entered the independence period. Indeed, for a decade or so, there were some quite impressive gains in these newly minted nations—gains in economic growth, in education, in healthcare. Eventually, however, that first taste of freedom turned sour and, by and large, the expectations were disappointed, for reasons both internal and external.

In the middle of the 1970s, the international economic climate, perhaps punctuated most dramatically by the so-called "oil shocks"—the sudden rises of prices of this critical ingredient of any modern economy—the international climate turned inhospitable, and everything economic in Africa contracted.

Rulers—usually the same nationalists who had led the struggles to gain independence—responded by tightening their grips on power. They lacked the resources anymore to simply reward or buy off, if you like, opposition—reward supporters and buy off opposition. All over the continent, one-party states, military coups, and, it has to be said, a very high level of corruption became the order of the day.

In numerous places, there were real shooting wars. Angola and Mozambique's independence from Portugal did not signal the end of warfare in those countries, and they entered on to often decades-long (or more) civil wars. Liberia, Sudan, the eastern Congo, Sierra Leone—in one place at least, Rwanda, it was worse than that, and the emergence of a genuine genocide shocked Africa and the world.

Eventually, however, phoenix-like, at the end of the 1980s and into the early 1990s, there was a second wave—Africa's second democratization took place. Again, ordinary people as well as extraordinary people all over the continent forged what may be the basis for a new political dispensation. South Africa probably represented, of course, with its conversion from the rigors of white supremacy under apartheid into a democratically elected government in 1994, the most remarkable case of all.

So where does that leave us in the 21st century's first decade? I stated at the outset of the course, and I'll say it again, I refuse to be—I will never be—Pollyanna or Pangloss. I can make a good case, I think, for a quite dismal African future. Where is the financial and social capital for genuine development going to come from? What is the realistic alternative to continued reliance on commodity exports—and what are the likely returns for those exports? Isn't Africa going to have to wait another epoch for its turn as China and India bloom into developed powers?

As if this weren't enough, what about HIV/AIDS? What else is out there? Maybe just staying alive is going to be challenge enough.

I can wax scriptural on you: As one corrupt leader shall be removed, so shall another be visited upon us. It's almost too easy to find examples—a country like Zambia or Kenya, where the expulsion or rejection, if you like, of one leader raises again the hopes and expectations, often to find that those are disappointed by the replacements. All of this can, indeed, lead to a conclusion that the glass is not just half-empty—it's draining.

As you've probably guessed, that's not where my heart is. But professors are supposed to use their heads—and I think that there's plenty of evidence to suggest the possibility of something, not perhaps so grand as an "African Renaissance," the phrase popularized by South Africa's President Mbeki, but something like measurable progress.

First of all, the ideas of fundamental political accountability and basic political freedoms—freedom to speak, to write, and to organize—have, I think, been entrenched. That doesn't mean that they are enjoyed without fetter everywhere, but the idea of insisting upon those—that those should be the norm—has, I think, been firmly established.

In this sense, the democratic revival of the late 1980s and early 1990s, despite its setbacks, has made a lasting mark. There are virtually no one-party states or military regimes on the continent. That would have been a hard thing to imagine in 1985 or 1990. This change, in turn, is the key to exposing corruption and bringing it to within tolerable limits.

The idea of taking Africa's farmers—and maybe especially Africa's *women* farmers—its female farmers—seriously has also gained ground. On it depends, more than anything else, Africa's long-range food security, a subject not to be taken lightly anywhere.

In Uganda and Senegal, vigorous public education spearheaded by upfront public roles of presidents and leaders has made a real dent and, in fact, has rolled back, contained, and reversed even a calamity so widespread as HIV and AIDS.

In 2005, agreement was finally reached with institutions like the World Bank, the International Monetary Fund, the African Development Bank—institutions largely dominated by the richest countries of the world, often called the G8, or what have you—arrangements were finally made for a substantial measure of debt restructuring and, in fact, debt relief and forgiveness for a dozen or more African nations.

This is not something, obviously, that can happen every year, every five years, or every 10 years, but it does represent a fresh start. These, after all, were debts that were incurred through poor decisions made by people on both sides of the equation in Africa and in the developed world in a previous generation, and yet the burdens have saddled a continent where half the population is under 15.

I can't promise that restructuring of debt is going to lead to a takeoff in Africa's prospect, but I can virtually guarantee that without it, you won't see that takeoff.

In the digital age, a case like Ireland, another place where a lot of people referred to it as a basket case 10 to 20 years ago, there's been substantial evidence in education for a new era. I mean the digital age has sparked a boom. Perhaps that will offer a model. What if such education were offered to Africa's young, and often very enthusiastic, learners?

I would like to close, then, with some profiles, as I mentioned at the outset, of some real people. I'm going to mention four. I'm going to draw them from each corner of the continent: from West Africa, from southern Africa, from East Africa—persons whom I think do offer us an instance of hope.

You probably have never heard of Hamilton Naki. I had not. Hamilton Naki died in May of 2005 in Cape Town, South Africa. He had grown up very near to where Nelson Mandela grew up in the so-called eastern Cape Transkei region of that country. At the age of 14, he had gone to Cape Town, where he got a job at the University of Cape Town, at first tending the grass around that elite and basically whites-only institution, around the tennis courts.

He eventually caught on at the medical school and began to assist some of the professors there in the care and the anaesthetization of animals used for medical students to learn and to practice surgery. It was there that doctors began to observe his own skills: his ability to join tiny blood vessels with amazing delicacy and accuracy. He apparently would often quietly finish operations medical students had started.

In 1967, Dr. Christiaan Barnard asked Hamilton Naki to assist him in the world's first heart transplant. This was illegal. It was illegal for a black South African to be in a whites-only hospital in an operating theater, but it was done anyway. He was apparently a critical part of that dramatic achievement.

As Barnard said in an interview in 1993: "He has skills I don't have. If Hamilton had had the opportunity to perform, he would probably have become a brilliant surgeon." In 2003, he finally received an honorary medical degree from the University of Cape Town.

Somebody who did become a doctor—although a doctor of history, not of medicine—was someone from the other part of the continent, Emmanuel Akyeampong from Ghana. He was born in Kumasi, the historic home of the Ashanti kingdom in Ghana. He eventually went overseas to the United States and earned a doctorate in African history. His brilliance, in fact, has catapulted him to a position as professor of history at none other than Harvard University.

You might be sitting here thinking that Akyeampong is another example of another of Africa's problems: brain drain. Not so fast. He has maintained his home in Ghana. In fact, his wife and seven-year-old daughter are there. He's got one of the world's longer commuting marriages.

He's become the voluntary U.S. president of something called the African Pub Broadcasting Foundation. The idea here is to offer a continent-wide service that would parallel the roles played by NPR and PBS—that is, independent sources of information, news, and so forth—across the continent. The first project that Akyeampong intends to tackle is the possibility of combining AIDS education messages with information and entertainment through such a network. As he puts it: "Africa is ready to step forward."

Let's return to East Africa, southeastern Africa, to the country of Mozambique and a young man not yet 30 years old, Erik Charas. He left Mozambique in the midst of its civil war and got a degree at the University of Cape Town in electrical engineering, but returned. Erik is an employee at a non-profit organization which has a disarmingly simple solution to a basic human health problem. There are three million children who die each year of vaccine-preventable diseases, but vaccines generally need to be kept cold. They need to be kept at 46 degrees Fahrenheit or less.

What Charas has done with his fellow employees at the organization he works for called VillageReach is to take propane-driven refrigerators to various clinics and villages in Mozambique's rural areas where, therefore, the vaccines can be stored safely—they will not go bad—and where children can begin to be inoculated against preventable diseases like diphtheria, hepatitis B, and so on.

My final example is a remarkable woman indeed. Her name is Wangari Maathai. She was born in 1940 in central Kenya. That means that she grew up during the Mau Mau emergency that we looked at in a previous lecture. She came to the United States around the time of Kenya's independence in 1963 and got bachelors and masters degrees in this country.

In 1971, from the University of Nairobi, Wangari Maathai became the first East African woman from any country in that region to obtain a Ph.D., in this case in Veterinary Anatomy. By the mid-1970s, she had begun working with women's movements in Kenya and looking at the needs of rural Kenyan women: the lack of firewood, the lack of clean drinking water. She related this to the spread of commercial plantations that she had seen since she was a youth, which destroyed the biodiversity and capacity of forests to conserve water.

She started the Green Belt Movement. The Green Belt Movement since that time has planted on the order of 30 million trees on farms, school yards, church yards, all through the East African country of Kenya.

Her efforts often led her to clashes with commercial interests, the owners of plantations, and with the former despotic regime of President Daniel arap Moi. She was denounced and persecuted, but persevered. She was part of the demand for democratic reform that eventually led to Moi's departure in 2002 and multiparty elections. She was elected to parliament with 98% of the vote in December 2002 and is now the assistant minister for environment, natural resources, and wildlife.

She has spoken out on the disproportionate burden of women with HIV/AIDS and against age-old traditions even of her own culture, such as female genital mutilation or female circumcision.

For her efforts, Wangari Maathai in 2004 was awarded the Nobel Peace Prize. I would like to close by reading a little bit from her acceptance speech. She noted that historically her people had been persuaded to believe that because they are poor, they lack not only capital but the knowledge to address their challenges. But in this simple process of planting trees, they discover they must be part of the solutions.

She addressed her fellow Africans at the end and said: "As we embrace this recognition, let's use it to intensify our commitment to our people, to reduce conflicts and poverty and thereby improve their quality of life. Let us embrace democratic governments, protect democratic rights, and protect our environment. I am confident we shall rise to the occasion. I have always believed that solutions to most of our problems must come from us."

Ladies and gentlemen, I thank you for the journey, and I close you with this. Thirty years ago, I went to Africa and got hooked on its reality and its history. I know that many of you have either taken or contemplated such a journey. If you're still contemplating it, I leave you with one simple word: *Go*.

Thank you and goodbye.

Timeline

c. 4–3 million B.C. .... Emergence of *Australopithecus*, possibly the first in the hominid line of evolution, culminating in modern humans in East/Southern Africa.

c. 1.5 million B.C. .... Emergence of *Homo erectus* in Africa, definitely a human ancestor.

c. 100,000 B.C. .... Emergence of *Homo sapiens*, "man the wise," in Africa.

c. 40,000 B.C. .... Emergence of *Homo sapiens sapiens*, fully modern humans, in Africa.

c. 5000 B.C. to A.D 1000
(depending on region) .... Closing of Late Stone Age, opening of Iron Age. Also—though not necessarily concomitant with Stone Age/Iron Age transition—closing of hunting/gathering age, onset of agriculture.

c. 3100–c. 350 B.C. .... Egypt of the pharaohs.

c. 2000–c. 100 B.C. .... Kingdom of Kush in the Nubian region of modern Sudan.

c. 750–650 B.C. .... Nubian (or 25th) dynasty rules Egypt.

c. 3rd–5th centuries A.D. .... Introduction of camel revolutionizes trans-Saharan trade.

Mid-4th century A.D. .... Aksumite (Ethiopian) monarch converts to Christianity.

7th century A.D. .... Rapid Arab/Muslim expansion across North Africa.

c. 7th–12th centuries A.D. .... West African savanna kingdom of Ghana. Islam begins to penetrate West African savanna.

Late 1st millennium A.D.............Emergence of trading states in Southern Africa, such as Mapungubwe.

c. 11th–15th centuries. ....Swahili city-states emerge on East African coast.

c. 12th–15th centuries ....Kingdom of Great Zimbabwe.

Early 13th century ....Ethiopian Christian monks begin building a series of churches carved out of solid mountain rock.

Early 13th century......................Sundiata founds West African savanna kingdom of Mali.

c. 1300.....................................Completion of stone buildings at Great Zimbabwe.

1324–1325 ....King (*Mansa*) Musa of Mali makes epic pilgrimage to Mecca.

Early 15th century......................Sonni Ali founds West African savanna kingdom of Songhai.

1492 ....Columbus's voyage marks the opening of the *Atlantic System* linking Africa, Europe, and the Americas.

1498 ....Portuguese circumnavigation of Africa, around the Cape of Good Hope and into the Indian Ocean.

1505 ....Portuguese sacking of the Swahili city-state of Kilwa.

16th–19th centuries.....................Atlantic slave trade brings millions of Africans to the New World.

1591 ....Moroccans—with firearms—invade and defeat Songhai.

1619 ....First Africans brought to Virginia.

1652 ....Dutch establish post at Cape Town.

1657	Dutch East India Company releases nine employees, who end up as the first white settlers in what becomes South Africa.
1658	Dutch import the first slaves *into* Cape Colony.
1779	First conflict between Europeans and Xhosa—part of the southern Bantu peoples—in "South Africa."
1795–1806	British take over Cape Colony.
1807	Britain outlaws international traffic in slaves; West Africa's era of "legitimate commerce" soon underway.
c. early–mid-19th century	Islamic reform movements—many involving *jihad*, or holy war— emerge in the West African savanna.
1818–1828	Shaka Zulu's decade in power, when he founds the modern Zulu kingdom.
1820	First British settlers come to Cape.
1836–1845	Afrikaner (or Boer) "Great Trek" out of Cape Colony and into the interior.
1867	Diamonds discovered at Kimberley.
1879	Zulu/British war; Zulu finally conquered.
c. 1880–1905	"Scramble for Africa." Almost all of Africa taken over by European empires; onset of Africa's colonial period.
1884–1845	Berlin Conference of European powers considers "ground rules" for the scramble for Africa.

1886	Gold discovered near Johannesburg.
1896	Ethiopian Emperor Menelik defeats Italian army at Adwa; Ethiopia avoids colonization.
1899–1902	South African, or Boer, War between British and Afrikaners; Afrikaners finally defeated.
1910	Union of South Africa formed.
1912	African National Congress founded in South Africa.
1913	South African Natives Land Act establishes separate white and black areas.
1914–1918	World War I; the only major non-European theater is in East Africa, where there are both British and German colonies.
1935	Italy succeeds (finally) in taking over Ethiopia.
1935–1945	Numerous labor strikes across the breadth of colonial Africa; examples of proto-nationalist urban unrest.
1938	Cocoa "hold-up" in Gold Coast, an example of rural protest.
1939–1945	World War II. Hundreds of thousands of Africans serve overseas on the Allied side; in the aftermath, Britain and France, particularly, adopt more aggressive "developmentalist" colonial policies.
1941	Allied forces expel Italians from Ethiopia.

1944	ANC Youth League formed in South Africa, with Mandela a founder.
1948	"Purified" Afrikaner National Party takes power in South Africa; officially imposes policy of apartheid.
c. late 1940s–1964	High tide of "African nationalism"; within a few years either side of 1960, most colonies become independent under African rule— *except* for the settler colonies concentrated in Southern Africa.
c. early 1950s	"Defiance campaign" in South Africa by ANC and other organizations.
c. early–mid-1950s....................	"Mau Mau" rebellion/emergency in Kenya.
1955	Congress of the People in South Africa; Freedom Charter adopted.
1957	Gold Coast wins independence from Britain, becomes the modern country of Ghana, the first sub-Saharan colony to gain independence.
1960	South African security forces kill 69 unarmed protestors at Sharpeville; African nationalist organizations in the country are banned; they, in turn, adopt armed struggle.
1960–1961	Independence of many countries, including the Belgian Congo; its first premier, Patrice Lumumba, is executed by rebels, and the country is engulfed in civil war.

c. early 1960s ....Armed liberation movements emerge in Portuguese colonies of Angola, Mozambique, and Guinea-Bissau.

1964 ....Nelson Mandela and others sentenced to life imprisonment for treason in South Africa.

1965 ....Military coup brings Joseph Mobutu to power in Congo-Kinshasa. He will rule for 32 years.

1965 ....White settler regime in Southern Rhodesia proclaims Unilateral Declaration of Independence from Britain.

1966 ....Coup in Ghana overthrows Kwame Nkrumah, the "Father of African Nationalism."

1967 ....Tanzanian President Julius Nyerere issues the Arusha Declaration, a blueprint for "African socialism."

1967–1970 ....Nigerian civil war; attempt by Biafra (southeastern Nigeria) to secede ultimately thwarted.

1972 ....Beginning of sustained guerilla war in Rhodesia (formerly Southern Rhodesia).

1974 ....Coup in Portugal leads to the end of Portuguese rule in Angola, Mozambique, and Guinea Bissau; in the first two, however, civil war supported by outside powers continues.

1974 ....Ethiopian Emperor Haile Selassie overthrown by radical military officers.

c. mid-1970s	"Oil shocks"—price rises for petroleum—signal decline in terms of trade and deepening crisis in many parts of Africa.
1976	Uprising in Soweto, a huge township outside Johannesburg, signals the arrival of a new, defiant generation in South Africa.
c. early 1980s	AIDS identified; the disease almost certainly had already been spreading in Africa and will eventually have a significant impact.
c. late 1980s and early 1990s	Wave of "democratization" sweeps over Africa, leading to the end of one-party and military regimes.
1990	Mandela released from South African prison; negotiations for a democratic constitution begin.
1994	Rwanda genocide leaves some 700,000 dead.
1994	In South Africa's first-ever democratic election, Nelson Mandela and the once-outlawed ANC sweep to victory.
2000	Government-sponsored "invasions" of white-owned land begin in Zimbabwe. Crisis continues today.
2004	Nobel Peace Prize awarded to Wangari Mathai, the Kenyan woman who has courageously campaigned for the environment and human rights.
2004	Thabo Mbeki reelected South African president in the third peaceful and open election since the fall of apartheid.

Glossary

African National Congress (ANC): The oldest of Africa's "nationalist" organizations, founded in 1912 in South Africa. Became the main opposition movement to segregation and apartheid and was banned in 1960. Went into exile and pursued armed struggle, then was legalized in 1990 and, with Nelson Mandela at its head, took power in South Africa's first free elections in 1994.

Afrikaans: The language, similar to Dutch but considered by linguists to be distinct, that developed after Dutch settlement in South Africa. Spoken mainly by Afrikaners and so-called "coloureds."

Afrikaner: A white South African of predominantly Dutch descent.

Age set (or age grade): A social unit determined not by kinship but by gender and the timing of one's birth. Thus, in a given community, males or females born within a few years of each other are part of the same male or female age set.

Aksum (or Axum): Ancient name for the state/kingdom later known as Ethiopia. Rulers converted to Coptic Christianity in the mid-4th century.

Apartheid: Afrikaans for "apartness," apartheid became the official policy in South Africa when the National Party took power in 1948. It carried the notions of social and political separation to extremes, even declaring certain black "homelands" to be "independent" of South Africa. But as with segregation, the dependence on black labor meant that genuine and complete separation was not an objective.

Asante (or Ashanti): A major state straddling the forest and savanna zones of central modern-day Ghana. The king or *Asantehene* remains a powerful figure in Ghana, though the kingdom is obviously subsumed into a larger unit.

Assimilation: The French colonial policy that allowed for the possibility of Africans becoming "black Frenchmen." Though often honored in the breach, it did result in Africans serving as parliamentary deputies in Paris, for instance.

Atlantic System: Refers to the complex linkages, arising during the era of mercantile capitalism, among the Americas, Europe, and

Africa. Important features include the European colonization of the New World, the rise of plantation sugar production, and the Atlantic slave trade, which brought millions of Africans to the Americas.

Australopithecus: Literally, "southern ape," a species appearing c. 3 to 4 million years ago in East and Southern Africa. Possibly the first in the hominid line of evolution, culminating in modern humans.

Bantu: Essentially a linguistic term, referring to a vast family of languages (actually a major subfamily of the even larger Niger-Congo category) spoken in central, eastern, and southern Africa. There are 400–500 distinct Bantu languages. The expansion of Bantu-speaking peoples is generally associated with the spread of ironworking and agriculture.

Bantustans: Originally the "reserves" (and comparable to American Indian reservations), Bantustans were the rural areas set aside for Africans, on a strictly "tribal" basis, in South Africa under segregation and apartheid. Eventually restyled as "homelands."

Biafra: The state-to-be that attempted to break away from Nigeria in the late 1960s but failed. See **Igbo**.

Boer: Dutch for "farmer," the term came to refer to predominantly Dutch-descended white settlers in South Africa. Eventually replaced for the most part by *Afrikaner*.

"Bushmen": See **Khoisan**.

Closed compound: The institution that emerged first at the diamond fields of Kimberley but became the ubiquitous form of housing for migrant African workers all through Southern Africa. The laborers were housed in hostels within fenced complexes, fed en masse, and tightly controlled.

Colonialism: A subcategory of imperialism, colonialism represents the open, formal rule of one country by another. It is based, ultimately, on conquest (or preemptive surrender). It was colonialism, not simply foreign domination or imperialism, that befell most of Africa at the start of the 20th century.

"Coloured": A South African term, often misunderstood, especially by Americans, who might assume it is an old term for "blacks"; in South Africa, these were, and to some extent still are, separate categories. The descendants of several populations contributed to make up the "coloureds": indigenous Khoisan of the Cape region; imported slaves from the Indian Ocean rim; and to a lesser extent, Afrikaners. Often equated with "mixed race" but most of the "mixing" took place long ago, especially in the 17th and 18th centuries.

Coptic: A branch of Christianity, distinct from Roman Catholic, Greek Orthodox, Protestant, and others. Centered in Egypt and Ethiopia, where a particular strain developed.

De Beers: Cecil Rhodes's diamond mining corporation, which achieved a virtual monopoly of the production and marketing of diamonds, first in South Africa and, later, worldwide.

Developmentalist states: After World War II, Britain and France undertook much more aggressive initiatives to develop their colonies socially, economically, and even politically, under the direction of the colonial state apparatus. Essentially, African nationalists inherited such states and certainly accepted the central state role in development, now, in theory, to benefit all "the people."

Ethnic group: A form of identity; an answer to the question: Who are "my people"? Properly used, the word *tribe* in Africa would refer to an ethnic group. But ethnicity is not set in stone or rigidly bounded; it changes over time and overlaps with other identities. No single criterion always works to determine ethnicity or distinguish between ethnic groups, but the "best bets" in Africa would be language difference and geographical place of ancestral origin. Still, it is a matter of self-perception—and of being perceived.

Female genital mutilation (FGM): Female "circumcision," actually covering a range of practices from excision of part or all of the clitoris to removal of most genital organs.

Freetown: The town in Sierra Leone that became the site where "recaptives"—would-be African slaves intercepted by British anti-slaving ships—were resettled. It became a site of cultural immersion in Western-style education and Christianity, and many of the recaptives returned to their original homes as African modernizers.

Frente de Libertação de Moçambique (FRELIMO): The main liberation movement that fought Portugal in Mozambique; led by Samora Machel.

Frente Nacional de Libertação de Angola (FNLA): An armed liberation group, based largely in the Kongo region of northern Angola, that emerged in the 1960s in Angola.

Fulbe (or Fulani or Peul): Largely pastoralist peoples spread over a wide east-to-west swath of the West African savanna and Sahel. In the 18th and 19th centuries, they were often behind Islamic reform movements and *jihads*.

Ghana: Earliest major state in the West African savanna, c. 7th to 12th centuries A.D. Linked to trade routes, involving especially gold and salt, across the Sahara Desert to the Mediterranean. The modern country of Ghana took its name from this kingdom, though in fact, today's Ghana lies well to the southeast of the old one.

Great Rift: The major tectonic plate disturbance running right down the eastern side, the "spine" of Africa. It is geologically associated with East Africa's Great Lakes region, with the Rift Valley of Kenya and Tanzania, and with major mountains, such as Kilimanjaro, Kenya, and the Mountains of the Moon.

Great Trek: The relatively sudden exodus of thousands of Afrikaners (Boers) out of the Cape Colony and into Southern Africa's interior, where they founded two new republics, the Transvaal and the Orange Free State. In many respects, it was a rebellion against British authority in the Cape Colony.

Great Zimbabwe: Usually refers to the greatest stone ruins in Africa south of the Nile region, located in the southwest of the modern country of Zimbabwe. These were ruins of a city, the capital of a kingdom with the same name.

Hausa: A very large ethnic group in the savanna belt of northern Nigeria. There were several major Hausa states; some of these were taken over by Fulbe Islamic reformers waging *jihad*, or holy war, in the early 19th century.

Homelands: See *Bantustans*.

Hominid: The line of evolution culminating in modern humans; possibly includes *Australopithecus* and definitely includes *Homo habilis* and *Homo erectus*.

Homo erectus: A species of the hominid line, a direct ancestor of modern humans, appearing some 1.5 million years ago in Africa and spreading throughout Africa and, indeed, into much of the Old World.

Hutu: An ethnic group that constitutes the substantial majority population of both Rwanda and Burundi. Dominated to some degree for centuries by Tutsi, the domination was much sharpened by Belgian colonial rule, which openly favored Tutsi over Hutu. Hutu extremists launched the 1994 genocide in Rwanda, which resulted in hundreds of thousands of Tutsi (and moderate Hutu) deaths.

Igbo: The principal people of southeastern Nigeria. The Igbo took to Western-style education with alacrity during the colonial period. Resentment of Igbo domination of business and clerical positions all over Nigeria boiled over into pogroms against them in 1966. In response came an attempt to secede from Nigeria and found the new nation of Biafra, which touched off the Nigerian civil war of 1967–1970, ending with defeat of the secession effort.

Illicit diamond buying (IDB): A term used for illegal removal and sales of diamonds.

Imperialism: An emotive term subject to many interpretations, to say the least. Very broadly, it is the power and/or influence exerted by more powerful countries over less powerful ones. This definition permits a delineation of various kinds of imperialism—economic or cultural, for instance, as well as colonialism, the direct takeover of the less powerful place—as subcategories.

Indirect Rule: The British policy in colonial Africa of ruling "through the chiefs," though in fact, all the empires made use of authority figures drawn from the subject population.

Industrial capitalism: Related, obviously, to the Industrial Revolution, beginning in Europe in the late 1700s. If the sailing ship was the symbol of mercantile capitalism, the factory and the railway serve as symbols of industrial capitalism.

Interahamwe: The Hutu "militias" that carried out much of the slaughter during the 1994 Rwanda genocide.

Khoikhoi: See **Khoisan**.

Khoisan: A term referring to the original indigenous peoples of Southern Africa who, for many thousands of years, lived primarily in small, mobile, hunting/gathering groups. Eventually, some of these took up the keeping of livestock and became known as Khoikhoi (or "Hottentots"). Those who still lived by hunting/gathering became known as San (or "Bushmen").

Kush: A major kingdom—possibly the oldest state in Africa save for ancient Egypt—that emerged in the Nubian region of the Upper Nile. In some respects quite Egyptian in style, in others—such as its still-undeciphered script—quite distinct. At one stage, it occupied Egypt as the so-called Nubian or 25th dynasty.

Mali: The grandest of the West African savanna empires, c. 13th–15th centuries A.D. The story of its founder, Sundiata, is the great epic of the region. A later king, or *mansa*, Kankan Musa, made a famous pilgrimage to Mecca in 1324–1325. This is the source of the name for the modern country of Mali.

Matrilineal: See **unilineal descent**.

Mau Mau: Insurgents in Kenya in the 1950s comprised mainly of the Kikuyu ethnic group who wished to rid Kenya of white settlers. They attacked not only white settlers but any Kikuyu they deemed to be collaborators.

Mercantile capitalism: Useful label for the era, c. 1500–1800, when European powers and firms sought profit and advantage from transporting commodities—including people defined as commodities, that is, slaves—from one part of the world to another for resale. The symbol of the age might well be the sailing ship. It has implications for history of imperialism and colonialism.

Meroe: City located at the confluence of the Nile and Atbara Rivers in Nubia, a later capital of the kingdom of Kush. Known as a center of iron production.

Mfecane: A Zulu word literally meaning "hammering" or "crushing," it came to refer to the period, c. 1800–1840, of turbulent transformation of the southern Bantu world. Larger and more powerful kingdoms and armies and reconfiguration of the ethnic map through movements of conquerors and refugees resulted from it.

Monoeconomy: An economy based on export of one (or, perhaps, two or three) key commodities. Colonial rule in Africa tended to promote this kind of economy, which continues after independence.

It generates considerable dependence on price and demand for the given product.

Movimento Popular de Libertação de Angola (MPLA): An armed liberation group, originally Marxist in orientation, that emerged in the 1960s in Angola.

Nubia: A region of the Upper Nile, corresponding with the southernmost parts of modern Egypt and northern parts of modern Sudan. Home to early and major African states and cities, such as Kush and Meroe.

One-party state: The alternative to competitive party systems that many African countries moved to in the 1960s–1980s. It was based, in theory, on consensus building, as in traditional villages, and made a reasonable stab at that in some cases but, in others, was simply a cloak for authoritarian rule and suppression of dissent.

Pass laws: Laws requiring that Africans carry booklets documenting their right to be and/or work in an urban area.

Patrilineal: See **unilineal descent**.

Periplus: A remarkable document from the first century A.D., written in Greek in the Roman Egyptian city of Alexandria. Essentially a guide to the Indian Ocean for Mediterranean and Red Sea trading ships. It shows quite clearly that "Azania"—the East African coast—was already connected commercially with areas to the north.

Polygamy: Refers to marriage involving more than one spouse, of either gender. *Polyandry*—one wife, more than one husband—is virtually unknown in Africa. But *polygyny*—one husband, more than one wife—has a long and wide history. It is declining but is still present, especially among older and/or rural populations.

Recaptives: See **Freetown**.

Rwandan Patriotic Front (RPF): Military organization composed of Tutsi in exile, mainly in Uganda.

Sahel: Like *Swahili*, comes from the Arabic word for "shore," though in this case, it refers to the southern "shore" of an ocean of sand—the Sahara Desert. A strip of semi-desert between the Sahara and the West African savanna.

San: See **Khoisan**.

Savanna: A major type of environment in western, eastern, and southern Africa. High in elevation, gently rolling to flattish, alternately wooded and grassed, with seasonal rainfall. It has probably been home to more people, and their history, than any other.

Scramble for Africa: The headlong pursuit of colonies in Africa by European powers, including Britain, France, and Germany, between about 1880 and 1905.

Segregation: Usually understood to mean racial separation in a context of white supremacy, and certainly there is much truth to this. Nonetheless, I suggest a somewhat more subtle understanding. Segregation as a system (and a word) appears at about the same time—the early 20th century—in South Africa and the U.S. South. Not simply a throwback or crude survival from a rural past, it can be seen as a modernization of white supremacy in societies going through the transformations to urban, industrial life; societies actually becoming more *integrated* economically—though unequally. Dependence on black labor—especially in South Africa—meant actual, total separation was not in the cards.

Settler/nonsettler colonies: A simple distinction, but one with profound implications. Settler colonies saw a substantial number of people from the colonial mother country settling and intending for that settlement to be permanent. Nonsettler colonies were taken over and ruled by outsiders but did not see such settlement. In settler colonies, Africans were far more likely to lose their land, and struggles for independence were far more likely to become armed struggles.

Shona: The largest ethnic group in the modern nation of Zimbabwe, though there are several important subgroups. Ancestors of the Shona were responsible for Great Zimbabwe and a number of successor kingdoms.

Songhai (or Songhay, Songrai): Another of the major states of the West African Sudan, or savanna, c. 15th–16th centuries A.D. Its downfall came when the Moroccan army invaded—with firearms—in 1591.

Structural Adjustment Programs (SAPs): Economic plans often adopted by African countries as the price of obtaining assistance from donor agencies, such as the World Bank or International Monetary Fund. SAPs typically involve fiscal belt-tightening (including cuts in social services), currency devaluation, and a lowering of tariff barriers.

Sudan: A modern African country in the continent's northeast, but the broader meaning is a reference to the whole savanna belt stretching east-to-west across West Africa.

Swahili: Language and culture of the East African coast. Although the word comes from the Arabic for "shore," Swahili is a Bantu language that became a *lingua franca* in the East African interior as well. Influence from Arabia is best seen in the predominance of Islam here.

Syncretism: The blending of cultural practices in realms ranging from medicine to music. Important especially in religion, where one can see indigenous African religious ideas or practices combined with Islam or Christianity.

Terms of trade: Essentially, the ratio in the value of what goes out (exports) versus what comes in (imports). If the ratio turns favorable, it can mean prosperity; the opposite turn can mean decline.

Timbuktu (or Timbuctu, Timbuctoo): The symbol of remoteness in the Western world, but a quite real—and, for a considerable time, quite important—city of the West African Sudan, on the great bend of the Niger River and at the edge of the desert. During the heydays of Mali and Songhai, it was a center of commerce but even more of Islamic learning, supporting scholars, libraries, and a thriving book trade.

Tonga: An ethnic group that straddles the border—which is the Zambezi River—between Zambia and Zimbabwe. (There are other, quite distinct Tonga peoples in Malawi and Mozambique.) A classic example of a "stateless" society in precolonial times. (Included here because the lecturer, having conducted considerable research in Tonga country, will draw illustrations from there.)

"Tribe": Possibly the most misunderstood term about Africa in the Western world, as it often conjures up images of primitivism and savagery. In Africa, on the other hand, it is usually used in a more neutral way, to connote ethnic identity. See **ethnic group**.

Tutsi: A minority that constituted something of a precolonial aristocracy in Rwanda and Burundi and that was greatly favored during Belgian colonial rule. Postcolonial resentment of Tutsi exploded into the 1994 genocide in Rwanda, in which hundreds of thousands of Tutsi were killed. Tutsi-led exiles were nonetheless able to invade and take over the country, driving Hutu *génocidaires* into exile in turn.

União Nacional para a Independência Total de Angola (UNITA): An armed liberation group that emerged in the 1960s in Angola and was eventually supported by South Africa and the United States.

Unilineal descent: A system of determining membership in kinship groups—clans or lineages—by inheriting/passing on membership between generations. One inherits his/her membership from one parent only, and only one parent can pass on the group membership to his/her children. Thus in *patrilineal* systems, one inherits clan or lineage membership from one's father, and only fathers can pass on membership to their children. In *matrilineal* systems, one inherits membership from one's mother, and only mothers can pass it on.

Witwatersrand: Literally "white water ridge," the 40-mile-long gold-bearing reef near modern Johannesburg, South Africa. Gold, even more than diamonds, was the foundation of the country's development. Today, the "Rand" is a huge industrial megalopolis.

Yoruba: The main language and ethnic group of southwestern Nigeria. Organized into a number of separate and powerful kingdoms.

Zulu: Originally a small chiefdom in the Nguni region of South Africa, between the Drakensberg Mountains and the Indian Ocean. Especially under the rule of Shaka Zulu from 1818 to 1828, it became a much larger, more powerful nation, indeed legendary for its military prowess. Today, it is the largest single ethnic group in South Africa.

Biographical Notes

Achebe, Chinua (1930–). Probably the best-known African writer to the outside world (though not one of Africa's Nobel Literature Prize winners, which include Wole Soyinka, Nadine Gordimer, and J. M. Coetzee). When his native Nigeria was still under British rule, Achebe published his first and still most famous work, *Things Fall Apart*, a moving and tragic portrayal of an African community facing ever-mounting intrusion by missionaries and colonialists. His subsequent novels offer indelible portraits of the African experience over the past century. His nonfiction includes 1984's *The Trouble with Nigeria*, a blistering critique of postcolonial African leadership.

Akyeampong, Emmanuel. Born in Ghana, Akyeampong completed his Ph.D. in African history at the University of Virginia in 1993 and is a professor of African history at Harvard. He has worked to develop a continent-wide African broadcasting corporation, similar to the American NPR and PBS.

Amin, Idi (or Idi Amin Dada) (c. 1925–2003). The Ugandan soldier who overthrew Milton Obote in 1972 in one of independent Africa's many coups. Large of girth and of personality, less so of intellect, Amin became almost a caricature of clownish African leadership, perfect fodder for those inclined to stereotype. There was little that was funny in his regime, however, as he led the nation to economic ruin and slaughtered opponents and intellectuals by the thousands. When he launched a ludicrous "invasion" of Tanzania in 1979, Tanzanian leader Julius Nyerere supported Ugandan exiles in a real counter-invasion that swept Amin from power and into exile.

Biko, Steve (1947–1977). The preeminent theorist and voice of South Africa's Black Consciousness movement, which above all, confronted the psychological burdens of racism and sought to erase feelings of inferiority or dependency among black South Africans. The young medical student was an inspiration to his generation. He was arrested many times, and following the last, he was beaten to death by security forces, resulting in his legendary martyrdom.

Botha, P. W. (1916–). The last of the Afrikaner old guard to hold power in South Africa, Botha's time as head of the country's government (1978–1989) was marked by halting, ultimately hollow reforms and fierce repression of the opposition. His departure following a stroke in 1989 cleared the way for F. W. de Klerk to free Mandela and otherwise liberalize politics.

Charas, Erik. An engineer from Mozambique who received his BS in electromechanical engineering from the University of Cape Town in 2000, Charas developed a propane-driven refrigerator to keep vaccines cool in rural areas where no electricity is available.

de Klerk, F. W. (1937–) A quiet insider for most of his career in South Africa's ruling party, de Klerk nonetheless became the focal point of a new Afrikaner generation that realized that apartheid could not continue. He replaced P. W. Botha as president in 1989 and moved quickly to legalize all political movements. Most dramatically, he released Mandela from jail. The pace of change outran his attempts to control it, but he became a deputy president under Mandela for a time after the election of 1994. He was awarded the Nobel Peace Prize jointly with Mandela.

Haile Selassie (or Ras Tafari) (1892–1975). "King of kings, Lion of Judah"—and the last emperor of Ethiopia. As regent (from 1916) and emperor (from 1930), Haile Selassie was an inspiration to many Africans on the continent and in diaspora, given that he was the ruler of virtually the only part of Africa to successfully resist colonial conquest. When Mussolini and the Italians invaded in 1935, his eloquent appeal to the League of Nations was ignored. Restored to the throne by Allied forces in 1941, he ruled—with an iron hand—until revolutionary Marxist army officers overthrew him in 1974, ending the 1600-year Ethiopian monarchy.

Houphouët-Boigny, Félix (1905–1993). Although usually included with Africa's classic "nationalist generation," Houphouët was a conservative figure in many ways, who barely called for independence before France bestowed it on his home country of Côte d'Ivoire (Ivory Coast). As the nation's first president for over three decades, he eschewed radicalism and pursued development in quite capitalist fashion—with considerable success, for a time. The Côte d'Ivoire's stability and growth was often cited as a "miracle," especially in comparison with such neighbors as Nigeria and Ghana. Alas, the decline set in before Houphouët's death in 1993, and the country descended into civil war, now in uneasy abeyance.

Ja Ja (1821–1891). The former slave who became an entrepreneur and modernizer during the so-called "legitimate commerce" era in the 19th century. In the Niger River Delta, Ja Ja became a power in the production and marketing of palm oil, needed as a pre-petroleum lubricant and soap ingredient in the West. In the 1880s, when he attempted to circumvent Europeans by getting his own ships, the British consul essentially kidnapped him and sent him into exile. The move was a precursor of approaching colonial conquest.

Kaunda, Kenneth (1924–). A deeply religious man, Kaunda was born the son of a Christian pastor who had moved from Nyasaland (now Malawi) into northeastern Zambia. Though not as highly educated as other leading nationalists of his generation, he was a schoolteacher who pressed the movement in Northern Rhodesia (now Zambia) to greater militancy. He became the country's first president at independence in 1964 and articulated his philosophy of "Humanism," meant to avoid extremes of left and right. He was never a dictator but became increasingly authoritarian as Zambia's copper-based economy went into a tailspin from the mid-1970s. Under pressure, he agreed to multiparty elections in 1991, which he lost badly, and to his credit, he left power graciously. His star has actually risen again as his successors have disappointed.

Kenyatta, Jomo (c. 1891–1978). Another towering figure of 20th-century African politics, Kenyatta began as an activist for his own Kikuyu people of central Kenya, who were hardest hit by settler expropriations of land in this British colony. He spent a number of years in Britain, earning a doctorate in anthropology at the London School of Economics and publishing his dissertation, *Facing Mount Kenya*, a comprehensive description—and defense—of Kikuyu ways. Kenyatta denied involvement in the Mau Mau uprising of the 1950s but was tried and imprisoned by the British, who nonetheless eventually concluded, as they had with Nkrumah, that they must deal with him. He went almost straight from jail to government leader and became Kenya's first president at independence in 1963. He was a conservative and autocratic leader in power, moving, as others had, to a one-party state. He died still in office in 1978.

Leopold II (1835–1909). The eccentric (to say the least) king of Belgium at the turn of the last century. With a combination of charm and subterfuge, he attracted many to his private, allegedly humanitarian project in Central Africa, the so-called Congo Free

State. His real object was rubber, which grew wild there and was needed in the burgeoning automobile and electrical industries. He never set foot in Africa himself, but his army of mercenaries enforced a brutal regime of forced rubber collection. Even in an age of imperialism, the excesses of Leopold's regime provoked an international outcry; some would call it the first human-rights campaign. Under pressure, he turned the Congo over to the Belgian government in 1908.

Livingstone, David (1813–1873). A remarkable and enigmatic person in several respects, Livingstone was the son of a Scottish factory worker who became a medical doctor. He eventually went to Southern Africa in the mid-1800s and began a series of quite incredible journeys, on foot, across the continent. He was a gifted naturalist and a shrewd observer of humanity and wrote books that aroused considerable interest in Africa in Victorian Britain. Livingstone was an advocate of "Christianity and Commerce"—but not *necessarily* colonial conquest for Africa.

Lobengula (c. 1836–1894). The second and last king of the Ndebele, a nation that started as a breakaway from the Zulu under Lobengula's father, Mzilikazi, and as a "kingdom on the march," eventually settled in the southwest of modern Zimbabwe. Lobengula's eventual misfortune was that his kingdom lay squarely in the path of Rhodes's ambitions to colonize the Rhodesias for Britain. He was deceived by Rhodes's agents into signing several "concessions," which he later repudiated. But a clash was inevitable, and it came in 1893 in a war with Rhodes's forces, which predictably ended with Ndebele defeat and with Lobengula's death under still-uncertain circumstances.

Lumumba, Patrice (1925–1961). A former mail clerk, Lumumba rose overnight to political prominence as Belgium moved, with some panic, to decolonize the Congo in the late 1950s. He became prime minister at the head of a shaky coalition as the Belgians left in 1960. His radicalism, which has made him a heroic martyr to some Africans of subsequent generations, earned him the wrath of the West at the height of the Cold War. Faced with several secession movements and foreign interventions, Lumumba was seized by rebels from the southern province of Katanga and murdered in early 1961.

Maathai, Wangari (1940–). The first East African woman to earn a doctorate in biology. When she returned to her home of Kenya after study in America in the late 1960s, she began organizing women through her Green Belt Movement to be stewards of the natural environment, specifically by conserving and planting trees. Her outspokenness in confronting the powerful earned her persecution by the former government of Daniel arap Moi. After Moi's departure, she was elected to Parliament in 2003 by an overwhelming majority and was appointed the Assistant Secretary for Environment, Wildlife, and Natural Resources in the new government of Mwai Kibaki. In 2004, she was honored with the Nobel Peace Prize.

Machel, Samora (1933–1986), and **Graca Machel** (1946–). Samora Machel was the brilliant and charismatic leader of FRELIMO, the main liberation movement that fought Portugal in Mozambique. He became the country's president after the Portuguese left in 1975 and instituted radical experiments in collective farming and the like, which met little success. He supported liberation movements in Zimbabwe and South Africa and, in return, became embattled with a rebel movement in Mozambique supported by South Africa. He was adopting much more pragmatic policies when killed in a still inadequately explained air crash in 1986. His wife, Graca Machel, was an impressive force in her own right in education and women's empowerment. Some years after Samora's death, she was remarried...to Nelson Mandela.

Mandela, Nelson (1918–). The symbol *par excellence* of the struggle against white minority domination—apartheid—in 20th-century South Africa. Trained as a lawyer, Mandela joined the African National Congress (ANC) and helped found the ANC Youth League in the 1940s. In the 1950s, he was instrumental in countless protest campaigns against the mounting apartheid impositions. He was tried for treason but acquitted in 1961, by which time the ANC was banned, and Mandela had concluded that armed struggle was unavoidable. He was convicted of treason and sentenced to life imprisonment in 1964. Released in 1990, he led ANC negotiations culminating in the country's first democratic elections in 1994, through which he became South Africa's first African president. He retired in 1999 after one term but remains active in the fight against HIV/AIDS and as a peacemaker in neighboring countries.

Mansa **Musa** (?–1337). With Sundiata, the most famous of the *mansas*, or kings, of old Mali. A more devout Muslim than some of his predecessors, his famous pilgrimage to Mecca in 1324–1325 put Mali on the map of the Muslim and medieval European worlds. He encouraged Muslim scholarship and literacy using the Arabic script in such places as Timbuktu.

Mbeki, Thabo (1942–).The son of Govan Mbeki, Mandela's fellow activist and prisoner, Thabo Mbeki practically grew up in the South African freedom movement, though largely in exile. By the 1980s, he was the ANC's shadow foreign minister. An eloquent intellectual, he lacks Mandela's popular touch but was clearly slated for a prominent position when South Africa's regime change became inevitable in the 1990s. He was elected deputy president under Mandela in 1994 and succeeded him as president in 1999; he won reelection easily in 2004. Although his prolonged denial of a connection between HIV and AIDS brought him sharp domestic and international criticism, South Africa has continued to enjoy growth and stability under his leadership.

Mobutu Sese Seko (1930–1997). Originally known as Joseph Mobutu, he rose through the ranks of the military in the Belgian Congo and emerged as the central military authority in the chaotic early days of the Congo's independence. In 1965, he carried off a bloodless coup and took power over the vast country. He held it for no less than 32 years, partly due to his own cleverness in using carrot and stick, partly due to considerable aid from the West, which saw him as a bulwark against communism and the only hope for stability. By many accounts, Mobutu became one of the richest men in the world, systematically draining his potentially wealthy country's resources and siphoning aid for his own pocket. He was finally overthrown in 1997 by insurrections emanating from the Great Lakes region in and around the country's east.

Moshoeshoe (1787–1870). Born nearly at the same time as Shaka but among the Sotho peoples of the high interior of what is now South Africa. Like Shaka, he was a soldier and statebuilder, though Moshoeshoe had a very different personality and much preferred diplomacy to warfare in pursuing his goals. He united a number of Sotho communities under his overall rule, first in response to the threat of insecurity posed by the "Mfecane." Moshoeshoe lived twice as long as Shaka, which meant that he had to face an entirely different threat in the second half of his life—the advance of the European frontier. He responded to it both diplomatically and militarily and with considerable success; in the end, he chose, reluctantly, to accept becoming a British "protectorate." This move prevented his kingdom of Lesotho being incorporated into modern South Africa.

Mugabe, Robert (1924–). Born on a Catholic mission station in northern Zimbabwe (when it was Southern Rhodesia), Mugabe became active in nationalist politics of his home country after returning from a stint teaching school in Nkrumah's Ghana. Jailed for a decade in 1965 by the white-settler-dominated regime of Ian Smith, upon his release, he quickly rose to the head of the Zimbabwe African National Union, the political/guerilla movement based next door in Mozambique. When the intensifying liberation war forced negotiations and an election in 1980, he became Zimbabwe's first president and remains in power today. When his position seemed threatened in 2000, he initiated seizures of white-owned land and a political crackdown; today, the country is in political and economic crisis.

Muhammad Ture (?–1528). The best-known king of the Songhai Empire in the West African savanna, ruling from 1493 to 1528; founder of the *Askiya* dynasty. He is credited with centralizing administration, reviving the trade in gold and salt (as well as cotton, kola, and horses), and, like *Mansa* Musa of Mali before him, making the *hajj*, the pilgrimage to Mecca.

Naki, Hamilton (1926–2005). South African who, despite a lack of formal education, worked as an assistant to South African surgeons and became known for his ability to join tiny blood vessels with amazing delicacy and accuracy. Dr. Christiaan Barnard, with whom he worked, greatly admired Naki's skills. In 2003, Naki finally received an honorary medical degree from the University of Cape Town.

Nkrumah, Kwame (1909–1972). The "Father of African Nationalism." Nkrumah, born in the British West African colony of the Gold Coast, studied at universities in America before returning home after World War II. He quickly attracted a political following, especially among younger Ghanaians impatient with Britain's pace of reform. He also articulated a genuinely pan-African vision of

Africa's regeneration. With his motto of "seek ye first the political kingdom," he continually stepped up demands on the British, who eventually concluded that they must deal with him. He led the Gold Coast to independence—with the changed name of Ghana—in 1957, the first sub-Saharan colony to gain it. In power, Nkrumah pursued grand projects of development at home and abroad and became increasingly autocratic, banning opposition and jailing opponents. The military overthrew him in 1966, and he died in bitter exile in Guinea.

Nyerere, Julius (1922–1999). A genuine intellectual with a popular touch, Nyerere became the central figure in Tanganyika's nationalist movement after studying at the University of Edinburgh (and translating Shakespeare into Swahili). He became the first president of the country (whose name changed to Tanzania when it merged with Zanzibar in 1964), a post he held until 1985. *Mwalimu* ("the teacher") Nyerere's Arusha Declaration of 1967 was an eloquent platform of African socialism and self-reliance, but he enjoyed little success in fostering economic development. His version of the one-party state was one of the few that allowed for debate and competition, but he eventually abandoned the model anyway and set a powerful example by living modestly and stepping down from power voluntarily.

Rhodes, Cecil John (1853–1902). Born in England, Rhodes went out to what would later become South Africa as a young man and soon made his way to the diamond fields of Kimberley. Through his company, De Beers, Rhodes oversaw the conversion at Kimberley from a "rush" to a modern, deep-level mining industry, employing costly technology and many thousands of miners. A man of great political as well as financial ambitions, he became prime minister of the Cape in 1890 and served until 1896. Afterward, with a new firm, the British South Africa Company, backed by a royal charter, he financed and orchestrated the conquest of two territories named for him, Northern and Southern Rhodesia, and added them to the British Empire. Buried in the Matobo Hills of Zimbabwe (formerly Southern Rhodesia), he endowed Rhodes Scholarships to Oxford in his will.

Samori Ture (c. 1830–1900). A member of the *juula* (Muslim merchant class) in the western Sudan (the savanna belt of West Africa), but better known for his extraordinary military skills, Samori built a new empire around himself in the 1870s. As the French expanded eastward from their base in Senegal, Samori actually re-created his empire several hundred miles to the east and left the French a scorched earth to occupy. Eventually, the French caught up to Samori and met a fierce resistance that more than earned their respect. But he was captured in 1898 and exiled to Gabon, where he died two years later. He is considered a national hero in no less than three modern West African countries.

Savimbi, Jonas (1934–2002). A charismatic figure, Savimbi led an Angolan political and military movement, UNITA, for more than 30 years. Based among the ethnic groups of central Angola, UNITA was one of three movements competing for power when the Portuguese departed in 1975. When the rival MPLA, with Cuban and Russian support, prevailed in the capital, Savimbi, backed by South Africa and the United States, launched a seemingly endless civil war. It came to an uneasy close only with Savimbi's death in an MPLA raid early in the new millennium.

Senghor, Léopold (1906–2001). A Senegalese intellectual and gifted poet, Senghor first attracted attention in the 1930s with his poems and essays expounding *negritude* and ideology promoting blackness, *africanité*, as positive, marked by warmth, emotion, intuition. A Catholic, he proved an adroit builder of political alliances in predominantly Muslim Senegal. Becoming a deputy in the French assembly after World War II, he emerged as the obvious choice to lead the country to independence and served as its premier from independence in 1960 to his voluntary retirement in 1980.

Shaka Zulu (1787–1828). His father was monarch of the small Zulu chiefdom in the region between the Drakensberg Mountains and Indian Ocean, in the eastern part of today's South Africa, but he rejected the child Shaka, who was raised by his mother, Nandi. He first distinguished himself as a soldier and commander under Dingiswayo, who had begun the processes of political consolidation and military intensification associated with the "Mfecane." With Dingiswayo's support, he seized the Zulu throne after his estranged father's death in 1816 and, upon Dingiswayo's own death in 1818, took his place as head of a larger confederation. Shaka aggressively expanded and unified this political grouping, converting the meaning of *Zulu* from a small chiefdom to a major kingdom. His exceptional military and statebuilding skills brought him great success for a time, but his was a complex personality. After the death of his mother, his judgment faltered, and he was assassinated by plotters, including his half-brothers and personal aides, on September 24, 1828.

Smith, Ian (1919–). The hard-line white-settler leader who came to power in Southern Rhodesia in 1962, just as the Central African Federation, which for a decade had combined Southern and Northern Rhodesia and Nyasaland, was collapsing. Determined to resist the British government's plans to hand over power to the African majorities in her colonies, Smith's government made its own Unilateral Declaration of Independence from Britain in 1965. He banned African nationalist parties and imprisoned their leaders, including Robert Mugabe. By the early 1970s, Smith's government faced a serious guerilla war, which raged until he reluctantly accepted elections in 1980, bringing Mugabe to power. Unrepentant, he remains a vocal and tireless critic of the black government.

Smuts, Jan (1870–1950). A Cambridge-educated intellectual, Smuts, a South African Afrikaner, was also an able military man, as he showed in fighting Britain in the South African or Boer War of 1899–1902 and in World War I, when he fought *for* Britain in East Africa. He became prime minister of South Africa in 1919, lost the office in elections of 1924, returned to share power as deputy prime minister in 1933, and rose to prime minister again in 1939, when South Africa, by the thinnest of margins, entered the war on the Allied side. Though Smuts had been one of the builders of segregation, he was viewed as too soft and moderate by "purified" Afrikaner nationalists, who defeated him in 1948—and began the imposition of apartheid.

Sundiata (or Sundjata, Sunjata, Son-jara) (c. 1210–c. 1260). The founder king of the major West African savanna empire of Mali in the 13th century. The story of Sundiata is the basis of the most famous epic from Africa, transmitted in its considerable length orally for several centuries and eventually recorded, translated, and published in many versions. Sundiata illustrated personally the symbiotic nature of religious conversion—described as a devout Muslim in some contexts, still clearly concerned with older, land-based spirits in others.

Tippu Tip (or Hamed bin Muhammed) (c. 1830–1905). An Arab/Swahili trader and warlord who established a trading/raiding state in what is now western Tanzania and southeastern Congo in the later 19th century. He carried out considerable depredations in search of ivory and slaves, which were moved east to the coast and Zanzibar. He eventually became a sort of regional governor for a time under Leopold's Congo Free State before retiring to Zanzibar in 1891.

Verwoerd, Hendrik (1901–1966). The most elaborate theorist of grand apartheid in South Africa. Before and after becoming prime minister in 1958, Verwoerd envisioned a future South Africa in which black Africans would have no role other than certain forms of labor; their social and political "futures" would be strictly away in the barren reserves (later *Bantustans* or "homelands"). He had absolutely no patience with opposition, banning the ANC and other parties in 1960. His government tried Mandela and sent him to prison for life. He was dramatically assassinated in parliament in 1966 by a deranged white man.

Bibliography

Essential Reading:

Achebe, Chinua. *Things Fall Apart.* New York: Anchor Books, 1994. First published in 1958 and undoubtedly the best-known book by an African writer in the wider world. Considered by some "God's gift to African studies," the novel gets "inside" an African culture—the Igbo of Nigeria—and shows the destructive impact of the onset of colonial and missionary activity.

Cooper, Frederick. *Africa since 1940: The Past of the Present.* Cambridge: Cambridge University Press, 2002. An exceptional book, distilling a great deal of learning into a single, rather slim volume. To my mind, the best single introduction to contemporary Africa, incredibly lucid and persuasive.

French, Howard. *A Continent for the Taking: The Tragedy and Hope of Africa.* New York: Vintage Books, 2005. Perhaps the best of several recent fine books on contemporary Africa (such as that by Bill Berkeley). French was the *New York Times* correspondent in Africa for many years. Very informative and never over the top but written with a passionate intensity born of both affection and disgust.

Gilbert, Erik, and Jonathan T. Reynolds. *Africa in World History: From Prehistory to the Present.* Upper Saddle River, NJ: Pearson Prentice Hall, 2004. The most recent basic textbook on African history and quite impressive indeed. The colloquial style, obviously designed to appeal to undergraduates, may not be to everyone's taste, but the summations of evidence, debates, and arguments are up to date and quite stimulating.

Mandela, Nelson. *Long Walk to Freedom: The Autobiography of Nelson Mandela.* Boston: Little, Brown & Co., 1994. Parts of Mandela's memoir were originally written and hidden while he was in prison; others are drawn from interviews and essentially ghostwritten. But it is all riveting, one of the great stories of the 20th century, from his boyhood to his inauguration as South Africa's first democratically elected president

Reader, John. *Africa: A Biography of the Continent.* New York: Vintage Books, 1999. A sweeping look at the entire history of Africa as a landmass and a stage for human history. The first parts are best, where Reader presents rather complex information and theory from geology and natural history in a quite understandable way.

Shillington, Kevin. *History of Africa*. Rev. ed. New York: St. Martin's Press, 1995. A serviceable textbook that packs a great deal of information into a reasonable space, with many useful illustrations and maps.

Thompson, Leonard. *A History of South Africa*. 3rd ed. New Haven, CT: Yale University Press, 2001. The best one-volume history of South Africa—thorough, informative, and gracefully written by the late, distinguished authority.

Supplementary Reading:

Achebe, Chinua. *Anthills of the Savannah*. Garden City, NY: Anchor Press/Doubleday, 1987. The last great novel by Africa's most famous writer, a piercing—and wickedly funny—portrait of political corruption and the heroic efforts of a few to resist it. Bears more than a passing resemblance to the author's native Nigeria.

———. *The Trouble with Nigeria*. Exeter, NH: Heinemann Educational Books, 1984. A razor-sharp nonfiction indictment of his country's leadership, from the pen of the great novelist and poet.

Anderson, David. *Histories of the Hanged: The Dirty War in Kenya and the End of Empire*. New York: W.W. Norton & Co., 2005. "Mau Mau," the armed uprising against the British in 1950s Kenya, continues to fascinate fine historians, and Anderson's new book, based on much previously unused archival data, is a premier example. The sheer ferocity of Britain's counterattack on a movement that killed a total of 32 white settlers may astonish.

Armah, Ayi Kwei. *The Beautyful Ones Are Not Yet Born*. Oxford: Heinemann, 1988. First published in 1968 and undoubtedly based on the fall of Kwame Nkrumah, it remains a classic statement, in novel form, of the disappointments of independence.

Asante, Molefe Kete. *Afrocentricity*. Trenton, NJ: Africa World Press, 1988. A summary of one version of Afrocentric approaches to Africa and the African diaspora.

Ayittey, George. *Africa Betrayed*. New York: St. Martin's, 1992. An African commentator places the blame for the continent's plight squarely on its African leadership.

Berkeley, Bill. *The Graves Are Not Yet Full: Race, Tribe and Power in the Heart of Africa*. New York: Basic Books, 2001. An excellent and heartfelt examination of the actual nature of several of Africa's crises, from a brilliant reporter.

Bernal, Martin. *Black Athena: The Afroasiatic Roots of Classical Civilization.* Two volumes. New Brunswick, NJ: Rutgers University Press, 1987–1991. A study that, to say the least, proved controversial. Bernal argues that classical Greece in particular owed most everything to Egypt and the Near East.

Boahen, Adu. *African Perspectives on Colonialism.* Baltimore: Johns Hopkins University Press, 1987. Considered reflections from the great Ghanaian historian (and briefly president).

———— (with J. F. Ade Ajayi and Michael Tidy). *Topics in West African History.* 2nd ed. Barlow, Essex, UK: Longman, 1986. Slim but informative volume introducing basic material on West African history.

Bratton, Michael, and Nicolas van de Walle. *Democratic Experiments in Africa: Regime Transitions in Comparative Perspective.* Cambridge: Cambridge University Press, 1997. Probably the most authoritative look at the wave of democratization that swept over Africa in the late 1980s and early 1990s. Clear and comprehensive.

Bundy, Colin. *The Rise and Fall of the South African Peasantry.* Berkeley: University of California Press, 1979. Based on his truly seminal article of 1972, Bundy's book shows that innovation and market response among South African small farmers was not enough to prevent their marginalization in the name of white supremacy.

Caputo, Robert. *Kenya Journal.* Washington, D.C.: Elliott & Clark, 1992. A remarkable photographic journey through Kenya.

Cell, John. *The Highest Stage of White Supremacy: The Origins of Segregation in South Africa and the American South.* Cambridge: Cambridge University Press, 1982. A stimulating comparative history of segregation that argues that it was a modernization of white supremacy in the context of industrialization and urbanization—not simply a leftover from slavery or the frontier.

Coulson, David. *Namib.* London, UK: Sidgwick & Jackson, 1991. Astonishing photographs of an astonishing place, the stark desert along the coast of southwest Africa.

————. *The Roof of the World.* New York: Holt, Rinehart, & Winston, 1983. Another beautiful but also informative book of photographs and commentary on the mountain ranges of Southern Africa.

Crush, Jonathan, Alan Jeeves, and David Yudelman. *South Africa's Labor Empire: A History of Black Migrancy to the Gold Mines.* Boulder, CO: Westview Press, 1991. By far the best short introduction to the overwhelming importance of labor migration in Southern Africa.

Curtin, Philip. *The Atlantic Slave Trade: A Census.* Madison: University of Wisconsin Press, 1969. Many of Curtin's works over a long and distinguished career deserve attention. This was, as some might say, *the* pioneering effort to be truly serious in counting the volume of the Atlantic slave trade. Roundly criticized, it has proven to be not terribly far off the mark.

Davidson, Basil, ed. *African Civilization Revisited: From Antiquity to Modern Times.* Trenton, NJ: Africa World Press, 1991. A most valuable collection of primary documents on Africa from antiquity to, essentially, the 19th century.

————. *The African Slave Trade.* Rev. and expanded ed. Boston: Little, Brown, & Co., 1980. A revision of his 1961 classic *Black Mother* and a digestible one-volume history of the Atlantic slave trade, from the most revered and respected popularizer of African history.

Decalo, Samuel. *Coups and Army Rule in Africa: Motivations and Constraints.* 2nd ed. New Haven, CT: Yale University Press, 1990. A fine study of military coups. Argues that they cannot be explained by theories of redressing abuses or corruption but, basically, by the less flattering quest for power.

De Kiewiet, C. W. *A History of South Africa, Social and Economic.* Oxford: Clarendon Press, 1941. Probably the oldest academic work in this bibliography. Despite some outdated terminology ("natives," for example), it remains a powerful history and was groundbreaking in its departure from white settler narratives.

Des Forges, Alison. *"Leave None to Tell the Story": Genocide in Rwanda.* New York: Human Rights Watch, 1999. Probably the closest thing to a definitive account of the 1994 Rwanda genocide. Comprehensive and informative.

Diop, Cheikh Anta. *The African Origin of Civilization: Myth or Reality.* New York: L. Hill, 1974. This is *the* classic argument that Egypt should be seen as black African in origin and the fount of other African, as well as European, civilizations.

Elphick, Richard, and Hermann Giliomee, eds. *The Shaping of South African Society, 1652–1840.* First Wesleyan Edition (revision of 1979 original edition). Middletown, CT: Wesleyan University Press, 1989. The most comprehensive volume on the old Cape Colony under, first, Dutch, then, British rule. Essays on every aspect of colonial society from acknowledged authorities.

Equiano, Olaudah. *The Interesting Narrative of the Life of Olaudah Equiano, Written by Himself.* Edited with an introduction by Robert J. Allison. Boston: Bedford Books of St. Martin's Press, 1995 (first published in the United States in 1791). The ultimate ex-slave memoir, as fascinating today as when first published. Kidnapped in what is now Nigeria, Equiano survived the middle passage to the West Indies, was eventually emancipated, and became an eloquent voice for abolition.

Fredrickson, George. *Black Liberation: A Comparative History of Black Ideologies in the United States and South Africa.* Oxford: Oxford University Press, 1996. The sequel to his *White Supremacy* and, obviously, the other side of the coin. Equally impressive.

———. *White Supremacy: A Comparative Study in American and South African History.* Oxford: Oxford University Press, 1981. A pioneering study in comparative history, illuminating numerous segments in the histories of both countries.

Gann, L. H., and Peter Duignan, eds. *Colonialism in Africa. 1870–1960.* London: Cambridge University Press, 1969–1975. Five-volume collection on all aspects of the colonial period, edited by two conservative scholars. Includes many fine essays.

Giliomee, Hermann. *The Afrikaners: Biography of a People.* Charlottesville: University of Virginia Press, 2003. This will be the definitive history of the Afrikaners, from the fine South African historian.

Gourevitch, Philip. *We Wish to Inform You that Tomorrow We Will Be Killed with Our Families: Stories from Rwanda.* New York: Farrar, Straus, and Giroux, 1998. The best known of the journalistic treatments of the 1994 Rwanda genocide and certainly a book to hold one's attention, even if in horror.

Hamilton, Carolyn, ed. *The Mfecane Aftermath: Reconstructive Debates in Southern African History.* Johannesburg and Durban, South Africa: Witwatersrand University Press and University of Natal Press, 1995. A superb collection of essays that treat all aspects of the so-called "Mfecane" disruptions of the 19th century. Several respond to the radical revisionism of Julian Cobbing, who argued that it was largely the European-run slave trade rather than African statebuilding that was responsible.

————. *Terrific Majesty: The Powers of Shaka Zulu and the Limits of Historical Invention.* Cambridge, MA: Harvard University Press, 1998. Hamilton, one of the foremost authorities on Zulu history, shows that images and opinions of Shaka, founder of the Zulu kingdom, have always been varied and contradictory and defy neat categorization into white versus black or colonialist versus indigenous.

Hargreaves, John. *Decolonization in Africa.* 2nd ed. New York: Longman, 1996. An excellent survey of the whole process of ending colonial rule in Africa.

Hochschild, Adam. *King Leopold's Ghost: A Story of Greed, Terror, and Heroism in Colonial Africa.* Boston and New York: Mariner/Houghton Mifflin, 1999. Written in an exceptionally engaging style, a story at once horrifying—in its accounts of the greed and brutality behind the Belgian king's founding of the modern Congo—and inspiring—in its portrayals of the many who courageously exposed the abuses.

Hunter, Susan. *Black Death: AIDS in Africa.* New York: Palgrave Macmillan, 2003. For the lay reader, this is the best survey of the impact of the pandemic on Africa.

Iliffe, John. *Africans: The History of a Continent.* Cambridge: Cambridge University Press. 1995. In the view of some, the best one-volume history of the continent, written by a distinguished senior historian. Comparable in sweep to John Reader's book, though more academic in style.

Jeal, Tim. *Livingstone.* London, UK: Heinemann, 1973. Still probably the best biography of the remarkable and enigmatic David Livingstone.

Kapuściński, Ryszard. *The Emperor: Downfall of an Autocrat.* New York: Harcourt Brace Jovanovich, 1983. An astounding portrait of an absolute ruler and his fall: Haile Selassie of Ethiopia.

————. *The Shadow of the Sun.* New York: Vintage Books, 2002. Absolutely fascinating pieces of reportage from various parts of the

African continent, from the gifted, courageous, and legendary Polish journalist.

Kaunda, Kenneth. *Zambia Shall Be Free: An Autobiography.* London, UK: Heinemann, 1962. A book that is still inspirational and captures the hopes of the nationalist era, from the man who became Zambia's president—for 27 years.

Kenyatta, Jomo. *Facing Mount Kenya.* New York: Vintage Books, 1965. The doctoral dissertation of the man who became the first president of independent Kenya. First published in 1938, *Facing Mount Kenya* remains fascinating and invaluable because it can be read on many levels: (1) as a thorough and informative ethnography, (2) as a proto-nationalist polemic, and (3) as a rationalization of patriarchy.

Laye, Camara. *The Guardian of the Word.* Translated from the French by James Kirkup. New York: Aventura, 1984. Perhaps the most accessible version of West Africa's greatest epic, the story of Sundiata, founder king of Mali. Written in novel style by a great African novelist, based on his recording of the famous *griot* (oral historian) Babu Conde.

Lefkowitz, Mary. *Not Out of Africa: How "Afrocentrism" Became an Excuse to Teach Myth as History.* New York: Basic Books, 1996. The most convincing response to Bernal, Asante, and others who attribute origins of "Western civilization" to Africa or the Near East.

Maloba, Wunyabari O. *Mau Mau and Kenya: An Analysis of a Peasant Revolt.* Bloomington: Indiana University Press, 1993. Solid account of the legendary Mau Mau rebellion.

Mamdani, Mahmood. *Citizen and Subject: Decentralized Despotism and the Legacy of Late Colonialism.* New York: Oxford University Press, 1997. Mamdani's argument that the legacies of various forms of "Indirect Rule" hold the key to Africa's political crises is not altogether convincing, but the book is very stimulating indeed.

———. *When Victims Become Killers: Colonialism, Nativism, and the Genocide in Rwanda.* Princeton, NJ: Princeton University Press, 2001. A nuanced study of the Rwanda genocide by one of the most influential and creative scholars in African studies today, originally from Uganda.

Marcus, Harold. *A History of Ethiopia.* Updated ed. Berkeley: University of California Press, 1992. A standard, comprehensive history by the late authority.

Martin, Phyllis, and Patrick O'Meara, eds. *Africa.* 3rd ed. Bloomington: Indiana University Press, 1995. A collection of survey articles, of varying quality, designed for introductory students.

Meldrum, Andrew. *Where We Have Hope: A Memoir of Zimbabwe.* New York: Atlantic Monthly Press, 2004. The journalist Meldrum went to Zimbabwe in 1980 intending to stay three years. He fell in love with the place and stayed on, but his fearless writing about the ruling party's growing despotism led to his expulsion in 2003. Moving and informative.

Meredith, Martin. *Our Votes, Our Guns: Robert Mugabe and the Tragedy of Zimbabwe.* New York: PublicAffairs, 2002. A searing portrait of promise gone wrong, from a veteran observer of Africa.

————. *The Past Is Another Country: Rhodesia, UDI to Independence.* London, UK: A. Deutsch, 1979. A clear and informative overall history of Zimbabwe's turbulent path to independence.

Miller, Joseph. *Way of Death: Merchant Capitalism and the Angolan Slave Trade, 1730–1830.* Madison: University of Wisconsin Press, 1988. The *opus magnum* of a very respected scholar and, possibly, the most detailed examination of the slave trade in a particular African locality.

Minter, William. *King Solomon's Mines Revisited: Western Interests and the Burdened History of Southern Africa.* New York: Basic Books, 1986. A critical and well-researched history of Western involvement in Southern Africa over the past century plus.

Nkrumah, Kwame. *The Autobiography of Kwame Nkrumah.* New York: International Publishers, 1971. First published in 1957, the year Nkrumah led Ghana to independence. Still a valuable source for understanding the first generation of triumphant nationalists.

Northrup, David, ed. *The Atlantic Slave Trade.* 2nd ed. Boston: Houghton Mifflin, 2002. Superb selection of excerpts from all the main authorities on the slave trade.

Nzongola-Ntalaja, Georges. *The Congo from Leopold to Kabila: A People's History.* London and New York: Zed Books, 2002. Somewhat heavy with radical jargon but a thorough and revealing history from a respected Congolese scholar, a former president of the U.S. African Studies Association.

Oliver, Roland. *The African Experience: Major Themes in African History from Earliest Times to the Present.* New York: HarperCollins, 1991. Another fine one-volume history from an eminent authority. May be a bit denser than books by Reader or Iliffe.

Omer-Cooper, John. *The Zulu Aftermath: A Nineteenth-Century Revolution in Bantu Africa.* Evanston, IL: Northwestern University Press, 1966. A classic in modern African studies that stands up quite well decades later, despite attacks on it.

Pakenham, Thomas. *The Boer War.* New York: Random House, 1993. A magisterial history of the conflict in South Africa between the British and the Dutch-descended white Afrikaners.

———. *The Scramble for Africa, 1876–1912.* New York: Random House, 1991. A comprehensive and clear narrative of the European colonization of virtually the whole continent at the turn of the 20th century.

Parrinder, Edward Geoffrey. *Religion in Africa.* Baltimore: Penguin Press, 1969. (A revised and updated version was published in Britain by Sheldon Press in 1976 as *Africa's Three Religions.*) Despite being published some time ago, this volume remains a useful overview of indigenous religion, Christianity, and Islam in Africa over the long run.

Peires, Jeffrey. *The Dead Will Arise: Nongqawuse and the Great Xhosa Cattle-Killing Movement of 1856–7.* Bloomington: Indiana University Press, 1989. A remarkable book about a remarkable and tragic episode: the millenarian response of the Xhosa peoples of South Africa, who under frontier pressure and inspired by a young girl's prophecy, slaughtered tens of thousands of their cattle in the vain hope of ushering in a "new age."

Ranger, Terence. *Are We Not Also Men? The Samkange Family & African Politics in Zimbabwe, 1920–1964.* Portsmouth, NH: Heinemann, 1995. Ranger is certainly among the most distinguished of living historians of Africa. Of his many books, this is perhaps the most appealing, the story of generations of a talented, well-known Zimbabwean family living through colonial rule; based on rich, privately held material, such as letters and diaries.

Robinson, David. *Muslim Societies in African History*. Cambridge: Cambridge University Press, 2004. A recent and welcome examination of the interplay between African cultures and Islam, with well-drawn case studies. From a distinguished scholar and quite readable.

Rodney, Walter. *How Europe Underdeveloped Africa*. Oxford, UK: Blackwell, 1997 (first published in 1972). The classic statement of "underdevelopment theory" as applied to Africa, from the late Guyanese scholar and activist. Indeed an overstatement, but one that nonetheless still packs a considerable punch and makes a number of telling points.

Sahlins, Marshall. *Stone Age Economics*. New York: Aldine de Gruyter, 1981 (first published in 1972). Includes Southern African San, or "Bushmen," in a wider survey of foraging lifestyles; argues that this was not a desperate, eke-out-a-living situation at all, but one providing a comfortable life with plenty of time for creativity and leisure.

Sibomana, André. *Hope for Rwanda: Conversations with Laure Guilbert and Hervé Deguine*. London and Sterling, VA: Pluto Press, 1999. An extraordinary book from an extraordinary man, dead far too young: Rwandan, Hutu, Catholic priest, crusading journalist, and humanist. Full of insights into Rwanda's tragedy yet not without hope, as the title suggests.

Sparks. Allister. *Beyond the Miracle: Inside the New South Africa*. Chicago: University of Chicago Press, 2003. Third in Sparks's trilogy and probably the best look at the realities, problems, and prospects of postapartheid South Africa.

———. *The Mind of South Africa*. New York: Ballentine Books, 1991. Sparks is arguably South Africa's premier journalist of recent times. This is the first part of his trilogy on his home country and certainly the one with the largest sweep: essentially an extremely readable history that ends just before Mandela's tide-turning release in 1990.

———. *Tomorrow Is Another Country: The Inside Story of South Africa's Road to Change*. Chicago: University of Chicago Press, 1996. Second in Sparks's trilogy, the ultimate inside account of the negotiations leading to Mandela's release and those that produced the new political regime in South Africa.

Thomas, Elizabeth Marshall. *The Harmless People.* New York: Knopf, 1959. The classic account of a community of San, or so-called "Bushmen," deep in the Kgalagadi (Kalahari) Desert.

Thompson, Leonard. *Survival in Two Worlds: Moshoeshoe of Lesotho, 1786–1870.* Oxford, UK: Clarendon Press, 1975. A master historian's definitive study of a towering figure of Southern African history. Moshoeshoe, king of Lesotho, lived through both the "Mfecane" and the coming of the European frontier. He was responsible for Lesotho remaining outside—though surrounded by—modern South Africa.

Thornton, John. *Africa and Africans in the Making of the Atlantic World, 1400–1800.* 2nd ed. Cambridge: Cambridge University Press, 1998. A comprehensive look at the Atlantic slave trade. Thornton portrays African leaders as active and capable agents in the system, not helpless victims, and is skeptical that the trade seriously handicapped Africa's development.

Van Onselen, Charles. *The Seed Is Mine: The Life of Kas Maine, a South African Sharecropper, 1894–1985.* New York: Hill and Wang, 1996. An awesome work that traces one sharecropper family in South Africa for a century, squarely in the context of developing segregation and apartheid.

Vansina, Jan. *Oral Tradition as History.* Madison: University of Wisconsin Press, 1985. One of many books by one of the deans of modern African historical studies and a real pioneer in legitimizing the use of oral sources for historical reconstruction.

Vickery, Kenneth P. *Black and White in Southern Zambia: The Tonga Plateau and British Imperialism, 1890–1939.* Westport, CT: Greenwood Press, 1986. A study of colonial Zambia illustrating something of a peasant "victory" over settler interests in the colonial period.

Wrong, Michaela. *In the Footsteps of Mr. Kurtz: Living on the Brink of Disaster in Mobutu's Congo.* New York: Perennial, 2002. A lively and fascinating, if depressing, account of Mobutu's regime.

Internet Resources:

"African History on the Internet," *Africa South of the Sahara.* http://www-sul.stanford.edu/depts/ssrg/africa/history.html.   A Stanford University site with hundreds of links to sources on African history. Searchable by more than 30 topics, including slavery, ancient civilizations and kingdoms, colonial period, and religion.

"African Studies Center—University of Pennsylvania," http://www.africa.upenn.edu. Solid basic information (maps, State Department summaries, and so forth) on each country in Africa, plus links related to that country.

"allAfrica.com," http://allafrica.com. The most comprehensive source for news from Africa, including stories from hundreds of African newspapers and media outlets. Numerous feature sections (business, sport, and others), as well.

"BBC News International Version-Africa." *BBC News.* http://news.bbc.co.uk/ 2/hi/africa/default.stm. The BBC News Africa site. Another outstanding source for information out of Africa. Widely used and respected in Africa itself.

"Mail & Guardian Online," http://www.mg.co.za. Site of the *Mail & Guardian*, South Africa's finest newspaper, with solid coverage of other countries in the Southern African region as well.